Advances in
LIBRARIANSHIP

Volume 10

Advances in
LIBRARIANSHIP

Edited by
MICHAEL H. HARRIS
*University of Kentucky
Lexington, Kentucky*

Volume 10

1980

ACADEMIC PRESS
A Subsidiary of Harcourt Brace Jovanovich, Publishers
New York   London   Toronto   Sydney   San Francisco

COPYRIGHT © 1980, BY ACADEMIC PRESS, INC.
ALL RIGHTS RESERVED.
NO PART OF THIS PUBLICATION MAY BE REPRODUCED OR
TRANSMITTED IN ANY FORM OR BY ANY MEANS, ELECTRONIC
OR MECHANICAL, INCLUDING PHOTOCOPY, RECORDING, OR ANY
INFORMATION STORAGE AND RETRIEVAL SYSTEM, WITHOUT
PERMISSION IN WRITING FROM THE PUBLISHER.

ACADEMIC PRESS, INC.
111 Fifth Avenue, New York, New York 10003

United Kingdom Edition published by
ACADEMIC PRESS, INC. (LONDON) LTD.
24/28 Oval Road, London NW1 7DX

LIBRARY OF CONGRESS CATALOG CARD NUMBER: 79–88675

ISBN 0–12–785010–4

PRINTED IN THE UNITED STATES OF AMERICA

80 81 82 83   9 8 7 6 5 4 3 2 1

Contents

Contributors .... *ix*
Preface .... *xi*
Contents of Previous Volumes .... *xiii*

AACR 2: Antecedents, Assumptions, Implementation
WESLEY SIMONTON

    I. Introduction 1
   II. Content of Catalogue Codes 4
  III. Assumptions—Tenets—Attitudes 18
  IV. External Influences 26
    V. The Future of AACR 2 28
       References 36

Academic Library Management Studies: From Games to Leadership
H. WILLIAM AXFORD

    I. Management and the Status Quo 39
   II. The Management Review and Analysis Program
       (MRAP) 43
  III. Beyond MRAP 51
  IV. Collection Use Studies and Management:
       Challenges to the Status Quo 57
       References 60

And Gladly Teach: Bibliographic Instruction and the Library
ARTHUR P. YOUNG

    I. Introduction 63
   II. Literature Reviews and Bibliographies 64
  III. Assumptions and Rationales 66
  IV. The Educational Environment 68
   V. Evaluation and Research 72
  VI. Instructional Patterns 76
 VII. Reflections................................... 80
       References 81

Library Materials Budgeting in the Private University Library: Austerity and Action
FREDERICK C. LYNDEN

    I. Introduction 90
   II. The Library Materials Budgeting Literature 91
  III. Environment and the Budgeting Process 96
  IV. Budget Formulation and Presentation 101
   V. Collection Development and the Materials Budget .. 116
  VI. Interlibrary Cooperation and the Materials Budget .. 131
 VII. Conclusion 139
       References 151

Individual Decision Theory: An Overview
JAMES D. SODT

    I. Introduction 155
   II. Background: Individual Decision Literature 156
  III. Optimism 156
  IV. The Subjective Expected Utility (SEU) Model 163
   V. Bayesian Models 174
  VI. Conclusion 182
       Selected Bibliography.......................... 183

Library Education in India, Pakistan, and Bangladesh

P. B. MANGLA

I.	Scope	191
II.	Brief Historical Background	192
III.	Library Education	195
IV.	Similarities and Variations	234
V.	Conclusion	236
	Selected Bibliography	238

Subject Index *241*
Cumulative Subject Index Volumes 1–10 .... *245*

Contributors

Numbers in parentheses indicate the pages on which the authors' contributions begin.

H. William Axford (39), deceased

Frederick C. Lynden (89), Rockefeller Library, Brown University, Providence, Rhode Island 02912

P. B. Mangla (191), Department of Library Science, University of Delhi, Delhi, India II0007

Wesley Simonton, (1), Library School, University of Minnesota, Minneapolis, Minnesota 55455

James D. Sodt (155), College of Library Science, University of Kentucky, Lexington, Kentucky 40506

Arthur P. Young (63), University Library, University of Alabama, University, Alabama 35486

Preface

These are difficult times for librarians. Spiraling inflation and steady or even decreasing funding pose formidable obstacles for all those committed to the delivery of quality information services to the citizens of a postindustrial world. The financial crisis gripping libraries has proven particularly jarring following so quickly on the heels of the euphoric "good times" enjoyed by library interests in the 1960s.

As the picture began to change in the early 1970s, information professionals generally reacted in one of two ways. First came the fatalistic paralysis which seemed to grip many, pushing them toward a cynical nihilism. In contrast, was the widely held naïve optimism which looked eagerly toward federal and state governments for substantial infusions of life-giving financial support. Neither of these views proved particularly productive. Of late, we are witnessing a more realistic assessment of the library future. The emerging view is critical but not cynical, conscious of what appear to be long-range constraints but cautiously optimistic about future possibilities, skeptical of "quick-fix" solutions but confidently pursuing innovations with real promise.

We now appear to have weathered the emotional trauma associated with our changed condition, and information professionals everywhere are moving in a cautious but positive manner toward the solution of problems associated with our need to operate under severe financial constraints.

Many of the papers that follow evidence this new direction. In the first, Wesley Simonton, one of the profession's best informed cataloging theorists, accesses the origins and nature of the second edition of the Anglo American Cataloging Rules. AACR 2 will likely garner more ink than any other development in librarianship over the next several years, and Simonton's thorough assessment should prove of real value to anyone wishing to ponder seriously the nature and implications of the new code.

In the second paper, H. William Axford takes an equally tough-minded look at one of academic librarianships most sacred cows—the management review and analysis program (MRAP). Axford questions both the premises and value of the management analysis orientation and then moves to a startling advocasy of collection use studies as a means of improving the management of library service. We are sorry to report that Bill Axford died on August 12, 1980.

In the following paper, Arthur Young assesses the state of the art in bibliographic instruction in libraries. In a thorough examination of the literature Young demonstrates the strengths and weaknesses of library instructional programs, and critically analyzes the research studies undertaken to determine the educational gains made through such programs. Quality instructional services require substantial financial support, and Young's paper should prove of use to all librarians interested in weighing costs against benefits in this area.

Frederick Lynden, in his paper "Library Materials Budgeting in the Private University Library," presents a detailed analysis of the way in which a group of private university libraries are coping with their eroding book budgets. Lynden's study, based on work he completed as a Council on Library Resources Fellow, combines the traditional literature survey with an original and critical research study of the libraries involved. His paper illustrates, better perhaps than any we have read, the slow and painful transition made by academic libraries from the prodigal 1960s to the austere 1970s.

The final two papers in this volume represent contributions to long-range projects treated regularly in these *Advances* over the past half-dozen years. In a paper on "Individual Decision Theory" James D. Sodt reviews interdisciplinary research on information-seeking behavior and decision theory. Sodt's paper represents one in a series of studies designed to translate major interdisciplinary research into terms and contexts of use to information professionals. In his essay Sodt dissects the major paradigms controlling work in this area, and unflinchingly illustrates the problems besetting the two principal models.

In the last paper in this volume, P. B. Mangla, the head of the library education program at New Delhi, surveys the origins and current status of library education in India, Pakistan, and Bangladesh. His careful and informed essay clearly outlines the considerable growth and the complex problems of library education in that area, and offers valuable comparative insights for librarians everywhere who are interested in library education.

Contents of Previous Volumes

Volume 1

The Machine and Cataloging
 George Piternick

Mechanization of Acquisitions Processes
 Connie R. Dunlap

Mechanization and Library Filing Rules
 Kelley L. Cartwright

Standards for Technical Service Cost Studies
 Helen Welch Tuttle

The Undergraduate Library Trend at Large Universities
 Robert H. Muller

The Changing School Library: An Instructional Media Center
 Chase Dane

Reference Service to Children—Past, Present, and Future
 Lillian K. Orsini

Progress in Bibliotherapy
 Ruth M. Tews

Effectiveness in Cooperation and Consolidation in Public Libraries
 Ralph Blasingame and
 Ernest R. DeProspo, Jr.

Library Planning: The Challenge of Change
 Robert E. Kemper

Acceleration of Library Development in Developing Countries
 Carl M. White

SUBJECT INDEX

Volume 2

Access to Information
 William S. Budington

Control and Dissemination of Information in Medicine
 David Bishop

The Computer in Serials Processing and Control
 Don L. Bosseau

Micropublication
 Allen B. Veaner

The Changing Role of the State Library
 Kenneth E. Beasley

Censorship, Intellectual Freedom, and Libraries
 Edwin Castagna

Reader Services to the Disadvantaged in Inner Cities
 Margaret E. Monroe

Oral History: Problems and Prospects
 Louis M. Starr

Armageddon in International Copyright:
Review of the Berne Convention, the Universal
Convention, and the Present Crisis in International Copyright
  Dorothy M. Schrader
AUTHOR INDEX—SUBJECT INDEX

Volume 3

On Beyond 999Z—Patterns of Library Service to Children of the Poor
  Binnie L. Tate

Youth as a Special Client Group
  James W. Liesener and Margaret E. Chisholm

The Emergence of the Community College Library
  Harriett Genung and James O. Wallace

Teaching Library Skills to College Students
  Miriam Dudley

Academic Library Buildings in the United Kingdom
  H. Faulkner Brown

Academic Library Buildings in the United States
  Ralph E. Ellsworth

Federal Grants and Public Libraries
  James G. Igoe

Anglo-American Code Implementation
  Elizabeth L. Tate

Catalog Use Studies and Their Implications
  James Krikelas

Converting Bibliographic Data to Machine Form
  Don Sherman

Archive and Manuscript Collections
  Robert L. Brubaker

AUTHOR INDEX—SUBJECT INDEX

Volume 4

MARC and Its Applications to Library Automation
  Roy B. Torkington

Selective Dissemination of Information
  Georg R. Mauerhoff

Circulation Automation
  Hugh C. Atkinson

Social Responsibility and Libraries
  Arthur Curley

Women in Librarianship
  Anita R. Schiller

The Use of Resources in the Learning Experience
  Johnnie Givens

Reading as Information Processing
  John J. Geyer and Paul A. Kolers

SUBJECT INDEX

Volume 5

International Information Systems
  Jacques Tocatlian

National Planning for Library and Information Services
  Foster E. Mohrhardt and Carlos Victor Penna

Statistics that Describe Libraries and Library Service
  Thomas Childers

Coordination of the Technical Services
  Helen Welch Tuttle

Trends in Library Education—United States
  Lester Asheim

The Technologies of Education and Communication
  Gerald R. Brong

Audiovisual Services in Libraries
  Irving Lieberman

Sound Recordings
  Gordon Stevenson

Joint Academic Libraries
  Richard D. Johnson

AUTHOR INDEX—SUBJECT INDEX

Contents of Previous Volumes

Volume 6

Performance Measures for School Librarians; Complexities and Potential
  Evelyn H. Daniel

Productivity Measurement in Academic Libraries
  Thomas J. Waldhart and Thomas P. Marcum

Relevance: A Review of the Literature and a Framework for Thinking on the Notion in Information Science
  Tefko Saracevic

The Impact of Reading on Human Behavior: The Implications of Communications Research
  Roger Haney, Michael H. Harris, and Leonard Tipton

Trends in Library Education—Europe
  Donald Davinson

The Role of Middle Managers in Libraries
  Beverly P. Lynch

AUTHOR INDEX—SUBJECT INDEX

Volume 7

Vocabulary Control in Information Retrieval Systems
  F. W. Lancaster

Major Developments in Classification
  Ingetraut Dahlberg

National Libraries in Developing Countries
  Simeon B. Aje

The American Library Association and the Library Association: Retrospect, Problems, and Prospects
  W. A. Munford

Popular Culture and the Public Library
  Gordon Stevenson

Public Library Use, Users, Uses: Advances in Knowledge of the Characteristics and Needs of the Adult Clientele of American Public Libraries
  Douglas Zweizig and Brenda Dervin

Personal Roles and Barriers in Information Transfer
  Anne Wilkin

The Applications of Citation Analyses to Library Collection Building
  Robert N. Broadus

AUTHOR INDEX—SUBJECT INDEX

Volume 8

Collection Development in Large University Libraries
  Rose Mary Magrill and Mona East

The Library of Congress in American Life
  John Y. Cole

Affirmative Action and American Librarianship
  Elizabeth Dickinson and Margaret Myers

American Indian Library Service
  Charles T. Townley

Advances in American Library History
  David Kaser

Trends in Library Education—Canada
  John P. Wilkinson

Continuing Education for Librarians in the United States
  Elizabeth W. Stone

SUBJECT INDEX

Volume 9

Intellectual Freedom in Librarianship: Advances and Retreats
  David K. Berninghausen

User Fees in Publicly Funded Libraries
  Thomas J. Waldhart and Trudi Bellardo

The Evaluation of Paraprofessional Library Employees
  Charles W. Evans

Measuring Library Effectiveness: A Review and an Assessment
Rosemary Ruhig Du Mont and Paul F. Du Mont

Operations Research in Libraries
Abraham Bookstein and Karl Kocher

Funding Support for Research in Librarianship
George W. Whitbeck, Jean Major, and Herbert S. White

Advances in Medical Librarianship
Donald D. Hendricks

Advances in Australian Library Services
Carmel Maguire

SUBJECT INDEX

AACR 2: Antecedents, Assumptions, Implementation

WESLEY SIMONTON

Library School
University of Minnesota

I. Introduction	1
II. Content of Catalogue Codes	4
A. The Authorship Principle	5
B. Form of Heading for Persons	10
C. Form of Heading for Corporate Bodies	11
D. Choice of Main Entry	14
E. Access Points	16
F. Description	17
III. Assumptions—Tenets—Attitudes	18
A. Explicit Statement of Principles	18
B. Recognition of User Needs	19
C. Provision of Options	21
D. Direct and Collocative Functions	24
IV. External Influences	26
A. The Influence of Technology	26
B. International Agreement	28
V. The Future of AACR 2	28
A. The Bibliographic Milieu	28
B. Implementation and Influence of the Code	31
References	36

I. INTRODUCTION

This paper is concerned with the major theoretical principles and substantive provisions of the second edition of the *Anglo-American*

Cataloguing Rules (1978) (AACR 2).* It seeks to relate the new code to the Anglo-American cataloguing tradition and, as appropriate, to other codes and major theoretical writings, particularly those of the past 30 years, including developments designed to secure or further international agreement on cataloguing rules and principles. The paper considers first the content and then the "point of view" (assumptions, tenets, and attitudes) of AACR 2 and other codes. This discussion of the content devotes considerable attention to the concept of corporate authorship, the major theoretical question raised by the new code, and summarizes varying points of view of the past 30 years on this and other important questions relating to choice and form of the entries under which documents are represented in library catalogues. Following a brief discussion of the influence of technology and of questions relating to international agreement, the paper concludes with an assessment of the code's future, based on issues and problems related to its adoption and implementation in American libraries. It is hoped that the paper will be useful both to the generalist (non cataloguer) for its identification and summary of major issues, and to the specialist (cataloguer), for its synthesis of widely scattered familiar materials. Footnotes have been used liberally in an attempt to keep detailed explanations, examples, and references to other sources from interrupting the flow of the text.

AACR 2 represents the work of many persons, particularly members of committees from Canada, the United Kingdom, and the United States, with final decisions made by the Joint Steering Committee for Revision of AACR, composed of representatives of each of the five corporate bodies identified on the title page as responsible for the work: the American Library Association, the British Library, and Canadian Committee on Cataloguing, the Library Association and the Library of Congress. Edited by Michael Gorman and Paul W. Winkler, it is presented as a second edition of the *Anglo-American Cataloging Rules* (1967) (AACR 1) and as a work that "continues" rather than "supersedes" the work of Seymour Lubetzky and C. Sumner Spalding, the successive editors of AACR 1, "having the same principles and underlying objectives as the first edition, and being firmly based on the achievement of those who created the work" (p. v.) and at the same time reflecting a number of developments of the last decade that have

---

*For detailed presentations of the objectives and major provisions of AACR 2, the reader is referred to Gorman (1978) and Simonton (1979).

necessitated a revision of the earlier work. It is proposed as a code "designed for use in the construction of catalogues and other lists in general libraries of all sizes." It is not "specifically intended for specialist and archival libraries," although it is "recommended that such libraries use the rules as the basis of their cataloguing" (p. 1).

The other major codes and theoretical writings considered here include the following works. Citations to these works utilize the acronyms listed below and are referred by rule numbers rather than page numbers unless so indicated.

1. The three codes adopted officially by the American library community, in 1908, 1949, and 1967: *Catalog Rules: Author and Title Entries* (1908) (AA), *A.L.A. Cataloging Rules for Author and Title Entries* (American Library Association, 1949) (ALA), and AACR 1. Of these, AA and AACR 1 are based on cooperative work with British colleagues and AACR 1 with Canadian colleagues as well. (The text of AACR 1 was revised considerably in the 12 years between its publication and that of AACR 2 in matters relating both to headings and description. For ease of reference, no acount has been taken of these changes in the text of this paper and all references to AACR 1 are to the text as published in 1967, even though several important changes were made soon after publication. It should also be noted that there are significant differences between the "North American text" and the "British text" of AACR 1; unless otherwise qualified, all references in this paper to AACR 1 are to the North American text.)
2. Lubetzky's discussion and criticism of the Anglo-American tradition: *Cataloging Rules and Principles,* 1953 (CRP) and his incomplete draft of a new code in 1960: *Code of Cataloging Rules: Author and Title Entry* (CCR).
3. The international agreement on cataloguing principles adopted in 1961: *Statement of Principles Adopted at the International Conference on Cataloguing Principles, Paris, October 1961* (the Paris Principles) (International Conference, 1976).
4. The most recent codification of the German theory of cataloguing: *Regeln für die alphabetische Katalogisierung* (1977) (RAK).
5. Two important European commentaries on the principles of cataloguing: Domanovszky's *Function and Objects of Author and*

Title Cataloguing: A Contribution to Cataloguing Theory (Domanovszky, 1975) and Verona's *Corporate Headings: Their use in Library Catalogues and National Bibliographies* (Verona, 1975).

II. CONTENT OF CATALOGUE CODES

Cataloguing and bibliographic activities related to the identification and description of a document* are based on questions relating to the conditions under which the document was produced. Every document represents the result of creative work of one or more persons, whose identity may or may not be known. If more than one person is involved, the collaboration may be synchronous (e.g., a work written jointly by two person(s) or asynchronous (e.g., a translation, adaptation, etc.) The person(s) may have some relationship with a corporate body which has some degree of responsibility for the creation and/or distribution of the document.

Traditionally, catalogue codes have provided directions for the following parts of the cataloguing activity:

1. Determination of the "entries" or "access points" at which a bibliographic description of the document is to be displayed in the catalogue
2. Determination of the form of the heading for each entry; a heading may be either
   a. The name of a person
   b. The name of a corporate body (including political jurisdictions)
   c. The name of the place (generally local) in which a corporate body is located, followed by the name of the body
   d. The name of a corporate body or political jurisdiction, followed by a form subheading, or
   e. The title of the document
3. Selection of one of the entries as the "main entry"
4. Description of the physical object

---

*The term "document" is used here in its generic sense and is intended to encompass all media.

A. The Authorship Principle

Catalogue codes have frequently been identified as codes for "author and title entries" because the identification of the author of a document is an important part of the cataloguing process. It follows, then, that a catalogue code must present, explicitly or implicitly, a definition of "author" if its conception of authorship is to be understood. The term is defined by the *Oxford English Dictionary* as "the person who originates or gives existence to anything," especially "one who sets forth written statements; the composer or writer of a treatise or book." In this regard the concept of "main entry" must be considered. "Main entry" is defined by AACR 2 as "the complete catalogue record of an item, presented in the form by which the entity is to be uniformly indentified and cited." Earlier definitions, such as that of AA—"the full or principal entry"—reflect the contemporary practice, which prescribed bibliographic descriptions of varying length at the several access points. In any event, one entry is selected as the main entry for each item catalogued and the direction to "enter under . . ." is to be read as "make main entry under . . ." In the simplest case of authorship—a document created by a single individual of known identity, with no relationship to a corporate body—all codes agree on the selection of the author's name as the main entry heading.

1. PERSONAL AUTHORSHIP

The term "author" as applied to persons has traditionally been used in a broad sense in the Anglo-American tradition. Accordingly, AA includes explicit recognition of editors, compilers of collections, cartographers, and composers as authors and AACR 2 identifies "writers of books . . . composers of music . . . compilers of bibliographies . . . cartographers . . . artists and photographers . . . [and] in certain cases performers," the major changes being the addition of performers, as proposed earlier in Lubetzky's CCR, and the deletion of editors and compilers.

2. CORPORATE AUTHORSHIP

Anglo-American codes, based on the tradition of Panizzi, Jewett, and Cutter, have extended the concept of authorship to corporate bodies without providing any extended rationale for the concept or indication of its scope. Thus, AA directs the cataloguer to "enter a work under the name of its author whether individual or corporate" (1), provides in its definition of author that "corporate bodies may be considered the authors of publications issued in their name or by their authority," and calls for entry under names of political jurisdictions of "official publications issued by them or under their auspices" (58). ALA continues these provisions and states that "the author is considered to be the person or body chiefly responsible for the intellectual content of the book." Lubetzky's phrasing of the concept is "enter under the name of the corporate body publications issued in its name" (CRP, p. 48).

In 1956 an international group defined corporate authorship as "the collective responsibility of a body of persons for the content of a document" and found recognition of the concept in 15 of 19 codes examined. The other four, all German codes, provided only "implicit partial recognition" of the concept (IFLA Working Group on the Coordination of Cataloguing Principles, 1956). Lubetzky's draft code (CCR) provides a clearer statement of the Anglo-American position than the earlier codes: "A work produced by, or issued in the name of, a person or corporate body is entered under the name of that person or corporate body" (p. xii). "A work which, explicitly or implicitly, represents an act, communication, or product of a corporate body is entered under the name of that body" (22). Lubetzky also addresses the question of the work of an individual issued by a corporate body, directing that such a work be entered under the name of the individual except in the case of a work (1) "prepared for and issued in the name of a corporate body"; (2) representing an "administrative, regulatory, or other official communication . . . which may successively be prepared by different individuals"; or (3) representing "an official statement made by an individual on behalf of a corporate body" (26) and presents a comparable rule (45) for works of government officials.

In 1961, the International Conference on Cataloguing Principles, attended by delegations from 53 countries and 12 international organizations, adopted the "Paris Principles," including agreement that main entry should be made under the name of a corporate body for works that are "necessarily the expression of the collective thought or activity of the corporate body" or works for which the corporate body is "collectively responsible for the content of the work" (9.1, 9.11 and 9.12).*

Gorman finds these two provisions for entry under corporate body to be an unsuccessful attempt to reconcile two opposing views:

> first, that a corporate body can be an author; secondly, that a corporate body cannot be an author but may serve as a useful identifying label for a work . . . The first depends on an application of the idea of corporate authorship, that is, it depends on an analysis of the relationship of the body to the content of the work. The second definition depends, to some extent, on the evidence of the title page and does not imply acceptance of authorship but acceptance of a degree of corporate responsibility that has to be combined with some title page evidence (Gorman, 1968, p. 12).

AACR 1 retains the Anglo-American concept of corporate authorship and devotes five pages (Rule 17) to an attempt to provide guidelines for the handling of "works issued by or bearing the authority of a corporate body, but with authorship or editorship specifically and prominently attributed to one or more persons."

Gorman (1968) suggests that "a work may be considered to be of corporate authorship if (a) it is *clearly* and *unambiguously* an official statement of the body, *or* (b) if the person(s) who wrote the work (whether known or not) were *acting as an agent* of the corporate body in order to further the activity of the body or to express its corporate thought" (p. 14).

Domanovszky (1975), in a classic presentation of the German position, defines "author" as "a person who has written the original version of a work," a definition he finds "in harmony with everyday language" (p. 116). He argues against extending the concept of authorship to corporate bodies, finding such action an "impardonable mistake" because the concept is unknown in everyday speech. He further asserts that the lack of a common sense of the meaning of the term leaves cataloguers free to establish a meaning, but that they have been unable to do so, creating to date only "quite vague definitions of the

---

*The term "corporate author" had been used in the draft statement of principles for the conference but proved unacceptable to a number of the delegations and was replaced by the phrase "entry under the name of a corporate body," thus foreshadowing the provisions of AACR 2 on corporate authorship.

concept, and even vaguer deliminations of the term 'corporate author' " (p. 120). He argues that the basic reason for the inability to agree on a definition of corporate authorship is that the variations of degree of corporate responsibilty are so many that it is impossible to identify a point on the spectrum at which a division can be made. He ends by recognizing the "really valuable contribution" of American librarians in "discovering the great value these names [of corporate bodies] are capable of attaining in the role of formal marks" and the "astonishing failure of another great cataloguing tradition, the German one, to appreciate this inestimable kind of formal marks. But at this point the merit of American cataloguers ends; most of their steps taken for exploiting the possibilities offered by corporate names . . . have been very unlucky, and their outcomes have thrown a great burden upon author-title cataloguing throughout the world" (pp. 125-126). The most recent German code (RAK) continues the German tradition of attributing authorship only to persons and introduces the concept of "*Urheber*" (originator) to identify corporate bodies that have either (*a*) created or (*b*) sponsored and edited an anonymous work, an anonymous work being defined as a work with no personal author named or ascertained. Main entry is made under the name of the "Urheber" only if certain formal criteria concerning the relationship of the name of the Urheber to the title of the work are met.*

Verona's analysis of corporate headings finds that the concept of corporate authorship is now widely accepted, but without any clear statement of its theoretical basis and with a great range in the extent of its use. Her "Suggestions for the Formulation of Agreements on Corporate Headings" include a definition of corporate bodies:

> All types of groups of individuals with a firm organization, as well as conferences and expeditions with a distinctive name, should be included in the meaning of the term "corporate body for cataloguing purposes"; no exceptions should be made for territorial authorities or commercial publishers [Verona, 1975, p. 155].

---

*"*Als anonymes Werk wird ein Werk bezeichnet, dessen Verfasser weder genannt noch ermittelt sind*" (17). "*Urheber*" is defined as "*Körperschaften . . . die . . . ein anonymes Werk oder Teile eines solchen Werkes erarbeitet oder veranlasst* **und** *herausgegeben haben*" (18). Kaltwasser (1975, p. 281) and Verona (1975, pp. 15-16) discuss the criteria for main entry under *Urheber* in some detail.

of corporate authorship:

> A work should be considered to be of corporate authorship if it may be concluded by its character or nature that it is necessarily the result of the creative and/or organizational activity of a corporate body as a whole, and not the result of an independent creative activity of the individual(s) who drafted it; in the context of this definition the term corporate body should be interpreted as applying to any type of corporate body, irrespective of whether it is an independent corporate body [Verona, 1975, p. 155].

and directions for handling the problem of personal vs. corporate author:

> With respect to scientific and technical works corporate authorship should be restricted to cases where there is no doubt that they are the result of the creative activity of a corporate body as a whole, and where no conflict with personal authorship might arise, as is the case with reports of the scientific results of an expedition, or with proceedings of a conference. Monographic works dealing with a particular scientific, technical, economic, etc. topic and approved, commissioned, edited, issued, sponsored or published by a corporate body should be considered to be of personal authorship, irrespective of the number of personal authors involved and regardless of the fact whether the personal authors are named in the publication or can be ascertained [Verona, 1975, p. 155].

AACR 2 (21.1B2) retains the Anglo-American concept of a corporate body ("an organization or a group of persons that is identified by a particular name and that acts, or may act, as an entity"), introduces a definition of "name" ("Consider a corporate body to have a name if the words referring to it are a specific appellation rather than a general description"), and is more liberal in including commercial publishers. However, the concept of corporate authorship is no longer recognized,[*] having been replaced by one of responsibility, in which works "emanating from" (i.e., issued by, caused to be issued by, or originated by) a corporate body are to be entered under the name of the corporate body if the document (1) is of an administrative nature; or (2) consists of the text of one of a number of specified "legal and governmental works" such as laws, treaties, etc.; or (3) records "the collective thought of the body" or the "collective activity" of a "prominently

---

[*]Indeed, at "Author," the Glossary directs the user to "Personal Author."

named" conference, expedition or event" falling within the definition of a corporate body." A vestige of corporate authorship may be found in the provision for main entry of sound recordings, films, and videorecordings under the name of a performing group in certain cases.*

The foregoing discussion of the concept of authorship, personal and corporate, has identified major differences in the Anglo-American and German cataloguing traditions. Fewer differences are to be found in the rules for form of heading for persons and corporate bodies, to be considered next.

B. Form of Heading for Persons

The major questions concerning form of headings for persons relate to (1) the selection of a single form from among a number of variant forms and (2) the decision whether to use a uniform heading, i.e., the same form of name on all occasions. Major changes have occurred in the rules on both of these points in the last 30 years. ALA prescribes use of the author's name in full and in the vernacular in most cases and, for an author known by more than one name, prefers (1) the most authentic or (2) the best known if the most authentic is little known. In any case, a single form of name is used, without variation, in all headings (82).

The Paris Principles accept the concept of a uniform heading but prefer the fullest form of the author's name "most frequently identified in editions of his works" unless another form has become established in general usage (8.2 and 8.21). AACR 1 also prefers the name by which the author is "commonly identified." prescribes the use of the "fullest form that has appeared in a prominent position" in the author's works, and calls for spelling out forenames represented by initials in the case of authors with "common" surnames, e.g., "Eliot, Thomas Stearns" (43). The only provision for the use of more than one

---

*Rule 21.1B2 calls for entry under the name of the performing group for those films and recordings "resulting from the collective activity of a performing group as a whole where the responsibility of the group goes beyond that of mere performance, execution, etc." The only example provided is of a recording by the Rolling Stones, in which authorship is clearly involved. Paul Winkler has suggested that the rule is also intended to cover "authorship in the sense of improvisation, as with a recording by a jazz group or in the sense of a group of actors who improvise a drama that is filmed" (Winkler, 1979).

form of name for an author writing under more than one name is presented as a footnote alternative. AACR 2 continues to emphasize the name by which the person is "commonly known," gives further emphasis to the name "that appears most frequently in the person's works" (22.2A), leading to "Eliot, T.S.," and prescribes the use of different pseudonyms as headings for different works in the case of an author with no predominant form of name (22.2C3).

C. Form of Heading for Corporate Bodies

The heading for a corporate body may consist of

1. The name of the corporate body alone
2. The name of the corporate body, preceded by the name of a larger body to which it is subordinate
3. The name of the corporate body, preceded by a place name or the name of a political jurisdiction

In deciding on the form of the name of the corporate body to be used in the catalogue, it may be necessary to consider one or more of the following options: (1) the form found in the body's publications, (2) the official name, (3) a conventional form of name (e.g., "Westminster Abbey" rather than "Collegiate Church of St. Peter in Westminster"), and (4) the form given in reference sources. General decisions may also be necessary with regard to the following questions:

1. Possible modification of names (e.g., "M. Robert Gomberg Memorial Committee" modified to "Gomberg (M. Robert) Memorial Committee")
2. The form of qualifiers used to distinguish two or more corporate bodies (Loyola University) or political jurisdictions (Paris) with the same name
3. The use of the earlier, later, or successive names (for those corporate bodies whose name has changed)
4. The language of the heading: that of the country of the corporate body or that of the cataloguing agency*

*The question arises primarily with corporate bodies that are treated as subordinate units of political jurisdictions. The traditional Anglo-American practice has called for a "bilingual heading" (Koel, 1979) such as "Germany. *Heer.*" instead of either "Deutschland. Heer." or "Germany. Army."

With the possible exception of corporate authorship, no problem has proved so vexing for cataloguers. For Jewett, in an earlier age, the solution was simple: The heading for all corporate bodies, including governments, was to be "the name of the body, the principal word to be the first word, not an article" (Jewett, 1853, Rule XXII). Lubetzky, however, writing exactly a century later, found that "the tortuous course we have followed in the past seventy-five years in dealing with the problem of corporate entry," including attempts to define types of corporate bodies such as "societies" and "institutions," with differing rules for their names, had led to a "maze of rules in the apparent belief that although the cataloger may have to grope his own way, he will lead the reader surely to the desired destination" (Lubetzky, 1953, pp. 35, 33).

In his unfinished code of 1960, Lubetzky directs that a corporate body be represented "under the name by which it is identified in its works . . . in the language and form used by it" (27a). A subordinate body is to be entered under its own name unless the name implies subordination or is not "complete, unambiguous . . . or sufficient without the name of the other body" (33a). Government publications are to be "treated the same as other works of corporate authorship" (41) with the exception of certain aspects not found in other works of corporate authorship, for which special rules are provided. For the first time, a code based on the Anglo-American tradition does not provide for the use of a form subheading for such materials as laws, treaties, and constitutions, which are to have as their heading simply the name of the jurisdiction concerned (42-43). A jurisdiction "generally known by a conventional name is entered under this name, preferably in English" (46). The code distinguishes between government agencies created to exercise "legislative, administrative, or judicial authority" and those created to serve "educational, cultural . . . and other non-regulatory functions," with the former to be entered under the name of the jurisdiction and the latter under their own names unless that name implies subordination or is not complete without the name of the jurisdiction (47a).

The provisions of the Paris Principles relating to headings for corporate bodies are quite similar to those of Lubetzky's code, except that the language "best adapted to the needs of the users of the catalogue" is to be used if there are official names in several languages (9.42) and for the names of "states and other territorial authorities" (9.44). The concept of "subordinate function" is presented as a criterion for indirect entry (9.61) and the rule on subordinate units of government (9.62) is presented as a subdivision of a general rule on subordination.

The basic provisions of the Paris Principles formed the framework for the preparation of AACR 1, but one significant departure from the Paris Principles was incorporated in the North American text as a result of the "economic circumstances obtaining in many American research libraries" (AACR 1, p. 141). This departure provides for exempting local churches and "certain other corporate bodies," including educational institutions, libraries, galleries, and five other named types from the rule calling for entry of corporate bodies under their names in favor of the earlier practice, which prescribed entry under the name of the place in which the body is located (98-99). The effect of "economic circumstances" may also be seen in the adoption by the Library of Congress of the policy known as "superimposition," whereby the new rules have been applied only to newly established corporate bodies and the headings for corporate bodies already represented in the catalog normally have not been changed, whether or not the heading agrees with the provisions of AACR 1.

AACR 1 specifies that subordinate bodies are to be entered directly under their own names unless the name implies subordination and makes an attempt to clarify "implies subordination" by identifying six types of name (69-70). For government bodies, AACR 1 echoes CCR in providing that agencies exercising the basic legislative, judicial, and executive functions are entered as subheadings under the heading for the government and that other bodies "created and controlled by the government" are to be entered if possible under their own names. It is suggested that because of varying definitions of the executive functions of government, the rule is most effectively framed in terms of a negative definition and six types of bodies with some kind of relationship to government are identified for which the heading will be constructed according to the rules for corporate bodies generally, without regard to their relation to government.

Verona's major proposals relating to form and structure of corporate headings call for using the form "most frequently occurring on the corporate body's publications . . . in the language normally used by the corporate body," with conventional names and modified forms avoided. Successive names are to be used in the instance of change of name and place names are to be added as an identifying characteristic "whenever possible and suitable." Names of territorial authorities are to be recorded in their original linguistic form, in accordance with the recommendation of the International Meeting of Cataloguing Experts of 1969. She suggests direct entry for subordinate bodies even when their names imply subordination or are grammatically linked to the name of the parent body, with indirect headings being restricted to "subordinate units whose name consists merely of a generic term such as secretariat, library, archives, etc., or whose name is so general that it might be used for a subordinate unit of any type of corporate body." Organs of states and other territorial authorities are to be treated as are all other corporate bodies, with preference for entry directly under the name of the organ and with the name of the territorial authority added as an identifying characteristic where necessary and suitable [e.g., "Geological Survey (United States)"] (Verona, 1975, pp. 156–157).

AACR 2 follows the prescriptions of Lubetzky's CCR and the Paris Principles in accepting the basic concept of preference for entry under the name of the corporate body and gives greater prominence to the concept of the "predominant" form of the name than AACR 1. It also permits fewer modifications of and omissions from the name than AACR 1. With regard to subordinate bodies, a general rule specifies five types of names requiring entry under the name of the larger body. These are quite comparable to the six types identified in AACR 1. For government agencies, the decision on direct entry or entry under jurisdiction is no longer based on the general criterion of "legislative, judicial, and executive functions"; instead a general rule is presented calling for entry directly under the name of the agency unless it begins to one of 10 types, of which 3 are based on the nature of the name and 7 are based on function (including legislative, judicial and executive). Form subheadings for legal and liturgical materials are no longer to be used, following the practices of Lubetzky's code and the Paris Principles.

D. Choice of Main Entry

Cataloguing codes vary in the degree to which they present, at a single point, the alternatives for choice of the main entry, with indication of relative priority. The most succinct statement of recent years is Lubetzky's:

A work produced by, or issued in the name of, a person or a corporate body is entered under the name of that person or corporate body; a work of multiple authorship is entered under the person or body represented as chiefly responsible for it; a work of complex, changing, doubtful, or unknown authorship is entered under title (Lubetzky, 1960, p. xii).

AACR 1 indicates that

Choice of entry has been treated as a problem of determination of authorship responsibility. Hence the general rules of entry are framed around an analysis of the various patterns in which this responsibility may be distributed between persons, between corporate bodies, and between persons *and* corporate bodies (p. 5).

and provides a set of general principles prescribing (1) entry under author or principal author "when one can be determined," (2) entry under editor or compiler in the absence of an author or principal author, and (3) entry under title in the case of "other works whose authorship is diffuse, indeterminate, or unknown" (AACR 1, pp. 9–10).

AACR 2 presents no explicit list of choices and priorities, but the rules themselves and the accompanying examples suggest the following implicit statement of practice:

The main entry for a work other than a sound recording, film or videorecording is made under the name of a person (or a surrogate thereof), under the name of a corporate body or under the title of the work, according to the following rules, in order of priority:

1. A work emanating* from a corporate body and exemplifying one or more of a group of specified categories of publications is entered under the name of the corporate body.
2. A work emanating from a corporate body, not exemplifying this group of publications, and a work not emanating from a corporate body is entered under the name of the sole or principal personal author if one can be assumed or determined.
3. A work of undetermined principal authorship with no more than

---

*A work is considered to have emanated from a corporate body if it has been "issued by that body *or* . . . caused to be issued by that body *or* if it originated with that body" (21.1B2).

three authors named on the chief source of information is entered under the name of the first author.
4. All other works are entered under title, including:
   a. Works of unknown or diffuse responsibility,
   b. Collections and works produced under editorial direction,
   c. Works accepted as sacred scripture by a religious group.

The rules for entry of films and recordings follow the same general principles, with the addition of provision for entry under principal or first-named performer (including a group) for an item containing the works of more than one author or composer.*

E. Access Points

The term "access point" has been introduced in AACR 2 to replace in part the earlier term "entry." It is used to refer to any "name, term, code, etc., under which a bibliographic record may be searched and identified" (Glossary). In general, AACR 2 is more liberal than AACR 1 in suggesting added entries as access points and provides for an added entry in many cases in which a cross reference would have been made under earlier practice.

*As indicated, this statement is based on the rules and the examples, taken together. As noted in the General Introduction,

> The examples used throughout these rules are illustrative and not prescriptive. That is, they are intended to illuminate the provisions of the rule to which they are attached, rather than to extend those provisions. Neither the examples nor the form in which they are presented should be taken as instructions unless the accompanying text specifically states that they should (0.14).

There are occasions, however, in which the cataloguer must consider the practice suggested in an example as prescriptive, such as the case of a work that asserts personal authorship and also qualifies for main entry under a corporate body. The rules provide no directions for choice of main entry for such a work, but an example ("A room-to-room guide to the National Gallery/by Michael Levey") (21.4B) provides entry under corporate body. Because the rule for corporate main entry follows that for personal main entry, it follows that there is no priority inherent in the earlier appearance of a rule. Further, the code itself provides no guidelines for choosing between conflicting rules. The Library of Congress has commented obliquely on this question: "We do not follow the order implied by rule 22.16's coming before rule 22.18" (Library of Congress, 1979c, p. 9).

F. Description

The rules for description are presented in Part I of AACR 2, reflecting the asserted sequence of operations "in most present-day libraries and bibliographic agencies," in which a description of the item is prepared before the determination of access points.* The rules are based on the uniform framework of the *ISBD(G): General International Standard Bibliographic Description,* developed by the International Federation of Library Associations and Institutions in response to a request from the Joint Steering Committee. The major changes from AACR 1 are:

1. Greater attention to the description of nonbook materials and their integration in a general framework for the description of all library materials [ISBD(G)].
2. The introduction of prescribed punctuation intended to signal the introduction or conclusion of a particular element of the description.
3. An insistence that "the description of a physical item should be based in the first instance on the chapter dealing with the class of materials to which that item belongs" (0.24). The most notable example of this principle is that which emphasizes the microform characteristics of a printed monograph rather than those relating to the original publication as the basis of the primary description of the item.
4. The optional provision, following the title proper, of a term ("general material designation") to identify the medium of publication, e.g., "map," "graphic," "microform." Two lists of these terms are provided, one for use by British agencies and one for use by North American agencies.
5. The provision, obviously as an option, of three "levels" of description, with the direction to "base the choice of a level of description on the purpose of the catalogue or catalogues for which the entry is constructed" (1.0D).
6. The requirement, in most instances, of the inclusion of a statement of responsibility in the description (AACR 1 mandates the

---

*Of the codes in the Anglo-American tradition considered here, the only other one to present the rules in this sequence has been that of Jewett, for reasons that may be related to technological considerations, as discussed later in this article.

omission of a statement of responsibility when the form of name in the statement is the same as that in the heading and in several other instances).*

III. ASSUMPTIONS—TENETS—ATTITUDES

An assessment of a catalogue code must consider not only its content, as reflected in decisions and rules on substantive matters relating to authorship, main entry, access points, and description, but also its underlying assumptions, tenets, and attitudes, explicit or implicit. These are discussed here under the following headings:

1. Explicit statement of principles
2. Recognition of user needs
3. Provision of options
4. Direct and collocative functions

A. Explicit Statement of Principles

The long-standing influence of Cutter's definition of the objects of a dictionary catalog:

1. To enable a person to find a book of which either
   - A. the author
   - B. the title   is known
   - C. the subject
2. To show what the library has
   - D. by a given author
   - E. on a given subject
   - F. in a given kind of literature
3. To assist in the choice of a book
   - G. as to its edition (bibliographically)
   - H. as to its character (literary or topical) (Cutter, 1904, p. 12)

may be seen in the adoption of quite similar statements in the Paris

---

*For example, the AACR 2 description of an item presented as an edition of Charles Dickens's *Bleak House* will include a statement of responsibility ("/Charles Dickens") which would not have been included in a description based on AACR 1 rules.

Principles (2.1 and 2.2). However, most codes have not included an explicit statement of principles and an IFLA working group of the mid-1950s found that "most of the catalogue codes in current use are not based on any clearly defined principles, and the attempt to deduce such principles from them is rendered difficult by their internal inconsistencies" (IFLA Working Group on the Co-ordination of Cataloguing Principles, 1956, p. 290). Lubetzky demonstrated this shortcoming in relation to Anglo-American codes in his *Cataloging Rules and Principles* of 1953 and presented in the introduction to his *Code of Cataloging Rules* of 1960 a clear statement of "the objectives which the catalog is to serve, the method by which these objectives are to be achieved, the basic aspects of the problem of cataloging, and the general principles which underlie the rules" (p. ix).

AACR 1 and 2 are, in turn, progressively less explicit than the CCR in identifying the principles on which they are based. The AACR 1 states that its underlying principles are based on the Paris Principles, with certain specified major departures, and presents brief statements of the general principles that underlie the rules for entry (pp. 9–10) and the rules for description (pp. 189–190). AACR 2 is limited to references to other sources. The authors assert that it is in even closer conformity with the Paris Principles than AACR 1 and note that the rules in Part I, Description, are based on the general framework of the General International Standard Bibliographic Description. There is, however, no statement of general principles related to the choice of entry or access points.

B. Recognition of User Needs

It is frequently asserted that the excellence and utility of a catalogue code will be increased in the degree that the author(s) take account of the "approach" and "needs" of the (nonprofessional) user of the catalogue, and of the amount of information brought to the catalogue by that user, in the formulation of the rules and principles of the code. This point of view is traditionally traced to Cutter, specifically to his admonition that "the convenience of the public is always to be set before the ease of the cataloguer" and his assertion that

> Strict consistency in a rule and uniformity in its application sometimes lead to practices which clash with the public's habitual way of looking at things. When these

habits are general and deeply rooted, it is unwise for the cataloguer to ignore them, even if they demand a sacrifice of system and simplicity (Cutter, 1904, p. 6).

These statements of Cutter are quoted in the preface of AA in defense of its provision of exceptions and alternatives and with the hope that the rules for societies and institutions, "while open to the charge of inconsistency . . . will serve to bring the vast majority of these bodies under the heading where they are most likely to be looked for in English and American libraries" (p. ix). They are repeated in ALA as justification for "exceptions or qualifications . . . prescribed when too strict an application of a general rule would result in a heading not giving the most direct approach" (p. xx). In recent years, such practices have been canonized by Ranganathan in the "Canon of Sought— Heading or Canon of Relevance":

> The decision whether an entry
>   with a particular type of heading, or
>   with a particular choice for that heading, or
>   with a particular rendering of that choice, or
>   with a particular added entry arising out of it,
> should be based on the answer to the question: "Is reader or library staff likely to look for a book under the particular type or choice of rendering of heading?" (Ranganathan, 1955, p. 63).

The term "sought heading" is increasingly used, particularly by British writers, in the sense of "the heading that most catalogue users will consult for a particular entry" (Gorman), 1977 p. 594). Preference for sought headings may be seen in AACR 2 in its provisions for use of title-page forms of names, for the use of multiple pseudonyms used by a single author, and in the provision for main entry under performer.*

Deference to the supposed, albeit unidentified, needs of users may

---

*The Library of Congress has observed that:

> Another benefit expected to follow adoption of AACR 2 concerns the user's retrieval of bibliographic information. AACR 2 has been formulated to provide headings that are more often in conformity with names as they appear in works and citations than is now the case, thereby reducing the time that users lose when they encounter cross-references rather than the catalog entries they seek. The increased convenience and time savings of accessing a data base that produces a greater number of sought headings is an advantage compounded by the total use of the catalog (Library of Congress, 1978, p. 652).

also be seen in the provision for making an added entry "under the heading for a person or corporate body or under a title if *some catalogue users might suppose* that the description of an item would be found under that heading or title rather than under the heading or title chosen for the main entry" (21.29B, italics added), repeating a provision of AACR 1 in essentially the same words.

Other writers have been less inclined to emphasize the user's point of view. In commenting on Cutter's views, Minto asserted that "the 'public's habitual way of looking at things' is by no means a constant way and is liable to change" and pointed out that in the preparation of the Anglo-American code of 1908 the American committee sought to follow Cutter by seeking to determine the heading where a work is "most likely to be looked for" and the British committee were "more in favour of adopting a consistent principle and abiding thereby" (Minto, 1909, pp. 296–297).

Pettee, commenting on code revision in the 1930s, predicted that:

> The form of name . . . will be determined by the best international or English usage, and will not be some guess at the catchword form which the reader would naturally expect. Thomas Hyde's principle, that the consistency of the catalog should take precedence over the convenience of the reader in looking for a particular book, is a sound doctrine. The "ease of the cataloguer" is not in question. This serves the "ease of the reader" best in the long run (Pettee, 1936, p. 288).

More recently, Tait, commenting on the rules for institutions in the 1908 code, finds it ironic that

> These special rules and exceptions . . . introduced into the code in deference to Cutter's convenience of the public principle . . . merely make our catalogues more involved and difficult to follow by the persons we are allegedly trying to help (Tait, 1969, p. 71).

C. Provision of Options

From Jewett to Ranganathan, the production of identical—or at least comparable—records for a given item by all cataloguers handling the item has been seen as one of the desirable, if not essential, results of a catalogue code.

> It should be remembered that a principal objective of the rules is to secure *uniformity;* and that, consequently, some rules which may seem unnecessarily burdensome,

and, in certain applications, even capricious, are all things considered, the best; because they secure that uniformity, which is not otherwise possible of attainment, and without which, the catalogues could not be comprehended in a general system (Jewett, 1853, pp. 18–19).

Whoever the cataloguer, the catalogue should be the same (Ranganathan, 1959, p. 14).

Uniformity of practice depends on two variables: (1) the degree to which a single solution for a problem is presented (i.e., Are options presented? To what extent is the cataloguer to exercise judgment?), and (2) the clarity of the rules (Are varying interpretations possible?). For Jewett, the answers to the first questions are simple:

> The rules for cataloguing must be stringent, and should meet, as far as possible, all difficulties of detail. Nothing, so far as can be avoided, should be left to the individual taste or judgment of the cataloguer. He should be a man of sufficient learning, accuracy and fidelity, to apply the rules (Jewett, 1853, p. 8).

Echoes of Jewett may be found in Gorman:

> The license to make . . . modifications can lead to lack of standardisation and to the petty local variations which are unacceptable financially, cooperatively, and bibliographically (Gorman, 1977, pp. 590–591).

and in Domanovszky:

> Statements or rules concerning main entries should not contain the "in case of doubt" clause; they should be drawn up in a clear and definite manner excluding even the possibility of a doubt worth mentioning. The cogency of this precept increases, naturally, in proportion to the importance and to the degree of generality of the matter dealt with by the statement or rule (Domanovszky, 1975, p. 125).

The authors of AACR 2, however, have chosen to provide a number of alternatives and options, asserting that "different solutions to a problem and differing levels of detail and specificity are appropriate in different contexts" (p. 2). These alternatives and options are of two kinds—those which "should be decided as a matter of cataloguing policy for a particular catalogue or bibliography agency and . . . exercised either always or never," and those which "should be exercised case by case" (p. 3). They also assert "the necessity for judgment and interpretation by the cataloguer . . . based on the requirements of a particular catalogue or upon the use of the items being catalogued" and "recognition of the fact that uniform legislation for all types and sizes of catalogues is neither possible nor desirable" (p. 3).

A final judgment of the clarity of the rules can only be made after an extended period of application by cataloguers in a variety of library environments. In the meantime, the first public discussion of the provisions of AACR 2 (the International Conference on AACR 2, held at Florida State University, Tallahassee, Florida, March 11-14, 1979) was noteworthy for the frequency of admonitions that there is need to "observe the intent of the rules" and that national bibliographic agencies must "interpret the rules" and "issue clarifying examples." Varying interpretations have been presented for the rules relating to: (1) the form of heading for certain government agencies: direct under their own name or as subordinate to the government; (2) the form of heading for a government agency with a name likely to be used in another government; (3) the headings for successive governments with the same name; (4) the headings for authors using more than one form of name in their works and for (5) the meaning of the phrase "collective thought" in relation to works emanating from corporate bodies.*

---

*These interpretations derive primarily from Hagler's detailed comparison of the two editions and from statements from the Library of Congress regarding their plans for implementation. The sources for the varying interpretations are presented below:

1. In commenting on the rule for government agencies entered subordinately (24.18), which prescribes 10 types of agencies that are to be entered subordinately, Hagler states:

> Type 1 and Type 2 offer the inevitable problem of interpreting their scope, since it will never be possible to draw up a satisfactory list of words . . . which automatically provide the "clue" to organizational incorporation or subordination . . . It is reasonable to assume that only national bibliographic agencies can accept responsibility for making such interpretations, for agencies within their own countries (Hagler, 1979, p. 98).

2. With regard to the problem of the government body with a name likely to be used by a comparable body of another government (e.g., Council on International Economic Policy) Hagler notes that two examples show "that the intent of AACR 2 is to *restrict* as much as possible the entry of agencies under the name of a government" (Hagler, 1979, p. 99).

3. Hagler has suggested that the rule relating to differentiation of governments with the same name (24.6A) is intended to cover only governments "*simultaneously* identified by the same name," although the wording of the rule includes no such limita-

D. Direct and Collocative Functions

From Cutter to AACR 2, authors and originators of catalogue codes have recognized, implicitly or explicitly, two objectives, best expressed by Lubetzky:

> to enable the user of the catalog to determine readily whether or not the library has the book he wants
> to reveal to the user of the catalog, under one form of the author's name, what works the library has by a given author and what editions or translations of a given work (Lubetzky, CRP, p. 36).

As many writers have pointed out, there may be an inherent conflict between these two functions, frequently labeled "direct" and "collocative," respectively, for any item being catalogued. The conflict arises from the fact that entries or headings designed to enable the user to locate readily and directly the record for a particular "book" may not be the entries or headings best suited to collocating or assembling all of the intellectual productions ("works") of a single author or all of the editions of a given work, because rules designed to achieve the first objective concentrate on the physical object and, more particularly, the title page, and rules designed to achieve the second objective concentrate on the intellectual content of the document, without regard to the phrasing of a particular title page. Problems arise because of varying identifications of an author and varying identifications of a work. Two

---

tion (Hagler, 1979, p. 96). This interpretation has been reinforced by a statement from the Library of Congress (1979c, p. 18).

4. The Library of Congress, in discussing the question of whether the heading for an author who produces works under more than one name should be the name by which the author is commonly identified, the author's real name, or multiple headings representing the author's various names, suggests that "an author who uses more than one name and is not predominantly known by any one name will be represented in the catalog under multiple headings" (Library of Congress, 1978, p. 648), whereas the rules as written call for multiple headings only in the case of "a person using pseudonyms . . . [and] not known predominantly by one name" (22.2C3).

5. Tucker notes that the term "collective thought" used in determining entry for works emanating from corporate bodies is subject to a wide range of interpretation, with some catalogers likely to view it as a very restrictive concept and others likely to view it much more loosely (Tucker, 1980, p. 199).

classic examples will illustrate the two sources of the conflict. The mathematical works of Charles Lutwidge Dodgson have generally been issued under his real name and his literary works under his pen name, Lewis Carroll. Are all of his works to be assembled at one point in the catalogue or are the mathematical works to be entered under Dodgson and the literary works under Carroll?

The second example relates to the individual works of an author and presents the case of a work by Emerson, now best known under the title "American Scholar" but originally published under the title "An Oration Delivered before the Phi Beta Kappa Society." Are these to be assembled at one point under the heading for Emerson or treated as two different titles under Emerson? The choice between the two objectives, when they are in conflict, has been expressed as a choice between favoring the "bibliographic unit" (i.e., the physical object) or the "literary unit" (i.e., the intellectual content). Verona (1963) has presented the case for the bibliographic unit and Lubetzky (1963) the case for the literary unit.

Catalogue codes vary in their degree of explicit recognition of the conflict between the two objectives and statement of preferred unit. ALA states that "the finding list function of the catalog is extended beyond what is required for location of a single book to the location of literary units" (p. xx), with footnote reference to Pettee's classic statement that "The book in hand is considered not as a single item but as a representative of a literary unit" (Pettee, 1936, p. 270). CCR presents the two methods and prescribes preference for the literary unit as being

> consistent with the essential purpose of a publication, which is to present a certain work and with the essential interest of the users of a publication, which is in the work presented by the publication. It is also a method calculated to produce a catalog which is systematic in structure and efficient in use (p. xi).

Rule 7 of CCR mandates the use of a single uniform title to assemble, under the name of an author, editions of a single work with varying titles. Neither the Paris Principles nor AACR 1 addresses the question directly but the general preference for title-page information in the latter would seem to indicate an implicit preference for the bibliographic unit. AACR 2 again does not address the problem directly and limits more sharply than AACR 1 the use of outside sources of bibliographic information. Further implicit evidence suggesting that the bibliographic unit is predominant in AACR 2 may be seen in the fact that the use of uniform titles is presented only as an option. ["Although the rules . . . are stated as instructions, apply them according to the policy of the cataloguing agency." (25.1)] Explicit favoring of the finding list function of the catalog is found in provision for use of multiple pseudonyms used by an author, if none predominates, instead of selecting one of these or the real name as a uniform heading for an author (22.2C3). AACR 2 attemps to maintain the distinction between "book" and "work," using the term "item" ("a document or set of documents in any physical form, published, issued, or treated as an entity, and as such forming the basis for a single bibliographic description") (p. 567) in Part I, Description, and the term "work" (not defined) in Part II ("The rules in Part II apply to works and not generally to physical manifestations of those works") (20.1).*

IV. EXTERNAL INFLUENCES

A. The Influence of Technology

The preface of AACR 2 identifies "particular attention to developments in the machine processing of bibliographic records" as one of the guidelines governing the revision of AACR 1 from the beginning of the project, but Gorman finds "a number of questions posed by automation that remain unanswered by AACR 2" because "all the returns are not yet in on bibliographic records in machine systems" and "AACR 2 could not take the effects of library automation fully into account because those effects have yet to be completely assessed and understood" (Gorman, 1978, p. 210). This position is echoed in the General Introduction of AACR 2, which, in discussing the possibility of presenting the rules in the framework of "alternative headings" instead of "main and added entries," indicates that the former was not embodied in the rules "largely because of the lack of time to explore the considerable implications of such a change" (0.5). In contrast, Malin-

---

*Domanovszky (1975, pp. 94–97) provides a trenchant analysis of the problems deriving from the failure of codes to maintain a clear distinction between the two concepts.

conico (1980) has argued that there is little causal relation between technology and cataloguing principles:

> There is, of course, a very pronounced correlation between technology and the form and effectiveness of a library catalog, and technology can either assist or hinder a transition from one set of principles to another, but, technological advances have not had, and cannot have, any influence on the principles on which bibliographic control is based. We can, of course, modify our basic objectives to articulate more smoothly with facilities made possible by advanced technologies, but this is better characterized as capitulation rather than progress in harmony with a new ambience.

> The objectives of bibliographic control, and the functions to be served by a library catalog exist independently of the medium chosen to achieve those objectives (pp. 25–26).

> The effects of automation on bibliographic control will be made evident in the formats for machine representation of bibliographic data, and the nature of the systems implemented to manipulate those data; not in the codes developed to record and control bibliographic data. Computers will simply make it easier to accomodate principles that can only be developed in isolaton from them; they cannot create new principles . . . The bibliographic principles articulated by Cutter and refined by Lubetzky . . . exist independently of any technology, hence, cannot be modified by changes in technology (p. 27).

However, influences of computer technology are unmistakable in AACR 2, most notably perhaps in the emphasis on construction of a self-sufficient description of the physical object, including a statement of responsibility (Gorman, 1978; Malinconico, 1980).* Malinconico has also found examples of attempts to structure headings in such a way as to permit easier manipulation by computers, with less than completely satisfactory results (1980, pp. 32–35).

*Tait (1969, p. 32) has suggested that Jewett insisted on the repetition of the author's name in the title transcript because of technological considerations related to the stereotyping medium in which he was working rather than for bibliographic completeness. The modern parallel is striking—machine-based systems work more easily with descriptions that are complete in themselves and do not require the addition of the heading to indicate authorship or responsibility.

Tait has also asserted that the disagreement between American and British practice on change of name in the 1908 code was influenced by technology:

> The British, with their eyes on the needs of the printed book catalogue, were naturally in favour of the earliest form of name; while the Americans, exploring the greater flexibility of the card catalogue, were more generally in favour of the later or more current forms (Tait, 1969, pp. 48–49).

B. International Agreement

> One of the dreams which have long inspired librarians concerns the desirability of reaching agreement on a set of cataloguing rules which would enable catalogue entries to be universally understood and accepted and used together in our library catalogues and in bibliographical work. What was once a dream is becoming in the modern world, with its ever-growing stream of publications, its ever-increasing libraries, its ever-larger number of institutions devoted to the dissemination of literature and documentation, a matter of urgent practical importance (Francis, 1963, p. 17).

So Sir Frank Francis viewed the question of securing international agreement on cataloguing principles in 1961, a recurring question since publication of the Anglo-American code of 1908 (Chaplin, 1956).

If catalogue entries are to be "universally understood," agreement is necessary on: (1) rules of description; (2) the concept of "authorship" and the extent to which it is to be applied in the determination of access points, including main entry; and (3) the form of heading for personal and corporate names. With regard to the first, the present decade has seen agreement on general principles of description and their application to several bibliographic forms and media, including monographs and serials. On the score of authorship, AACR 2 has moved closer to the Paris Principles in deleting editors and compilers from the ranks of authors. It remains to be seen whether the extension of authorship to performers will be accepted by other countries. Elimination of the word "author" in rules related to works issued by corporate bodies has brought AACR 2 closer to the German tradition. Moreover, AACR 2 has moved closer to the Paris Principles by eliminating the exceptions to the rules that have resulted in entry under place rather than name for a large group of corporate bodies (exceptions found in the North American text only), but the basic problem remains as to whether names of corporate bodies, particularly those of territorial authorities, are to be presented in the language "best suited to the needs of the users of the catalogue" or in the original language.

V. THE FUTURE OF AACR 2

A. The Bibliographic Milieu

Any consideration of the future of AACR 2 must begin with a description of the present bibliographic milieu, that is, the present status of files of bibliographic records, in libraries. The present account is necessarily a very brief one, limited to American libraries.*

The basic medium for displaying the bibliographic records maintained by American libraries remains the card catalog, usually in dictionary form. The records in the catalog usually have been prepared under a number of codes and reflect varying, sometimes contradictory, principles of choice of main entry and choice and form of headings. The records have been influenced by administrative considerations, the most notable being the Library of Congress decision in 1967, followed by most libraries, to adopt the policy of "superimposition." The records are unit records, in the sense that the same physical description of a given item is presented at each access point. This single physical file, including in many research libraries considerably more than one million cards, is increasingly viewed as an expensive, cumbersome device, which should be replaced as soon as possible by some less expensive, more manageable device, preferably in an automated mode.

An ever-increasing number of libraries have created and/or maintain a second file which generally consists of a subset of the file represented by the card catalog. The second file is limited to bibliographic records in machine-readable form. These records normally include a higher proportion of recent imprints than the total file and are more likely to have been prepared in accordance with the principles of a single code (the North American text of AACR 1) but they also reflect the policy of superimposition. They are likely to have originated as unit records, but they may now exist in a different format, that of the "index register," in which a major file provides complete bibliographic information relating to an item, with a number of indexes (e.g., author, title, subject, series) appended to it in which less complete information about the item is provided.† The machine-readable file may be available for consultation in an on-line mode or it may exist only in an archival status with limited general availability. In both of these files—the card catalog and the machine-readable file—a considerable percentage of headings represent forms which conflict with those prescribed by AACR 2 [e.g.,

---

*Of the many influences presently operating to cause substantial changes in the bibliographic milieu, particularly of research libraries, only those directly created by or related to AACR 2 are considered here.

†The major file may be arranged either in order of cataloguing, a form suggested by the Library of Congress for the *National Union Catalog,* or in order of classification symbol, as at the University of Toronto (Blackburn, 1978), thereby providing a subject access additional to that traditionally provided by alphabetical subject headings.

"American Federation of Labor and Congress of Industrial Organizations" (AACR 1) and "AFL-CIO" (AACR 2)].*

The influence of the Library of Congress (LC) on the individual library is quite strong, both in matters relating to the record for a given item, with libraries increasingly reluctant to review individual LC records, and in matters of the broadest import relating to the form and structure of the bibliographic file, with libraries increasingly dependent on computer-based networks utilizing standardized formats and procedures. The available technology presents a wide variety of media for displaying the bibliographic record, from the traditional card catalog through the book catalog and computer output microfilm to terminals at which the file may be consulted on-line.

This, then, is the environment into which AACR 2 is to be introduced in January 1981. From that date, the four major national cataloguing agencies of the Anglo-American world—the British Library, the Library of Congress, the National Library of Australia, and the National Library of Canada—will apply the code to newly catalogued items and will publish their interpretations of the rules.† The Library of Congress has announced a policy of "gradual adoption" of the code, under which certain existing headings that are not in agreement with AACR 2, but that are judged to be "compatible" with AACR 2 headings, are to continue to be used unchanged.‡ The British Library has stated that

---

*In its first review of the changes necessitated by the implementation of AACR 2, the Library of Congress reported that changes would be required in 37% of the headings and 49% of the records in the MARC data base. A later report provided revised figures of 17 and 22%, respectively, resulting from the adoption of certain options and decisions not to adopt three changes suggested by examples in AACR 2: "Department" for "Dept.," "House of Representatives" for "House," and "United Kingdom" for "Great Britain."

†The first such statement from the Library of Congress (Library of Congress, 1979c) consists of 18 pages devoted primarily to the rules for form of heading, including geographic names. The editorial schedule for this article has precluded consideration of any later statements from the Library.

‡Examples and further details of the Library's early decisions are provided in Simonton (1979). The most recent announcement from the Library reveals that it has "now concluded that 'House' may be regarded as the conventional name for the 'House of Representatives' and that our current heading is consequently in accord with AACR 2, not merely compatible." The Library has also found that "there is at least some evidence for calling 'Great Britain' the conventional name for the 'United Kingdom of Great Britain and Northern Ireland'," with the result that this heading is also judged to be in accord with AACR 2 (Library of Congress, 1979b, p. 5).

AACR 2: Antecedents, Assumptions, Implementation   31

it will adopt the new code with no modifications (Downing, 1980, p. 220), and the National Library of Canada has announced only one exception to AACR 2 rules for personal name headings [relating to the relative placement of forenames and titles of honor and address (National Library of Canada, 1979, p. 13)].

B. Implementation and Influence of the Code

The dissemination by the four national cataloguing agencies of records with headings that may conflict with headings in existing card catalogues will require libraries to make decisions relating to the bibliographic records and the medium in which they are displayed.* If a library wishes to continue its existing card catalogue, it must either

1. Review each item received and change any existing or new heading for which there is a conflict (this policy will be necessary if the traditional practice of assembling the works with which a single person or corporate body is associated at a single point in the catalogue is to be maintained), or
2. Review each item, file old and new forms of a heading separately if there is a conflict and link the forms by a reference, or
3. File new records without review, accepting the resulting dispersal of entries for a single person or corporate body with no attempt to relate them to one another.

The difficulty of accepting any of these alternatives has led most libraries to consider seriously the option of introducing a new catalogue, probably in a new form, most likely on-line. If this option is adopted, the following questions must be addressed:

*It should be noted that many of the changes occurring after January 1981 will be caused by the abandonment at that time by the Library of Congress of the policy of superimposition, rather than by changes from AACR 1 to AACR 2. For example, the first list of "revised headings for 1981" issued by the Library of Congress includes several examples of entries given as examples in AACR 1 that were not adopted by the library because of the superimposition policy, including "Homer," "Stendhal," and "Wodehouse, P. G." (Library of Congress, 1979d). It should also be noted that only conflicts in the form of a heading will require action. For many monographic works there will be a difference in the choice of main entry under the two codes (e.g., title rather than corporate body) that can be assimilated without any necessary action on the part of the library.

1. Is the old catalogue to be "frozen" (sealed as is, with no provision for making changes to the records) or "closed" (necessary changes made to the records, but no new items added)?
2. If the catalogue is closed, will it be on the basis of date of imprint or date of cataloguing? (If it is frozen, only the option of date of cataloguing exists.)
3. How are serials to be handled?*
4. Should the "index register" format, with varying detail of bibliographic description at different access points, be adopted?
5. To what extent should varying entries in the two catalogs (e.g., "AFL-CIO" and "American Federation of Labor and Congress of Industrial Organizations") be linked?†

In view of the complexity of the milieu, it is tempting merely to repeat the view of a greater authority, writing in a less complicated time, and assert that "It would be a gratuitous presumption to attempt to prognosticate the effect of these rules on our cataloguing practice" (Sayers, 1909, p. 472); a few words will nonetheless be attempted on three topics of major importance: principles of authorship in AACR 2, options in AACR 2, and the likelihood of international agreement.

It is difficult to predict the extent to which AACR 2's lack of a general theory of authorship will affect cataloguing practice and the implementation of the code. With the abandonment of the concept of corporate authorship, the cataloguer can now use "authorship" only to refer to works for which the main entry is to be made under the name of a person. The rule prescribing the conditions under which main entry is to be made under the name of a corporate body now consists of specifying certain kinds of works as the basis of the decision rather than the conditions of creation of the document. Gorman has asserted that the new code, in rejecting "the nebulous notion of corporate authorship,"

---

*The question of the handling of serials is a complex one that has not been considered here because of lack of space. A great percentage of serials will have a different main entry under AACR 2 (there will be many changes from entry under corporate body to title main entry) and it is difficult to conceive of leaving entries for current serials in a "closed" catalog.

†The Library of Congress has presented the latest statement of its plans for freezing its catalogs in January 1981 (Library of Congress, 1980). The major source of information on plans of other libraries is the *Alternative Cataloging Newsletter,* published by the Milton S. Eisenhower Library of Johns Hopkins University.

has identified "the instances in which corporate main entry is useful and the instances in which it is not, free from the restraint of an untenable theory" (Gorman, 1978, p. 219). He has not defined "useful," however, and the student of codes may find AACR 2 difficult to understand and explain because of the variation between conditions of authorship and categories of publication as criteria for determining main entry. Will the practitioner find the code easier to use? Not, certainly, when seeking guidance in determining the main entry for a work of personal authorship that also qualifies as one of the kinds of publications that are to be entered under the name of a corporate body. Only by example does the code give guidance on this question. It is also difficult to predict the effect of the increase in number of works with main entry under title rather than under corporate body on single-entry bibliographies and on bibliographic citation practice.* The lack of a clear statement of preference between the direct and the collocative function and the prescription of uniform titles only as an option will probably result in a tendency toward emphasizing the direct, with a resulting weakening of the collocative ability of the catalogue unless the policies of the national cataloguing agencies favor liberal provision of uniform titles.

In considering AACR 2's provision of options, Sayers's words may again be judged appropriate: "[The inclusion of certain alternative rules] enhances the work as a book of reference, but makes its application a matter of much discretion" (Sayers, 1909, p. 469). Peter Lewis, Chairman of the Joint Steering Committee for Revision of AACR, has noted the elimination of certain "authorised divergence of practice, enshrined in the existence of two texts" (i.e., the North American and British versions of AACR 1) as a positive result of AACR 2. He has also asserted that "the exercise of options and divergences from the standards are luxuries that no one can now afford" (Lewis, 1978, p. 3). However, AACR 2 does present many options and already it is necessary to consult a number of supplementary sources to determine present practice in the application of the rules. To date, the only major

---

*One effect of this change has already been seen in the realization that many series added entries will now consist solely of the title proper, even for generic titles, such as "technical report." Recognition of the need to individualize such titles has led to the joint proposal of the Library of Congress and the National Library of Canada for a rule interpretation providing for a "unique serial identifier" (Library of Congress, 1979a).

disagreement on options among the four national cataloguing agencies reported in the literature relates to a rule for romanization, on which the British Library has taken an initial, "not yet finalised" position which is in conflict with that of the other three agencies (British Library, 1979). The British Library will also evidently be less generous than the Library of Congress in adding to a place name entry the name of a larger place name, preferring to do so only when the place name "is so obscure that the addition of the larger geographic place name is needed for purposes of identification" (British Library, 1979, p. 6), whereas the Library of Congress will add the larger place name to all cities and towns and to certain other place names (Library of Congress, 1979c, p. 15). The degree of agreement among the four agencies on January 1, 1981 will obviously be great but perhaps not complete.* If any of the four agencies applies any of the options relating to choice or form of heading on a "case by case" basis, an even greater body of "case law" will be developed. The Anglo-American cataloguing world has not yet been able to produce a code capable of being applied without benefit of a considerable body of supplementary commentary, and experience counsels that the conditions of authorship and dissemination of documents are so complex as to preclude easy answers to complex bibliographic problems. Nevertheless, it must be recognized that the complexity of the cataloguing process in an individual library inevitably will be influenced by the complexity of the necessary supplementary documentation.†

*A report from a meeting in March 1979 of the four national cataloguing agencies indicates that agreement has not yet been reached on "questions of placement of titles of nobility and terms of address preceding forenames, spaces after initials in personal names, use of unused forenames, and use of 'Dept.' vs. 'Department' in corporate names" (Library of Congress, 1979e, p. 474).

†The Library of Congress has already devoted over six pages to an explication of the principles to be followed in applying the chapter on form of corporate names to new headings established after December 31, 1980 and another two pages to headings already established or to be established before January 2, 1981 (Library of Congress, 1979c, pp. 17–24). These directions prescribe, *inter alia,* a form of heading for one political jurisdiction which is at variance with an example provided in the code, e.g., "New York (State)" rather than "New York (U.S.: State)." This variation evidently derives from the application of an option relating to place name entries. Taken together with the Library's decision that "House" (for House of Representatives) and "Great Britain" will continue to be used, contrary to forms presented in examples in the code, it illustrates dramatically the necessity of interpreting an example only in the context of

In matters relating to international agreement, as noted earlier, AACR 2 has moved closer to the German tradition on corporate authorship and to the Paris Principles with regard to form of name of corporate bodies, but substantial differences remain between the practices of AACR 2 and the recommendations of the IFLA Working Group on Corporate Headings.* It is clear that with regard to the ultimate question of the use of the original (vernacular) language or that of the user of the catalogue, when the two differ, international uniformity can only be achieved by use of the original language, as recommended by the International Meeting of Cataloguing Experts (IMCE) in 1969 and by the IFLA Working Group; however, Verona has been able to identify only five codes that follow, even in part, the IMCE recommendations (Verona, 1975, p. 64). Downing has noted that the use of the vernacular was "considered very seriously by the editors and the Joint Steering Committee" in the preparation of AACR 2 (Downing, 1979, p. 66). As Malinconico (1978) has observed

> A cataloguing code which would prove universally acceptable might be conceived which prescribes the choice of entries, but it is more difficult to imagine a single code that could prescribe universally acceptable forms of entry. For example, it hardly seems to be in the interests of a German library user to refer to his country in catalogue headings as *Germany, Allemagne, Germania,* or *Tystland;* or to refer to the same country in a catalogue in an English, French, Italian, or Danish speaking country as *Deutschland* (p. 65).

However, it is possible to conceive of "a data structure in which

---

the rule to which it is appended and of recognizing that in practice the interpretations and decisions of cataloguing agencies will be at least as influential as the explicit rules and implicit directions of the code.

*The recommendations of the working group include: (1) a preference for the form of name used on the publications of the body or in established reference sources; (2) a single rule for subordinate bodies, calling for entry under the name of the subordinate body unless the name implies subordination or is insufficient without the name of the parent body; and (3) the use of qualifiers "whenever possible and suitable." They also introduce the concept of "organ," defined, in relation to territorial authorities, as "a corporate body exercising legislative, judicial, administrative, informational, military, or diplomatic functions", and call for the entry of organs under the name of the territorial authority, as opposed to "nonorgans," which exercise "educational, scientific, technical, cultural, medical, religious, social, commercial, or industrial functions" and which are to be entered directly (IFLA Working Group on Corporate Headings, 1978).

authority files are maintained separate from but linked to bibliographic files [with the result that] an automatic translation can be effected between the related practices" (Malinconico, 1978, p. 65). This, indeed, represents an area in which technological resources can be put to effective use in implementing the new code and furthering international exchange of bibliographic records.

The major strength of AACR 2 lies in its treatment of descriptive cataloguing. The code provides directions for description of documents in all present media, in an internationally accepted framework that is consistent between the media and that promises likely accomodation of future media, organized in a manner generally superior to that of AACR 1. In addition, the authors of AACR 2 have resolved the divergences within Anglo-American cataloguing practice that existed in the two versions of AACR 1. Unfortunately, cataloguers and other users of the new code will not find a general statement of principles of authorship and entry; they must adjust to a fundamental change in theories of corporate authorship and to an increased emphasis on "sought" headings; and they must accept the necessity of consulting a substantial body of supplementary documentation relating to options and interpretations if the goal of standardization of bibliographic records is to be achieved.

REFERENCES

Alternative Cataloging Newsletter. Milton S. Eisenhower Library, Johns Hopkins University, Baltimore, Maryland.

American Library Association. Division of Cataloging and Classification (1949). "A.L.A. Cataloging Rules for Author and Title Entries," 2d ed. American Library Association, Chicago, Illinois.

"Anglo-American Cataloging Rules" (1967). American Library Association, Chicago, Illinois.

"Anglo-American Cataloguing Rules" (1978). 2d ed. American Library Association, Chicago, Illinois.

Blackburn, R. H. (1978). Two years with a closed catalog. *In* "Freezing Card Catalogs," pp. 45–64. Association of Research Libraries, Washington, D.C.

British Library (1979). AACR 2 optional additions, options and alternative rules: the British Library's position. *British Library Bibliographic Services Division Newsletter* **13**, 2–7.

"Catalog Rules: Author and Title Entries" (1908). American Library Association, Chicago, Illinois.

Chaplin, A. H. (1956). A universal cataloging code. *Library Quarterly* **26**, 337–347.

Cutter, C. A. (1904). "Rules for a Dictionary Catalog," 4th ed. U.S. Government Printing Office, Washington, D.C.
Domanovszky, A. (1975). "Functions and Objects of Author and Title Cataloguing." Verlag Dokumentation, Munich.
Downing, J. C. (1979). Anniversary and birth: AA 1908 to AACR 2. *Library Association Record* **81**, 66–67.
Downing, J. C. (1980). International implications of AACR 2. *In* International Conference on AACR 2, Florida State University, 1979. "The Making of a Code." pp. 206–225. American Library Association, Chicago, Illinois.
Francis, F. (1963). Address. *In* "Report, International Conference on Cataloguing Principles, 1961," pp. 17–21. International Federation of Library Associations, London.
Gorman, M. (1968). "A Study of the Rules for Entry and Heading in the Anglo-American Cataloguing Rules, 1967 (British text)." Library Association, London.
Gorman, M. (1977). Changes in cataloguing codes; rules for entry and heading. *Library Trends* **25**, 587–602.
Gorman, M. (1978). The *Anglo-American Cataloguing Rules*, Second Edition. *Library Resources & Technical Services* **22**, 209–226.
Hagler, R. (1979). "Where's that Rule?" Canadian Library Association, Ottawa.
IFLA Working Group on Corporate Headings (1978). [Final recommendations.] *Cataloging Service Bulletin* **2**, 30–44.
IFLA Working Group on the Co-ordination of Cataloguing Principles (1956). Report on anonyma and works of corporate authorship. *Libri* **6**, 271–298.
International Conference on Cataloguing Principles, 1961 (1976). "Statement of Principles," Annotated ed. IFLA Committee on Cataloguing, London.
"ISBD(G): General International Standard Bibliographic Description: Annotated Text" (1977). IFLA International Office for UBC, London.
Jewett, C. C. (1853). "On the Construction of Catalogues of Libraries," 2d ed. Smithsonian Institution, Washington, D.C.
Kaltwasser, F. G. (1975). The new German "Rules for Alphabetical Cataloguing (RAK)" and their position in the international framework. *IFLA Journal* **1**, 276–284.
Koel, A. (1980). The corporate complex (including choice and form of entry. *In* International Conference on AACR 2, Florida State University, 1979. "The Making of a Code." pp. 164–175. American Library Association, Chicago, Illinois.
Lewis, P. (1978). Introducing the second edition of AACR. *Catalogue & Index* No. 51, 1–4.
Library of Congress (1978). AACR 2: background and summary. *Library of Congress Information Bulletin* **37**, 640–652.
Library of Congress (1979a). Unique serial identifiers. *Cataloging Service Bulletin* **5**, 4–9.
Library of Congress (1979b). Implementation of AACR 2 at the Library of Congress. *Cataloging Service Bulletin* **6**, 5–8.
Library of Congress (1979c). Rule interpretations for AACR 2. *Cataloging Service Bulletin* **6**, 8–26.
Library of Congress (1979d). Revised headings for 1981. *Cataloging Service Bulletin* **6**, 26–40.

Library of Congress (1979e). A report on the third meeting of ABACUS. *Library of Congress Information Bulletin* **38**, 474–476.
Library of Congress. (1980). Freezing the Library of Congress catalogs. *Library of Congress Information Bulletin* **39**, 61–64.
Lubetzky, S. (1953). "Cataloging Rules and Principles." Library of Congress, Washington, D.C.
Lubetzky, S. (1960). "Code of Cataloging Rules: Author and Title Entry." American Library Association, Chicago, Illinois.
Lubetzky, S. (1963). The function of the main entry in the alphabetical catalogue—one approach. *In* "Report, International Conference on Cataloguing Principles, 1961," pp. 139–143. International Federation of Library Associations, London.
Malinconico, S. M. (1978). The coordination of bibliographic control. *In* "Towards a Common Bibliographic Exchange Format?" (Proceedings of the International Symposium on Bibliographic Exchange Formats, Taormina, Sicily, April 27–29. UNIBID, London.
Malinconico, S. M. (1980). AACR 2 and automation. *In* International Conference on AACR 2, Florida State University, 1979. "The Making of a Code." pp. 25–40. American Library Association, Chicago, Illinois.
Minto, J. (1909). The Anglo-American cataloguing rules. *Library Association Record* **11**, 289–302.
National Library of Canada (1979). Proposed policy for the implementation of AACR 2. *National Library News* Special Issue, June, 12–14. (This issue also contains NLC preliminary list of preferred AACR 2 options, pp. 15–30.)
Pettee, J. (1936). The development of authorship entry and the formulation of authorship rules as found in the Anglo-American code. *Library Quarterly* **6**, 270–290.
Ranganathan, S. R. (1955). "Heading and Canons." S. Viswanathan, Madras; G. Blunt, London.
Ranganathan, S. R. (1959). International catalogue code. *Annals of Library Science* **6**, 13–20.
"Regeln für die alphabetische Katalogisierung: RAK" (1977). Dr. Ludwig Reichert Verlag, Wiesbaden.
Sayers, W. C. B. (1909). The Anglo-American cataloguing code. *Library World* **11**, 467–472.
Simonton, W. (1979). An introduction to AACR 2. *Library Resources & Technical Services* **23**, 321–339.
Tait, J. A. (1969). "Authors and Titles." Archon Books, Hamden, Connecticut.
Tucker, B. (1980). Implementation of AACR 2 at the Library of Congress. *In* International Conference on AACR 2, Florida State University, 1979. "The Making of a Code." pp. 191–206. American Library Association, Chicago, Illinois.
Verona, E. (1963). The function of the main entry in the alphabetical catalogue—a second approach. *In* "Report, International Conference on Cataloguing Principles, 1961," pp. 145–157. International Federation of Library Associations, London.
Verona, E. (1975). "Corporate Headings: Their Use in Library Catalogues and National Bibliographies." IFLA Committee on Cataloguing, London.
Winkler, P. W. (1979). Letter dated November 26.

Academic Library Management Studies: From Games to Leadership

H. WILLIAM AXFORD*

University of Oregon

    I. Management and the Status Quo 39
   II. The Management Review and Analysis Program (MRAP) 43
       A. Origins 43
       B. Methodology 44
       C. Results 45
 III. Beyond MRAP 51
       A. Management Studies and Change 51
       B. The Pittsburgh Study and the National Enquiry
           into Scholarly Communication 53
       C. Use and Value 54
 IV. Collection Use Studies and Management: Challenges
      to the Status Quo 57
      References 60

I. MANAGEMENT AND THE STATUS QUO

If it is assumed that the ultimate goal of a library management study is improved institutional performance through effective challenges to the status quo, it is difficult to escape the conclusion that the innovations in this field introduced in the present decade, most of which have their roots in the behavioral and mathematical sciences, have achieved at best only limited success. As a matter of fact, it is remarkable how impervious the academic library has been to such highly touted and publicized tools of the "new management science" as the program planning and budgeting system (PPBS), management by objectives

*deceased

(MBO), operations research (OR), zero-based budgeting (ZBB), or organizational theory based on McGregor's philosophy of human nature. It is not that these evaluative and performance-oriented concepts have failed to stimulate thought and research within the profession with respect to applications relevant to the problems of academic library management, or that they have failed to find advocates in our professional schools. The long-term budget crisis and continuing pressures from outside agencies for accountability that became the lot of higher education as the decade of the 1970s unfolded have made the tools of the "new management science" impossible to ignore. However, there is little hard evidence to show that on the whole their effect on the profession has been such as to result in a significant upgrading of resource utilization in academic libraries. In other words, the promised benefits of the "new management science" for enhancing the academic library's service capabilities within the constrictions imposed by diminishing or stable resources have been only minimally realized. What we have seen is isolated examples where this has occurred rather than a broad spectrum phenomenon. (For a more optimistic assessment, see Kaser, 1974.)

This state of affairs results in large part from what I have labeled on other occasions the profession's "cottage industry mentality," which, among other things, tends to see the practice of librarianship through the eyes of the artist rather than those of the pragmatist (Axford, 1979).

One of the most visible results of this attitude is a deep-rooted suspicion of any approach to library management that involves attaching costs to existing systems, procedures, and services, which expresses itself in rationalizations similar to the following: "You can't quantify service. *Ergo,* any attempt to do so is not only a waste of time and resources but it could lead to decisions based on data that are irrelevant to the problem." Behind such arguments lurks the fear, springing from the realization that attaching costs to services—or more properly, to systems and procedures that produce them—will inevitably result in disturbing challenges to the status quo. In this respect, academic librarians are, of course, not unique; rather, they reflect a general anxiety within the academy, particularly within those colleges and universities whose budgets are largely enrollment driven and where the specter of program evaluation and support based solely on student credit-hour production haunts the campus.

Another factor contributing to the generally anemic results produced in academic libraries by the new management techniques that came into vogue during the 1970s is the increasing number of technocrats produced by our professional schools who, like their kind in every field the world over, tend to be more interested in ideology, methodology, or process per se than in the results of their application. What this attitude translates into in the academic library—an institution noted for its allegiance to the status quo—is the appearance or promise of change rather than the reality—image building in the manner of Gerald Rafshoon, rather than a real enhancement of the library's capabilities for effective resource utilization. Staff studies proliferate and find their way into the literature, but in reality they have had little effect on line operations. What our technocrats, steeped (or is it dipped?) in the techniques of the behavioral or mathematical sciences, have produced is a kind of arid scholasticism that feeds on itself rather than a general improvement in the way academic libraries are managed. For example, a management study along PPBS lines may analyze the cost effectiveness of a number of alternatives to existing systems and routines but result in the adoption of none of them, irrespective of their relative merits; an MBO exercise may define or clarify and publicize goals but establish no ongoing mechanisms for measuring progress toward their realization; in a library living with a continuing budget crisis a personnel utilization study showing underutilization of the professional staff and recommending corrective measures may end up gathering dust on the shelf; and experiments with participatory management become more concerned with individual ego satisfaction or enhancement rather than its theoretical *raison d'etre*, which is increasing a library's ability to achieve its educational goals within the constrictions of existing and anticipated resources.

For management tools that focus on output in relation to input to be effective, that is, to produce results as well as studies or experiments in library governance, there has to exist somewhere within the library the will to use the data and insights they are capable of generating as levers for inducing change in what is basically a change-resistant environment. In other words, there has to exist what one prominent writer on management has called the "will to manage" and which another has defined as being, more than anything else,

> a confident eagerness to act vigorously and cheerfully without fear in the face of uncertainty, unfettered by any need to examine in every possible detail from every

possible angle and with every possible method of analysis all of the possible considerations and consequences at stake in any decision or action (Levitt, 1978).

Thus defined, the "will to manage" is essentially a matter of leadership, something not held in high esteem at present. Indeed, John Gardner has aptly described contemporary society as "one innoculated by an anti-leadership vaccine." How this attitude affects management in higher education has been eloquently described by President William Boyd (1979) of the University of Oregon. Elaborating on a comment made by his counterpart at Stanford University, he said that:

> "management may be the only dirty word left on campuses, where ordinary obscenities have become common currency and lost their power to offend or exhort."

This sad state of affairs in which leadership is deplored at a time when it is sorely needed if institutions of higher education are to conserve and enhance their role as the wellsprings of knowledge in a knowledge-dependent society is directly related to the downturn in the fortunes of higher education that began nearly a decade ago. Faced with diminishing resources, academic administrators have increasingly been faced with the unpleasant problem of having to choose between a limited number of alternatives with respect to future planning, none of which is palatable to the academic communities they serve in terms of the attitudes and expectations created by the post-World War II boom that lasted for almost a quarter of a century. The uncomfortable situation of academic library administrators, most of whom share with the teaching faculty a corpus of fundamental assumptions about the library that has its roots in this same growth period, is abundantly clear in the problems posed by an imbalance between serial and monographic acquisitions, the need to consider alternative means of housing growing collections as capital construction funds become increasingly scarce, and the persistent challenges to the status quo stemming from a technology-driven movement toward interdependency that is rapidly eroding traditional institutional autonomy in such sensitive areas as collection development and providing bibliographic access to local collections. In coping with problems of this nature and magnitude, it seems obvious that a determination to act is an essential precondition for the effective use of any management tool. Furthermore, it seems apparent that the weakness of this impulse within academic library management explains, to a large extent, the fact that the tools of the "new management science" have done so little to affect the status quo in academic libraries.

II. THE MANAGEMENT REVIEW AND ANALYSIS PROGRAM (MRAP)

A. Origins

An effort to address this problem—and one that must be the most ambitious project ever undertaken to upgrade the management of academic libraries—is the Management Review and Analysis Program (MRAP), developed and promoted by the Office of Management Studies (OMS) of the Association of Research Libraries (ARL) and originally funded by the Council on Library Resources (CLR). The origins of the program are significant. As the decade of the 1960s drew to a close, a number of prominent individuals became concerned over the profession's ability to manage the increasingly large and complex research libraries that constituted one of its most important legacies. The ultimate result was ARL's Management Review and Analysis Program. Three individuals played key roles in its conception and subsequent development, Fred C. Cole, former President of the Council on Library Resources; Warren J. Haas, the present Council President; and Duane Webster, the Director of ARL's Office of Management Studies. It was Cole's suggestion that prompted the ARL to establish in 1969 a Committee on University Library Management (Booz, Allen, and Hamilton, Inc., 1973). Warren Haas was its first chairman. With the continued support and encouragement of the CLR, the ARL moved quickly into a joint effort with the American Council on Education to study the status of university library management contracting for the services of the management consulting firm of Booz, Allen, and Hamilton. Within the present context, the most important results of this enterprise were the establishment of ARL's Office of Management Studies in 1970, and its subsequent collaboration with Booz, Allen, and Hamilton in a detailed study of the organization and staffing of the Columbia University Libraries, for it was in this crucible that the MRAP was forged. As the Director of the ARL's Office of Management Studies put it:

> the concept of [the] MRAP grew out of the Association's study of problems in university library management, my experience with the Columbia study of organization and staffing, a series of meetings with the ARL/ACE Joint Committee on Management and numerous discussions with [advisors to the OMS] such as Fred Cole, Jim Haas, Steve McCarthy and Bob Vosper.*

As can be seen, the MRAP's parentage is indeed impressive, including as it does three prestigious organizations in the field of higher education—the Association of Research Libraries, the Council on Library Resources, and the American Council on Education—one of the country's best known management consultant firms, and several of the best known figures in the research library community. Without question, it is its geneology as much as the nature of the program that gives the MRAP a status in the history of management studies of academic libraries that is unique. It also accounts for the fact that to date almost 25% of the membership of the ARL has participated in the program and a growing number of small and medium-sized college and university libraries are opting to participate in one of its derivations, the Academic Library Development Program (ALDP) (see Morein *et al.*, 1977).

B. Methodology

Beyond its origins and the number of participating libraries, the significance of the MRAP lies in the methodology by which it attacks the problem of improving the management of academic libraries. [The literature on MRAP is extensive and, to date, mostly positive (see e.g., Buckland, 1976; Johnson *et al.*, 1979; Stevens, 1975; Webster 1974; Webster and Gardner, 1975).] The fundamental assumption of the MRAP is that a self-imposed, highly structured, guided self-study (guided by the OMS) has the potential for developing within the participating library a collective will to and capacity for changing the manner in which the academic library has been traditionally managed, i.e., move it toward a more participatory form of management, and that this process, in and of itself, will result in a more effective use of resources.

*Letter from Duane Webster to the author, May 25, 1979.

In the terminology of the behavioral science in which the MRAP is rooted, the successful negotiation of an intricate exercise in problem identification and analysis, not unlike a laboratory maze, will lead to behavioral and attitudinal changes within the organization that will inevitably affect its performance in a positive way.

More specifically, the MRAP has two sets of internal goals, defined as those involving "process" and those having to do with "content," and an overarching public relations objective related to the library's image within the university. As for the process goals, the manual for the self-study is very specific. They are (1) to assess present management practices, (2) to secure a better understanding of management concepts and principles for participating staff, (3) to determine future actions for management improvement, (4) to create an open problem-solving climate, (5) to develop group process skills, and (6) to develop staff management and analytical capabilities. The content or issue-oriented goals to be examined within the framework of the self-study, in contrast, are left entirely to the library management. This is a crucial aspect of the MRAP as the Director of ARL's Office of Management Studies has noted, and its significance with respect to assessing the program's results will be dealt with later. Beyond these internal goals, "The program strives to secure for the library a more favorable image within the university community by underscoring [its] willingness to change [and be] accountable for the use of its resources" (Webster, n.d.). Given the historical background and sponsorship of the MRAP, this overarching program objective provides an interesting insight into the management of academic libraries as perceived within such organizations as the American Council on Education and the Council on Library Resources and among key figures within the Association of Research Libraries.

C. Results

What, then, have been the results to date of this intensive effort to improve the management of academic libraries—whose costs to participating institutions are by no means insignificant? (For instance, in a large research library the MRAP may involve as many as five F.T.E. for 18 months to 2 years.)

Despite the fact that in 1976 the Council on Library Resources (CLR) funded a study at the Pennsylvania State University to assess the impact of the MRAP (Johnson *et al.*, 1977), this is not an easy question to answer. There are several reasons that this is so. First of all, an underlying assumption of the program is that if the methodology of the self-study is rigorously and religiously followed, its projected benefits, in terms of a better managed library, will automatically materialize. Because of this faith in the efficacy of the exercise, the MRAP has no provision for assessing the short- and long-term results of its application in a participating library. Second, none of the ARL libraries that participated in the CLR study had anything significant in the way of pre-MRAP data bearing on management effectiveness that could provide benchmarks for assessing the program's results. Finally, the institutional goals for participating in the program, which are left to library management to define, generally have been so nonspecific as to preclude assessing the program's results in these terms. The authors of the CLR study cite the following example as typical: "The basic objective of [participation in the MRAP] is to improve the library's contribution in the academic process through better management and utilization of all resources" (Johnson et al., 1977, p. 7). This goal statement is in the best tradition of academic obfuscation, but as the authors note, "It is not particularly amenable to either measurement or assessment." Given these circumstances, the fact that the MRAP itself makes no provision for assessing its results, the fact that the participating libraries had no pre-MRAP data on the effectiveness of management practices, and the fact that the institutional goals for participation in the program were too general to permit an objective evaluation of the program on this basis, the authors of the CLR study had no other choice in assessing its results than a survey/questionnaire soliciting the "informed opinions" of "key informants." Consequently, what we have with respect to evaluating the MRAP as an instrument for upgrading the management of academic libraries is opinion rather than hard data, and even this by and large is so ambiguous as to leave the effectiveness of the program in doubt. On this subject, the authors of the CLR study had this to say:

> The data from the questionnaires and interviews when taken together indicate that overall, [the] MRAP was moderately successful in achieving the goals for the self-review established by the Office of University Library Management Studies. However . . . there was a diversity of opinion among library directors, managers and staff. Directors and managers consistently concluded more strongly in favor in all areas than did staff that [the] MRAP was a success (Johnson et al., 1977, p. 76).

Because the responsibility for investing in the program and implementing the recommendations that emerge from the self-study falls on library directors, a more optimistic estimate of the MRAP's results from this group as compared to staff should not be surprising. However, the differing perceptions between management and staff may reflect a basic weakness of the MRAP as a tool for improving the management of academic libraries, i.e., the possibility of differing expectations from a costly investment. On this point, the CLR study revealed a clear dichotomy between management and staff. Whereas the expectations of the former were focused on "management concerns and concrete results," those of the latter evolved around "communications, participation, personnel administration and staff development" (p. 81). This divergence of expectations seems to indicate that in practical application the philosophical linkage between the MRAP's "process" and "content" goals, i.e., achievement of the former will automatically lead to achievement of the latter, tends to break down, leading to polarized opinions on the part of management and staff as to the ultimate goals and consequently the value of the self-study process. When this occurs, and the CLR study clearly indicates that it does, the effectiveness of the MRAP in bringing about internal changes leading to the more effective use of resources is in doubt. Indeed, under these conditions, the self-study process may well be counterproductive.

This, of course, raises the larger question of why the potential of the MRAP for improving academic library performance seems to be modest at best. Fundamentally, it is a matter of the inherent limitations of the self-imposed, self-study to create a recognition of the need for change within an organization not noted for maintaining a constant and healthy skepticism regarding the efficacy of the means whereby it carries out its business. In this connection, the responses of library administrators to a question in the CLR survey dealing with performance are very revealing. When asked, "Would you say that the library is generally responsive to users?" they registered a plus 4.9 on a 5 point scale—about as close to a perfect score as you can get (Johnson et al., 1977, p. 32). Granted that "generally responsive" is an assessment open to some degree of flexibility in interpretation, the general level of satisfaction with the status quo shown by this response does not indicate the kind of critical management attitude that would lead library administrators to challenge it in any consequential way. Evidence for a general satisfaction with management performance also came to light in responses to a question regarding the effectiveness of goals and objectives formulation, organizational practices, leadership, staff development, budget and planning, personnel administration and general management. Except for two instances where one library director indicated a deficiency in the area of leadership and another in staff development, management performance was rated by library managers as highly effective or effective in all other categories (p. 124).

The belief that their libraries were "generally responsive to users" and that management performance rated good to excellent may account for the nonspecific nature of the goal statements, characterized earlier as academic obfuscation, proffered by library directors. Obfuscation within the context of an institutional self-study has been defined by one authority in the field as "invoking platitudes or high sounding generalizations that lead nowhere but that create the impression of genuine concern and interest" (Astin, 1976, p. 79).

All of this suggests that there has been a not insignificant element of gamesmanship on the part of library directors who have decided to invest in the MRAP, that is, possibly more interest in its external public relations value than its potential for inducing internal reform. Unfortunately, gamesmanship of this nature is a well-established fact throughout higher education as it attempts to respond to external pressures for change, and it would be highly naive to expect that library directors could remain immune from temptation. For instance, in a recent article in the *Chronicle of Higher Education,* Leon Botstein, President of Bard College, characterized much of the current debate on the Liberal Arts and the core curriculum as simply gerrymandering "structures so as to keep power and prestige intact" rather than a sincere effort to bring "real institutional change to colleges and universities." "Almost all of the new initiatives," he wrote,

> whether at Amherst, Harvard, Illinois Central or Gustavus Adolphus College focus on narrow educational abuses . . . . I suggest that these proposals on behalf of liberal learning are being used as a facile, acceptable front to shield us from addressing more serious social and cultural issues (Botstein, 1979, p. 17).

Botstein's comments on the nature of the present debates over curriculum reform point to the fact that image building, creating the illusion rather than the reality of change, is all too often, if not the conscious goal of the institutional self-study, its end result. Put another way, the publicity accompanying such an effort invariably speaks of a determination to come to grips with the critical issues confronting an institution, but the process tends to become bogged down with matters of considerably less substance and consequently considerably less threatening to the status quo. Most of the final reports of the MRAP study teams display this general characteristic. A good example would be in the area of planning where the recommendations concentrate on establishing the mechanisms for carrying out this function but seldom, if ever, make note of the specific issues, either local or national, that provide the focus without which such mechanisms become just another layer of expensive bureaucracy.

In one of the very few serious attempts to assess the institutional self-study as a mechanism for producing "truly consequential" changes in educational policy, D. R. Ladd commented on this tendency for issues of secondary importance to become paramount. After analyzing, among others, self-studies carried out by the University of California at Berkeley, the University of New Hampshire, the University of Toronto, Swarthmore College, Wesleyan University, Michigan State University, Columbia College, Brown University, Stanford University, and the University of California at Los Angeles, he concluded that "on the whole the educational policy changes proposed . . . often seemed to speak indirectly—if at all—to the deep malaise which presently [1970] affects so much of higher education" (Miller, 1979, p. 278). Ladd's ultimate assessment of the effectiveness of the self-study as an instrument either for inducing change or for encouraging greater faculty involvement in the development of educational policy was highly pessimistic.

> Unhappily, [he wrote] the results of these studies seem to lend support—at least in a negative way—to the efficacy of pressure politics as a way of bringing about change. There is little indication in any of the experiences to support the idea that the study-and-report technique is an effective way of gaining acceptance of the *need* for change *or developing enthusiasm for involvement in developing new policies.* [Emphasis added.] Where the study-and-report processes were intended primarily to challenge the *status quo*, they failed to do so. When the essential objective was to develop the details of a change in the *status quo* after the community had already accepted the need for some change or where pressures for change from outside the faculty were much in evidence, the study-and-report process was much more effective (p. 278).

Although Ladd found that the self-imposed self-study did little to generate faculty interest in determining new educational policies, one of the most obvious characteristics of the MRAP is its capacity for raising staff expectations that participation in the program will ultimately lead to greater involvement in policy decisions. Unfortunately, the post-MRAP experience seems to indicate considerable frustration on this score. For instance, the authors of the CLR study found that "by far the most negative comment [on the program] was the problem of implementation" (Johnson *et al.*, 1977, p. 94) Staff frustration over the fate of study team recommendations was also strongly, indeed in some cases, bitterly expressed, in 17 of the 19 responses the author received from members of study teams at 13 libraries to a letter soliciting, among other things, comments on staff expectations and the actual outcome of the program. One respondent attributed the incongruence between staff expectations and results to a misunderstanding of the ultimate goal of the program.

> It cannot be overemphasized, [he wrote,] that [the] MRAP was designed to study and recommend possible changes in certain library management areas and techniques/practices. That's all. The assumption was made after the fact by many of us—and this turned out to be naive and dangerous—that a change would occur because of the study and it would be positive, taking the form of management improvement which would automatically result in an improvement in academic library performance. We did not successfully internalize the fact that the program promised nothing except a self-study guided by amateurs, with some promise of formalization of findings.

Given the problems experienced with respect to implementing the recommendations of the study teams, this may, in fact, be a fairly accurate description of the end result of participation in the MRAP—"a self-study with some promise of formalization of findings." However, the fact remains that the program promises much more than this. The foundation on which it rests is the assumption that process automatically results in product.

In coming to any final conclusions regarding the effectiveness of the MRAP as a management tool, it should be borne in mind that it falls into the category of self-study that Ladd found to be the least effective in stimulating change in the way organizations behave, i.e., a self-study specifically designed to challenge the *status quo*, in this case the perceived or actual authoritarian nature of academic library management. It is a program that has been highly promoted on this basis for the better part of decade and tested in a substantial number of large research libraries and smaller institutions. Yet, to date, little has emerged from this extensive operational experience to lead me to change an opinion expressed in 1975 regarding its effectiveness in improving the management of academic libraries, i.e., "There is disappointingly little hard evidence to indicate that the MRAP has moved the participating libraries toward the kind of substantive internal changes, both attitudinal and structural, which would lead to better utilization of resources" (Axford, 1975, pp. 561–562). This is an opinion in which the authors of the CLR study concurred. "Although it might be difficult to agree on a definition of substantive," they wrote, [this view] "appears to be correct" (Johnson *et al.*, 1977, p. 99).

Nevertheless, the MRAP continues to be a first-priority program of the ARL, which has successfully sought funding from the Council on Library Resources and a private foundation to establish and promote a spinoff designed for the college or small university library, the Academic Library Development Program (ALDP). Under this program, ARL's Office of Management Studies will train upward of 100 consultants to assist academic libraries in conducting self-studies in a number of specified areas, e.g., collection development, management processes, library services. Given the questionable capacity of the self-study to produce what Ladd called "truly consequential changes" within organizations with a strong commitment to the status quo, it is hard to escape the conclusion that the allegiance it commands from such prestigious organizations as the ARL, and the CLR, and a large number of academic librarians results from a kind of Vietnam syndrome, that is, continued commitment to the self-study as a mechanism for improving the management of academic libraries as a matter of principle, or even ideology, irrespective of the fact that extensive operational experience points toward a significant incongruence between investment and results.

III. BEYOND MRAP

A. Management Studies and Change

A University of Southern California economist who rose to national prominence by promoting the idea that massive tax cuts would so increase people's incentive to work and invest that both federal revenues and the nation's economy would leap to new heights, has said that this concept is simply "a recognition that people change when their marginal incentives change." There is a lesson to be learned from this observation with respect to another type of academic library management study—one that first appeared in the early 1970s and is rapidly becoming a fact of life on campuses across the country. I refer to the periodic review of the performance of the library director, which can have national as well as local dimensions. This kind of management study is, of course, a part of the larger picture in which periodic performance review for all campus administrators followed on the heels of student evaluations of classroom performance and increasingly stringent promotion and tenure evaluations of the teaching faculty.

When competently administered, and when the purpose of administrative or management review is to help the individual improve his or her performance as well as to pass judgment on it, the process can be beneficial to the person evaluated, the library, and the community it serves. When badly handled, the administrative review can degenerate into an opinion poll where every individual's views are given equal weight irrespective of his or her competence to make judgments related to the complexities of library management. When this occurs, the director can be caught in a crossfire organized by special-interest groups whose knowledge of and interest in the larger issues confronting academic libraries may be limited, if not nonexistent, with the result that his or her professional credibility may be seriously and unjustifiably compromised.

Concern on this score has been expressed by the American Association of State Colleges and Universities, which has published some excellent "cautions" that could serve as guidelines for the process of administrative review (see Miller, 1979, pp. 179–182). The American Association of Administrators has taken similar action (see Jacobsen, 1979, p. 3). However, the concept of administrative or management review is still too new for such documents to be institutionalized on a broad basis and thus provide the kind of safeguards needed if the process is to achieve the desired results.

Given the anxiety-ridden atmosphere in which most academic library directors operate today, the marginal incentives for aggressively challenging the status quo are minimal if they exist at all. As a matter of fact, even raising for discussion the alternatives for coping with the most critical issues facing academic libraries is a risky business, as most of them are at variance with the past experience and present expectations of users and, to a certain extent, of the library staff itself. Under these circumstances, it is hard not to conclude that at least in the short run administrative review has the potential for inhibiting rather than encouraging the development of the management capabilities of library directors. The possibility of this occurring at institutions where the library director is not protected by tenure would be especially acute.

It has often been remarked that the academy tends to be considerably less interested in casting its agnostic gaze inward than in directing it outward into society at large. An outstanding exception to this generalization is the collection use study done at the University of Pittsburgh by Kent *et al.* (1978) which analyzed circulation records covering the period October 1968 through December 1975. It is not an exaggeration to say that the ramifications of this landmark effort for academic library administrators and college and university faculties will be of earth shaking proportions. As a matter of fact, the first tremors have already been recorded, and there is every reason to believe that before the 1980s pass into history, this form of management study will have proved to be the most effective change agent of all of the new management tools that have come into vogue during the 1970s.

Why is this so? After all, collection use studies have appeared in the literature for at least two decades without any visible effect on the way academic libraries are managed. Quite simply, the continued expansion of published knowledge, the long-term funding crisis of higher education, and quantum leaps in library applications of increasingly sophisticated computer technology have made it a management tool "whose time has come."

B. The Pittsburgh Study and the National Enquiry into Scholarly Communication

Perhaps the best way to illustrate the truth of this statement would be to dwell for a moment on the relationships between the Pittsburgh study and the report and recommendations of the National Enquiry into Scholarly Communications in the Humanities and the Humanistic Social Sciences, a $600,000 project funded by the National Endowment for the Humanities and the Ford, Mellon, and Rockefeller Foundations and sponsored by the American Council on Learned Societies (Scholarly Communication, 1979). Interestingly, this landmark document also came into being in response to the same set of circumstances as did the Pittsburgh study and the project was conceived at approximately the same time. Although they were independent efforts, and the focus of the National Enquiry was considerably broader, each in its own way was concerned with the same critical problem, i.e., the need for new approaches and new mechanisms for sustaining and enhancing the momentum of scholarship within the constrictions and the opportunities of a radically different set of political, economic, and technological realities than the one that determined the fortunes of higher education in the two decades immediately following World War II.

The central conclusion of the report of the National Enquiry is as follows, and it deals a devastating blow to the prevailing belief among scholars and librarians that the problems confronting academic libraries today, particularly the large research libraries, can or should be solved simply by massive increases in their budgets.

> It is true that many of the financial problems (but not necessarily the problems of performance) that plague the [present] system [of scholarly communications] could be eliminated through sharply increased subsidies for libraries, journals and scholarly presses that would allow each group to continue its activities unchanged. Such a "solution" is not only unrealistic . . . but even if possible, would be a serious mistake. The sheer size and rapid growth of scholarly and research material in all disciplines have created problems of performance that cannot be solved simply by more stable financing of current practice (p. 12).

As means for improving the performance of the system of scholarly communications, the National Enquiry recommended (1) the establishment of a national bibliographic system "to expand access to scholarly materials dramatically by freeing users from dependence on the local library and card catalog as the source of information on books, serials and other materials." (2) a national periodicals lending library as a mechanism for developing "more reliable and more cost effective methods of resource sharing," and (3) a national library agency to develop the components of a "national library system" (pp. 16–20).

C. Use and Value

All of these recommendations point toward a dramatic shift from the traditional reliance on local autonomy with respect to library resources to a growing interdependence among academic libraries and existing and new national library agencies. One of the critical management problems inherent in this transition, which, incidentally, is already well under way, is the identification of those materials so critical to the core teaching and research programs on the local campus that reliance on outside sources would be out of the question. Moreover, it is relative to this problem that the ongoing collection use study based on the data collection and analysis capabilities of automated circulation systems will play a critical role. In addition, such studies will provide extremely useful data with respect to weeding and alternative forms of local storage. Seen in its proper light, the collection use study is, quite simply, an empirically based, pragmatic, management response to the recommendations of the National Enquiry into Scholarly Communications, the most important of which called for the development of a national library system based upon the rapidly developing capabilities of libraries to provide quick and accurate bibliographic access to remote collections. In order for such an institution to achieve its goal of enhancing scholarly communications, national investment in the system must be accompanied by reductions in local expenditures for materials that are of secondary or tertiary importance. In making this distinction, moreover, the use equals value approach is the only one that can provide hard data to guide the difficult political process that will characterize the transition from almost total reliance on local resources to a growing dependence on a national library system. With respect to the use equals value concept, it should be noted that local use patterns do not necessarily speak to the intellectual quality of individual titles or their ultimate value to the larger world of scholarship. The concept has meaning only within the context of the intellectual energies prevalent on a given campus, as these undulate and evolve, as opposed to an idealized model of needs and the manner and extent of collection use.

The use equals value concept is obviously anethema to a great many scholars and librarians who still perceive the basic problem of scholarly communications in this country to be the magnitude of local investment rather than a critical need to modernize the system. Such individuals tend to view the ongoing circulation study as an instrument for assessing the quality of their "management decisions" in the area of collection development, which, of course, it is. Furthermore, they see it as an approach to collection development that is mechanistic, anti-intellectual and in fundamental conflict with the idea of a university. Hell may have "no fury like a woman scorned," but the intensity of the reaction of teaching faculty and librarians with collection development responsibilities when their judgement is called into question by the use of such an instrument must run a close second. Let us look at a couple of examples.

Immediately following the issuance of their final report by Allan Kent and his associates, the faculty library representatives at the University of Pittsburgh appointed a committee to draw up a response. The committee's report was subsequently endorsed by the whole group. It is difficult to summarize, but within the context of illustrating the depth of faculty feeling regarding the central finding of the use study, which was that almost 40%, or 14,697, of the monographs added to the Hillman Library in 1969 had not circulated outside the library in a period of 7 years, these are its salient points.

> The report submitted by Professor Kent and his associates is, in spite of the sheen of objectivity . . . a highly subjective and political document which should not be allowed to affect the . . . growth of the library at the University of Pittsburgh or any other institution seriously committed to the advancement of learning. . . . The figures serve as nothing but a red flag for administrators or other interested parties to wave in the face of an ill-informed legislature or public. . . . It fails to comprehend . . . either what a university is or to appreciate how sensible cost reductions can be achieved (Borkowski and MacLeod, 1979, pp. 64–65).

Echoing these sentiments, Jaspar G. Schad, Director of the Library/Media Resources Center at the University of Wichita has written:

> Despite its impressive array of statistical data and intricate formulas [sic], the study is based on incorrect assumptions and incomplete data that lead to meaningless conclusions. . . . Simply stated, the Pittsburgh Study does not demonstrate comprehension of the purpose of an academic research or university library (Schad, 1979, pp. 60, 62).

A. W. Astin, who has compiled a catalog of the games that academicians play when the status quo is seriously threatened, assigned responses to a serious research effort such as these to the category of "displacement and projection" which he defined as follows:

> The basic function of displacement and projection is to obviate the need for serious consideration of data for subsequent action by citing inadequacies in the data or services provided by the initiator of the project or the supplier of the data.
>
> One form of displacement, [he went on to say,] is caution. The game involves a litany of technical limitations in the data followed by a statement that it would be hazardous to attempt to formulate meaningful interpretations or generalizations concerning policy because of these limitations (Astin, 1976, pp. 81–83).

IV. COLLECTION USE STUDIES AND MANAGEMENT: CHALLENGES TO THE STATUS QUO

In spite of the outrage it provokes, the long-term collection use study, in all probability, will figure prominently in the management of academic libraries in the decade ahead. The reason is simple. As the report of the faculty library representatives at Pittsburgh pointed out, the work of Allan Kent and his associates is something that presidents, governing boards, and legislatures (none of whom is as ill informed as university faculties would like to believe) will find it impossible to ignore.

Of these groups, the institutional president and his or her immediate staff may play the most important role. For such individuals, the collection use study offers the possibility of some alleviation of the agonies associated with the dismemberment of programs; the long-range consequences of discharging young, untenured members of the faculty, many of whom may be of better quality than their older colleagues; and the prospects of ultimately having to terminate tenured faculty. Put another way, the collection use study, along with the growing capabilities of academic libraries for effective resource sharing embodied in the rapid development of large, automated bibliographic data bases which will ultimately be linked into a national data base, offer the possibility that local investment in collection development can be stabilized and possibly lowered, and, at the same time, provide access to a larger and richer reservoir of resources than any single institution would find it possible to provide.

Given the acute budget and space problems facing them in the next decade, it hardly seems possible that university presidents could miss the significance of the Pittsburgh study data indicating that in a large research library it is likely that around 40% of the monographs added to the collection in any given year will not circulate outside the library in the next seven. They certainly are capable of multiplying the 14,697 titles that fell into this category at Pittsburgh by the historical or current average price for a scholarly monograph (for the sake of illustration, let us say $10), project this yearly cost over a period of years, and get figures in the millions of dollars. Some of them may even attempt a rough and ready estimate of the labor costs just to convert a request to purchase into a document fully catalogued and ready for use and discover that it may equal or surpass the cost to purchase a scholarly work.

Whether the figure for titles not circulating over an extended period of time is 40% or 20% is really immaterial, as in either case the yearly cost in a large research library to acquire and process such material is in five figures—large enough, that is, to suggest to hard-pressed presidents that in the overall interests of the university tradeoffs may be possible given the improving capabilities of academic libraries for effective resource sharing. As a matter of fact, there is substantial evidence that at least one group of influential university presidents is becoming increasingly aware of this possibility and is moving politically to exploit it.

For instance, the presidents of those institutions that are members of the American Association of Universities (AAU) were in the thick of the effort that finally led to a bill being introduced in the United States Congress in September 1979 for the establishment of a national periodicals lending library. It is worthy of note that among this group there was a considerable level of frustration over the procrastination within the library community, including the Association of Research Libraries, to unite in support of a national lending library with broad collection development responsibilities, not simply periodicals. In a communication to the Executive Committee of the AAU at a point in time when squabbling among the various library special-interest groups seemed to preclude taking advantage of a favorable attitude among key members of the Congress, the chairman of that organization's Committee on Research Libraries noted that "a significant twitch has occurred in what we all feared might be a moribund project to create a federally financed national lending library." The "twitch" referred to was a meeting in Washington, D.C. attended by representatives of the Center for Research Libraries, the ARL, the Library of Congress, and the Council on Library Resources during which a broad, general agreement was reached on the desirability of a national lending library. The chairman of the committee concluded his letter with this observation: "We will have some difficult political arguments ahead of us, more likely from within the library community than from the world of elected officials, but I believe that we are going in the right direction as rapidly as we can go.*

Further evidence that the AAU presidents have begun to grasp the profession's technical capabilities for helping ameliorate their space and

---

*Letter from the chairman of the Committee on Research Libraries to the Executive Committee of the American Association of Universities, September 20, 1978.

budget problems in a manner congruent with sustaining quality teaching and research is to be found in the pressures they have applied to their library directors for membership in the Research Libraries' Information Network (RLIN), which is the operating arm of the Research Libraries Group. Behind this direct intrusion into the management of the country's largest research libraries by top-level institutional executives is more than the normal tendency of an elite group to band together in projects of common interest. Also operating is a recognition of RLIN's potential for stabilizing the costs of local collection development through cooperative acquisitions programs and automated bibliographic access to each other's collections.

As noted earlier, D. R. Ladd has called attention to the efficacy of external pressures in bringing about changes in the status quo. As far as the management of academic libraries is concerned, the collection use study carried out by Allan Kent and his associates is an excellent example of this process in action. Its methodology, the results of its analysis of a large body of circulation data, and its conclusions will continue to provoke controversy. More importantly, however, the odds are excellent that this kind of academic library management study will ultimately provoke fundamental changes in the way the academic library manages what has traditionally been its sine qua non, collection development. The economics of higher education as projected for the next decade strongly support this conclusion as does the report of the National Enquiry into Scholarly Communications. Furthermore, it seems possible that both the local and the national political environment will provide sufficiently attractive marginal incentives for academic library directors to eschew managerial gamesmanship for real leadership, the most important of which is the probability that they will not have to stand alone in trying to achieve acceptance within the scholarly community for basic changes in the mechanisms whereby it conducts its internal communications. Unlike the other examples of management studies treated superficially or in some depth in this review, the collection use study concerns itself with the long-term assessment of management decisions as they relate to collection development and space needs. Its methodology is to challenge the status quo with hard data on collection use patterns. For these reasons, it is likely that it will prove to be the most effective instrument for improving the management of academic libraries within the realities that these institutions will have to operate in the years ahead to come out of the sobering experiences of the 1970s.

REFERENCES

Astin, A. W. (1976). "Academic Gamesmanship: Student Oriented Change in Higher Education." Praeger, New York.

Axford, H. W. (1975). The interrelations of structure, governance, and effective resource utilization in academic libraries. *Library Trends* **23**, 551–571.

Axford, H. W. (1979). The great rush to automated catalogs: will it be management or muddling through. *In* "Requiem for the Card Catalog: Management Issues in Automated Cataloging (D. Gore, J. Kimbrough, and P. Spyers Duran, eds.), pp. 169–176. Greenwood Press, Westport, Connecticut.

Booz, Allen and Hamilton, Inc. (1973). "Organization and Staffing of the Libraries of Columbia University: A Case Study." Redgrave Information Corp., Westport, Connecticut.

Borkowski, C., and MacLeod, M. J. (1979). A faculty response from the University of Pittsburgh. *Journal of Academic Librarianship* **5**, 63–65.

Botstein, L. (1979). Liberal arts and the core curriculum: A debate in the dark. *Chronicle of Higher Education* July 9, p. 17.

Boyd, W. T. (1979). "Biennial Report to the University of Oregon Faculty." n.d., n.p.

Buckland, M. K. (1976). The management review and analysis program: a symposium. *Journal of Academic Librarianship* **1**, 4–14.

Jacobson, R. L. (1979). Professional growth, job security concern academic administrators. *Chronicle of Higher Education* August 13, p. 3.

Johnson, E. R., Stuart, H. M., and Ulisting, C. (1977). "An Assessment of the Impact to the Management Review and Analysis Program (MRAP)." Pennsylvania State University, University Park.

Johnson, E. R., Mann, S. H., and Whiting, C. (1979). Evaluating the impact of MRAP on several research libraries: Some thoughts on assessment. *In* "Library Research Round Table, 1977 Research Forums," (C. C. Curran, ed.), pp. 69–86. American Library Association, Chicago, Illinois.

Kaser, D. (1974). Evaluation of administrative services. *Library Trends* **22**, 257–264.

Kent, A., Montgomery, L., Cohen, J., Bulick, S., Sabor, W., Flynn, R., and Shirey, D. (1978). "A Cost–Benefit Model of Some Critical Library Operations in Terms of Use of Materials: Final Report." University of Pittsburgh, Pittsburgh, Pennsylvania.

Levitt, T. (1978). A heretical view of "management science." *Fortune* December 18, p. 52.

Miller, R. I. (1979). "The Assessment of College Performance: A Handbook of Techniques and Measures for Institutional Self-Evaluation." Jossey-Bass, San Francisco, California.

Morein, P. G., et al. (1977). The academic library development program. *College and Research Libraries* **38**, 37–45.

Schad, J. G. (1979). Missing the brass ring in the iron city. *Journal of Academic Librarianship* **5**, 60–62.

"Scholarly Communication: The Report of the National Enquiry" (1979). Johns Hopkins Press, Baltimore, Maryland.

Stevens, N. D. (1975). The management review and analysis program at the University of Connecticut. *Journal of Academic Librarianship* **1**, 4–10.

Webster, D. E. (n.d.). "A Description of the Management Review and Analysis Program." Association of Research Libraries, Office of Management Studies, n.p.

Webster, D. E. (1974). The management review and analysis program: an assisted self-study to secure constructive change in the management of research libraries. *College and Research Libraries* **35**, 114–125.

Webster, D. E., and Gardner, J. (1975). Strategies for improving the performance of academic libraries. *Journal of Academic Librarianship* **1**, 13–18.

And Gladly Teach: Bibliographic Instruction and the Library

ARTHUR P. YOUNG

Amelia Gayle Gorgas Library
University of Alabama

I. Introduction	63
II. Literature Reviews and Bibliographies	64
III. Assumptions and Rationales	66
IV. The Educational Environment	68
A. Perceptions and Commitment	68
B. Preconditions, Proficiencies, and Predictions	69
C. Measures of Library Proficiency	71
V. Evaluation and Research	72
A. Design and Assessment	72
B. Research: Gospel or Gossamer?	74
VI. Instructional Patterns	76
A. Organizational Setting	76
B. Levels of Instruction	76
C. Externally Stimulated and Self-Regulated Instruction	78
D. Mediated and Computer-Assisted Learning	79
VII. Reflections	80
References	81

I. INTRODUCTION

Bibliographic instruction is not new. Sporadic attempts to provide library patrons with self-help skills are traceable to the nineteenth century. The momentum was slow to build, however, and it has been only during the past decade that dramatic growth has been observed. There is abundant evidence that programs of bibliographic instruction have been adopted in many libraries and even elevated to the status of permanently funded services in some libraries. Dozens of conferences have been convened; the literature of bibliographic instruction has proliferated; national, regional, and state clearinghouses have been formed; nearly all library associations have created bibliographic instruction committees; and considerable foundation money has been dispensed. These indicators of accelerated interest in bibliographic instruction, in turn, reflect broader educational and library trends. Among these may be noted rising enrollments (until recently), curricular experimentation, mediated approaches to learning, expansion of outreach programs and personalized services, and the quest by many librarians in higher education for enhanced status within the academy.

In what follows the strivings, accomplishments, and failures of bibliographic instruction are chronicled and assessed, with special reference to the past 10 years. Principal topics encompass literature reviews and bibliographies; assumptions and rationales; research findings related to attitudinal factors, measures of library competence, and educational variables; evaluation and research; and the strengths and shortcomings of various instructional strategies. All types of libraries are considered, but the preponderance of literature on academic and school libraries invariably skews the emphasis. The corpus of literature is large and heavily endowed with polemical, nonevaluative specimens. Consequently, this review is necessarily selective and highlights that portion of the literature that stresses hypothesis testing, statistical inference, generalizability, and analyses of primary source material.

II. LITERATURE REVIEWS AND BIBLIOGRAPHIES

The literature of bibliographic instruction has steadily enlarged. Between 1967 and 1978, the number of entries indexed under "instruction in library use" in *Library Literature* increased each year, with an annual average of more than 75 items. Numerous other reports, proceedings, programs, and guides may be found in *Resources in Education*, the index to ERIC (Educational Resources Information Center) documents; *Current Index to Journals in Education*; and *Social Sciences Citation Index*. For theses and dissertations, the main sources are *Dissertation Abstracts International* and *Master's Theses in Education*.

At least four trends may be identified. The number of professional journals covering bibliographic instruction activities has expanded, although the subject continues to be poorly represented in the non-library press. Recently, more publications have appeared that focus on the need for measurable objectives and rigorous evaluation. If publication levels serve as a barometer of program activity, greater use of bibliographic instruction is occurring in elementary and high school libraries. The increase in doctoral dissertations on bibliographic instruction has added a qualitative dimension to the paucity of serious research, and perhaps signifies the acceptance of user education as a topic of continuing scholarly importance. Additional evidence of interest is confirmed by the publication of the proceedings of the Annual Conference on Library Orientation sponsored by Eastern Michigan University since 1972, and the appearance, in 1976, of a regular column on bibliographic instruction in the *Journal of Academic Librarianship*.

For an early survey of the library's educational heritage, consult the article by Butler (1942). The most comprehensive summary of library instruction literature, covering the years 1876–1958, is by Bonn (1960). Tucker (1979) examined instructional trends in academic libraries for the period 1876 to World War I. Snider (1965) includes a detailed section on library tests and the relationship between library use and academic performance. Use studies, library instruction, and research needs are ably treated by Henne (1966). Wendt (1967) examined the application of media and automated systems to bibliographic instruction for the period 1960–1967. British practices are spotlighted in the survey of academic libraries by Tidmarsh (1968). Davis (1970) has summarized the key studies on the relationship between library use and such variables as scholastic aptitude, academic achievement, and class level. Instructional applications and research studies are appraised in a discursive but discerning essay by Scrivener (1972). Ford (1973) reported on research studies on library use and effectiveness, user education, and client information needs. The research literature on bibliographic instruction was reviewed by Young (1974) and updated by Young and Brennan (1978). Two monographic surveys, with contributed chapters by prominent practitioners, capture the trends and diversity of bibliographic instruction activities in all types of libraries (Lubans, 1974, 1978).

Givens (1974), who traced curricular trends and librarians' educational response to them for the period 1930 to the early 1970s, concluded that many instructional programs were conceived in isolation and that much of the research had been noncumulative. Additionally, she admonished librarians to become more familiar with modern technology, educational psychology, and management theory. Stevenson (1977) analyzed 167 instructional studies pertaining to orientation, credit courses, staffing, faculty cooperation, design and evaluation, and alternative approaches. Although faculty cooperation was found to be the sine qua non of successful programs, librarians have not been able to garner widespread faculty support for user education activities. Considerable disillusionment with orientation and an increase in the use of skill exercises and seminar teaching were noted. The enthusiasm and approachability of the library staff, Stevenson postulated, may be even more critical than their academic or professional qualifications. Miller's (1978) review of bibliographic instruction in selected American colleges indicated that course-related instruction, as opposed to separate courses, was most popular; that a tentative relationship existed between library use and bibliographic instruction; that faculty status for academic librarians without commensurate expertise in cognate fields will not suffice; and that most user education programs were designed and implemented without adequate evaluation.

The authoritative guide to recent bibliographic instruction literature is the compilation by Lockwood (1979). Coverage is extensive for the period 1970–1977, with selected entries for earlier years. Books, articles, reports, and theses–dissertations are listed according to type of library or instructional approach; and an author index is furnished. Still valuable bibliographies of use studies and library instruction literature include those by Atkin (1971), Crossley and Clews (1974), Davis and Bailey (1964), DeWeese (1967), and Krier (1976). A continuing annual bibliography on the literature of bibliographic instruction, compiled by Hannelore Rader Delgado, has appeared in *Reference Services Review* since 1974.

III. ASSUMPTIONS AND RATIONALES

Simply expressed, all forms of bibliographic instruction are intended to furnish library users with some degree of familiarity with library services and to provide knowledge and skills needed for the identification and retrieval of relevant information. Underlying this statement of purpose is the rarely documented assumption that most library clients (real and potential) need, want, and will benefit from systematic exposure to library services and resources. Several librarians have even classified bibliographic instruction as a "survival skill" on the same level as literacy (Lubans, 1978). Lindgren's (1978) perceptive essay on the philosophical roots and rhetorical dimension of user education proceeds from just such a prima facie assumption of value. The ability to use libraries effectively is one of the "classic resources of the educated person," and that vision must be "communicated to others with merciless clarity" (p. 77).

Some commentators do not share the view that bibliographic instruction is a demonstrable virtue (Benson, 1979; Katz, 1974, 1978; McClure, 1974; Schiller, 1965; Wilson, 1979). The reservations focus on three major points of concern: (1) the validity of library instruction, especially as a component of reference service; (2) the alleged relationship between bibliographic instruction and library use/proficiency; and (3) the educational role of libraries and librarians.

Schiller (1965), in a seminal paper on the incompatibility of instruction and the direct provision of information, supported the latter function as the primary objective of reference service. Instruction is an unsatisfactory approach for many users because it short circuits the communication channels between clients and librarians. Katz (1974), too, is uncompromising about the priority role of reference service over instruction. Librarians must be "freed of the teacher–reference librarian ambivalence" because many librarians cannot teach. Further, self-help by amateurs is dangerous, instruction is often imposed on students unilaterally, and most users and nonusers do not care about learning the intricacies of the reference process. After 4 years, Katz (1978) remains an entrenched critic, proclaiming with funereal rectitude that "library education has failed." For a thoughtful corrective to the antiinstructionists, see the penetrating historical essay by Wagers (1978). He argues, persuasively to this writer, that James Wyer and Samuel Rothstein, two prominent interpreters of the reference tradition, have misread the past and constructed artificial dichotomies regarding instruction and direct service. Such pioneers as Samuel Green and William Warner Bishop, in fact, better understood the complementarity of instruction and the provision of information.

Benson (1979) is sharply critical of bibliographic instruction as perceived by many librarians. In a lively and insightful paper, he rejects library instruction as a "self-evident social good," and characterizes much of the bibliographic literature as resembling a "dialectic with the antithesis missing." And he insists that the assumption that instruction leads to more effective library utilization or to enhanced learning has yet to be demonstrated. Before these assumptions can be accepted, Benson cautions, those engaged in bibliographic instruction must depend less on anecdotal evidence, generate testable hypotheses, and produce scientifically defensible research.

Librarians' quest for the holy grail of faculty status has undoubtedly motivated some proponents of bibliographic instruction. According to Wilson (1979), the proposition that librarians are teachers "is an organization fiction disguising the truth" (p. 149). The librarian-as-teacher fiction fails to account for the differences between the bibliographic record and the primary literature and blurs the critical distinction between the professional act of teaching and the bibliothecal act of informing. The concept of librarianship as a teaching profession will not prevail, contends Wilson, because of confused premises and role dissonance. Librarians, while seeking the status of teachers, have obscured their unique role as information specialists.

IV. THE EDUCATIONAL ENVIRONMENT

A. Perceptions and Commitment

The perceptions of librarians, users, and teachers regarding the library's instructional mission have been probed in several studies. A British study found considerable role conflict and incompatible perceptions regarding the centrality of the librarian's educational role (Whitworth, 1970). Support for the introduction of bibliographic instruction was found among librarians, staff, and students in descending order. User attitudes toward bibliographic instruction have been explored in two papers by Lubans (1970, 1972). Twenty-seven nonusers at Rensselaer Polytechnic Institute indicated that their prior experiences with librarians and instruction were generally satisfying but resoundingly rejected the idea of taking an optional library instruction course. At the University of Colorado, 375 students were polled via a self-selecting sample. Slightly more than 50% of the respondents favored the availability of bibliographic instruction courses, but far fewer indicated that they would enroll in such a course. Fewer than one-third of the undergraduates and 60% of the graduate students believed that professors encouraged students to use the library. Only 21% of all respondents believed that faculty recognized library proficiency as a criterion in grading papers.

Contrasting faculty-librarian perceptions regarding the provision of bibliographic instruction were noted in a study of area specialist bibliographers (Stueart, 1971). The bibliographers ($N = 27$) were nearly unanimous in their commitment to instruction, but only two-thirds of the faculty ($N = 131$) and library administrators ($N = 77$) endorsed the idea. Academic librarians ($N = 136$), asked in a recent national survey to estimate the degree of institutional support for instructional programs, rated 77% of their library administrators as highly supportive but rated only 21% of their college administrations as strongly committed. Further confirmation of the soft support for bibliographic instruction was noted in the fact that only 11% of the respondents indicated that bibliographic instruction was formally represented in their library budgets (Lindgren, 1978). As these studies demonstrate, faculty, students, and nonlibrary administrators often assign a low priority to the value of library use and the acquisition of bibliographic skills. Overcoming this stasis is the most vexing challenge faced by library instruction personnel.

B. Preconditions, Proficiencies, and Predictions

Libraries are not autonomous agencies, and their educational role and effectiveness are often defined by interrelated variables. Four such factors—the relationship of library use to student attributes, the effect of library services on academic achievement, teacher familiarity with library skills, and the instructor's motivational role in stimulating library use—constitute significant aspects of the library's educational environment. Studies that have addressed these issues raise sobering thoughts about the permissible claims for library instruction and provide guidance for the design of instructional programs.

Despite persistent efforts over the last 50 years, researchers have not certified a strong causal relationship between library use and class level, academic achievement, or scholastic aptitude (Knapp, 1959; Mitchell, 1973; Thompson and Nicholson, 1941). Similarly, analyses of the impact of the availability and level of precollegiate library services on subsequent academic performance have not yielded significant positive correlations (Harkin, 1971; Ladner, 1966; Walker, 1963). Furthermore, the evaluation of contemporary library programs and their effect on subsequent student achievement has produced inconclusive findings. Hale (1969) used an experimental design on 50 high school students to study the impact of library instruction, maximum service, and opportunity for independent study on scholastic aptitude. Moderate gains were reported for the experimental section, whereas the control group, which was given service only upon demand, showed no appreciable improvement.

The dominant influence of the teacher in promoting library use has been documented in several important research investigations. Knapp (1959) reported that Knox College students borrowed over 90% of their books for course-related reasons. Hostrop (1968) concluded that the instructor is the primary determinant of student library use. Those "library-impelling instructors" who motivated students to use the library gave explicit assignments, required citations in papers, insisted upon high standards, and expressed a "fondness for books." Further confirmation of the instructor's pivotal influence on student library behavior may be found in the study by el-Hagrasy (1962) on the elementary school teacher and in Blazek's (1971) model study of high school teachers.

If the instructor is indeed the major influence on library utilization, then the extent of library knowledge possessed by prospective teachers is particularly important. Unfortunately, the evidence related to teachers' knowledge of libraries is depressing. Perkins (1965) administered two library proficiency tests to nearly 4000 college seniors enrolled in teacher training programs, and a low level of familiarity with library resources and how to use them was discovered. Lee (1971), in a variant replication of the Perkins survey within the state of Georgia, found similar results. Although most teacher training institutions favored a required segment on library orientation for teachers, few of them offered such courses. One must therefore conclude that any claim for bibliographic instruction involving the promotion of library use as the gateway to academic attainment cannot be sustained. Other rationales might be more appropriate and might include such objectives as improved retrieval efficiency, attitudinal modification, and the discriminative use of resources. The pivotal importance of the instructor in stimulating or discouraging library use has been documented beyond doubt. For this reason, it is vital that bibliographic instruction programs involve teacher participation to the maximum possible extent, and that instruction be related to course objectives and assignments.

C. Measures of Library Proficiency

Tests that measure student proficiency in library skills have been used as diagnostic tools to determine exemptions and remediation, and as a means to predict the relationship between library knowledge and various student attributes. Fewer than a dozen nationally distributed library tests have appeared over the past 40 years. Several of these tests have been statistically validated, but full standardization has not been achieved for any library proficiency instrument. One recent attempt to design and evaluate a library proficiency test for grades 4 through 12 was completed by Hyland (1978) in Ohio. The test was administered to 2670 students, and careful attention was paid to test construction techniques. The multilevel Peabody Library Information Test (1938–1940), developed by Louis Shores and Joseph E. Moore, and the Library Orientation Test for College Freshmen (1955) by Ethel M. Feagley are the two most frequently administered instruments (Bloomfield, 1974).

Extensive research has been conducted on the relationship of library proficiency to such variables as antecedent instruction, gender, academic achievement, scholastic aptitude, class level, and accreditation status (Cole, 1977; Corlett, 1974; Joyce, 1961; Lee, 1971; Louttit and Patrick, 1932; McDowell, 1977; Moore, 1940; Oakley, 1978; Riley, 1962; Snider, 1965; Woodington, 1978). A rather impressive positive correlation between library competence and cumulative grade-point average (.56) was reported by Snider (1965) at Southeastern Missouri State Teachers College. Scores on the library proficiency test surpassed the predictive power of such variables as high school grades and class standing. However, it is probable that library proficiency itself is a manifestation of more basic competencies, such as intelligence and problem-solving skills.

Presently available library tests may be faulted for many deficiencies: lack of standardization, excessive reliance on memory, faulty construction, and undue emphasis on cognitive assessment. Exclusive emphasis on the evaluation of cognitive knowledge by means of paper and pencil tests is artificial at best and invalid at worst. Because the terminal objective of many programs is to develop search skills, it is vital that performance measures be constructed to assess user negotiation abilities. Paper and pencil tests may be sound instruments for gross measures of library proficiency, but performance testing is required to determine whether user behavior has been modified (Kirk, 1975; Knapp, 1966).

V. EVALUATION AND RESEARCH

A. Design and Assessment

Managers increasingly recognize that the allocation of human and monetary resources to major social action and educational programs without evaluating progress and outcomes is unjustified. Evaluation, succinctly defined as "the measurement of desirable and undesirable consequences of an action intended to forward some goal that the actor values," may produce a number of benefits (Riecken, 1972, p. 86). Systematic evaluation, by requiring a needs assessment, the development of explicit objectives, consideration of alternative strategies, and the measurement of processes and effects, encourages more careful planning. This process, in turn, furnishes information to decision makers on successes, failures, and needed modifications. Information about program effectiveness provides the basis for accountability to the program's managers and clients. Beyond the assessment of program effectiveness and the rational allocation of resources, evaluation may also serve desirable political and scholarly ends (Abt, 1976; Weiss, 1972).

Evaluation methodologies may be categorized into two principal approaches. The scientific research model is intended to produce generalizable conclusions through the specification of research questions, the articulation of operational hypotheses, and the application of rigorous measurement tools, such as statistical formulas. A variety of research methods may be employed, including survey and experimental research, case studies, and historical analysis. Another research strategy, known as illuminative evaluation, depends less on the scientific model and more on subjective assessment (Harris, 1977; Taylor, 1978). This latter form of evaluation is less concerned with specifying and measuring outcomes than with assessing ongoing progress and interactions. It is an "eclectic" strategy, utilizing such techniques as participant observation and interviewing. This emphasis on formative assessment and the interpretation of interrelationships is a salutary corrective to the sometimes antiseptic nature of classical scientific research. Illuminative evaluation may enhance our understanding of processes, sequences, and reactions, but scientific research remains unchallenged as the preferred method for evaluating and codifying outcomes.

The problem of what to evaluate is a complex one and is closely related to the goals and objectives developed for a particular program. Assessment of the cognitive knowledge acquired during an instructional session, frequently through the administration of a pretest and a posttest, appears to be the most prevalent. Skill attainment, measured by some type of performance exercise, has been studied in several settings (Hacker and Rutstein, 1978; Kirk, 1975). Very little attention has been devoted to profiling informational needs prior to instruction, to soliciting attitudinal reactions, or to more precisely defining library use as a product of bibliographic instruction. Library use, for example, may be inversely related to library instruction. As proficiency increases, it may be that more discriminative selection results in reduced circulation (Benson, 1979). All of these variables, and their interactive relationships, merit further inquiry.

Exhortations in library literature concerning the need for more rigorous design and evaluation procedures are plentiful (Kirk, 1975; Stoffle, 1978; Vogel, 1972; Werking, 1978; Wiggins and Low, 1972). Several guidelines issued by the Association of College and Research Libraries (1975, 1977) have urged practitioners of bibliographic instruction to construct measurable objectives with explicit statements of behavior and performance criteria during the design phase of instructional programs. Without predetermined and measurable objectives, it is difficult to evaluate interim progress and final results. If generalizable outcomes are contemplated, explicit objectives and validated test instruments are imperative. Despite these preachments and the avalanche of examples in the social science literature, especially education, few library instruction programs have incorporated either measurable objectives or an evaluative component (Stoffle and Bonn, 1973; Ward, 1976; Young and Brennan, 1978). One can only surmise that this condition exists because few librarians have been trained in the use of scientific research or quantitative techniques and because there may be some reluctance to manipulate the environment, a process sometimes required in order to execute certain research designs.

B. Research: Gospel or Gossamer?

All disciplines depend upon the research process to establish boundaries of accepted theory and practice, and to challenge comfortable paradigms on the way to new frontiers. Moreover, this continuing process of inquiry and communication of findings must be subject to critical appraisal. The research literature on bibliographic instruction has been increasing at a modest rate, and this trend should be applauded. Regrettably, one cannot be overly sanguine about either the quality of many studies or the uncritical reception that has all too often prevailed. Examples from the research literature, some outstanding and several defective, serve to illustrate this observation.

Concerned with the lack of a cohesive research tradition and the application of accepted methodologies, Thomas Surprenant (1978) planned and executed a Solomon four-group experimental design to assess the relative merits of programmed instruction and the lecture method in teaching basic skills about the card catalog and other bibliographic sources. The two modes of instruction were also contrasted with three levels of learning (factual, conceptual, and application). Learning materials were pretested, the groups were randomly assigned, and inferential statistics were applied. Although the sample of 79 is small, Surprenant's cautiously stated conclusion that programmed instruction is slightly more effective than the traditional lecture is significant and should be considered by those engaged in bibliographic instruction. Other studies that rate high marks for conception, execution, and generalizability are those by Hardesty *et al.* (1979) on the acquisition of search skills; by Kuo (1973) on traditional and mediated presentations; by MacGregor and McInnis (1977) on a conceptual model to fuse library instruction and different levels of information sources; and by Smith (1978) on integrated instruction.

Some studies, in contrast to the aforementioned examples, do not survive scrutiny unblemished. Breivik (1977) conducted an experimental study at Brooklyn College to examine the effect of different instructional treatments (course-related, orientation, and no instruction) on disadvantaged students. Her analysis of disadvantaged clients and the library's need to reach them is excellent; however, the results of the study cannot be transferred beyond the test location because of the nonrandom selection of treatments and the absence of sufficient statistical information and interpretation. The impact of performance worksheets on library proficiency has been evaluated at Baylor University (Jennerich and Smith, 1979). Approximately 100 students were divided into four groups, three of which received a lecture, and the fourth a lecture and the worksheet. The claim of the worksheet's superiority is vitiated by the several methodological deficiencies. The low mean score on the experimental group's pretest is not explained and suggests an abnormality. Although t tests were applied to the data, further data manipulation with analysis of variance should have been considered. Because one control group scored nearly as well as the treatment group (no significant statistical difference), moreover, there is no justification for affirming the effectiveness of the performance exercise.

In another study, Phillips and Raup (1979) concluded that neither the lecture nor programmed instruction were superior strategies for teaching the use of periodical indexes. However, they failed to analyze data for a control group that received no instruction. In a critique and reanalaysis by Adams (1979), the control group data were compared to the experimental treatments, with the result that no group was demonstrably superior. The authors' findings were decimated. With the exception of studies by Terwilliger (1975) and Tucker (1979), very little historical research germane to bibliographic instruction has appeared. Terwilliger's review of the library–college concept is based upon extensive use of secondary sources and oral interviews with prominent exponents. However, the conspicuous lack of primary archival research weakens the study's authenticity and credibility.

Good intentions and honest efforts aside, there is still much room for improvement in bibliographic instruction research (and library research generally). Not only must the research itself improve, but the appraisal function, dependent upon consumer research literacy, must become more demanding and critical. As noted, not all research, however elegantly expressed or statistically saturated, meets scientifically defensible standards. Although empirically derived research is vital to the development of bibliographic instruction, consumer awareness of inappropriate designs, misapplied statistical tests, and misinterpreted conclusions is no less important. Beware the gossamer overlay of numerical authority; not all that is quantitative may be taken as gospel.

VI. INSTRUCTIONAL PATTERNS

A. Organizational Setting

Bibliographic instruction has developed rather pragmatically in the organizational sense. Most instructional programs are administered by reference departments and staffed by librarians who devote a part of their time to teaching. A few institutions have created separate instructional departments and have assigned full-time personnel. Separate instructional units are usually established in order to emphasize instructional services and to avoid the encrustations of more established units. Library instruction units, both integrated and autonomous, are not immune from interdepartmental jealousies and territorial disputes. Regardless of the organizational configuration, successful instructional programs are characterized by strong support from the library administration and by broad-based participation of the library staff (Dyson, 1975).

Most instructional units are staffed by librarians with reference experience. Technical service personnel and subject specialists do not participate in the design and delivery of instructional services to the extent that their competencies would indicate is desirable. The low level of participation by these librarians probably results, in part, from insufficient staff, lack of personal interest, and the isolationism of public service and technical processing departments. The almost exclusive staffing of bibliographic instruction programs with public service librarians and the failure of many libraries to adopt an instructional posture may also be explained by the minimal commitment of library education to the concept of bibliographic instruction. Only several graduate schools of library science offer a credit course on education for bibliographic instruction, and most of these have not been accepted as regularly offered courses (Dyer, 1978; Kirkendall, 1978; Stanton, 1978).

B. Levels of Instruction

Bibliographic instruction is offered in a variety of instructional levels and curricular arrangements. Four levels of instruction may be identified: orientation, basic instruction, subject-related instruction, and credit courses (Fox, 1979). Orientation, the most elementary form of bibliographic instruction, usually consists of a brief introduction to library facilities and resources. Orientation sessions may be conducted by library staff or completed as self-guided tours. Except for agreement that orientation should precede instruction, there is little consensus regarding the goals, value, and long-range impact of merely orienting patrons to the library (Andrew, 1975).

Basic instruction, usually 1 or 2 hours in duration, is often presented in conjunction with freshmen English courses. Many variations of this commonly used approach are reported in the literature. Colorado State University employs a library-use exercise which all freshmen students must complete (Hacker and Rutstein, 1978). At the University of Alabama, library science students are dispatched to English classes during the time when students are ready to prepare a bibliography and continue to serve as postinstructional consultants in the library following the presentations (Keever and Raymond, 1976). Diagnostic testing, self-learning modules, and immediate feedback are features of the individualized program used by Tarrant County Junior College (Lolley, 1978). The provision of library instruction to large numbers of first-year college students (and to elementary/secondary pupils) requires extensive cooperation from the teaching staff, a motivational context to ensure that instruction is related to curricular requirements, and imaginative materials.

Advanced library instruction may range from several hours in duration to an entire semester of library instruction germane to a particular course or discipline; and it may be taught by a librarian, a faculty member, or both. This form of instruction was the focus of Patricia Knapp's experimental library project at Monteith College during 1959–1962, and Earlham College's continuing program of course-integrated instruction (Kennedy, 1970; Kirk, 1971; Knapp, 1964). Knapp and her colleagues introduced and evaluated a 4-year sequence of integrated instruction in a liberal arts setting. Close faculty–librarian cooperation and sequenced, course-related assignments were major components of the Monteith project. Earlham College adopted the Monteith schema, modified it to suit local needs, and currently offers intensive, course-related instruction throughout much of the curriculum.

Separate credit courses in bibliographic instruction are becoming more prevalent. Ten campuses of the State University of New York offered credit courses during 1978. The average enrollment was 37 students per course, and the majority of courses were offered for 1 credit. All courses were registered with departments outside of the library, a significant indication that the library has not gained administrative acceptance as a full academic division (Roberts, 1978). A separate credit course was successfully implemented at the Yale Divinity School. Student/faculty response was encouraging, one student paper was published, and faculty are using graduates of the course to assist with research projects (Bollier, 1979). Proponents of credit courses defend them as important alternatives to brief, course-related instruction and as testimonials to the educative function of libraries. Detractors of such courses cite small enrollments and the consequent dissipation of valuable staff time (Fox, 1979).

Formal, group instruction is often supplemented by informal or individualized approaches. Point-of-use instructional presentations, designed for patron self-learning, are located near the bibliographic source or service which is explicated. A variety of media, including audiotapes, printed guides, slides, and signage, is utilized. Evaluation of the relevance and effectiveness of these presentations is being neglected (Olevnik, 1978). Group instruction often does not meet the needs of individual students, and other approaches may be required. One alternative is the term paper clinic, which frequently combines group instruction with individualized attention. Participants, usually upper-level undergraduates and graduate students, make appointments to discuss topic definition, search strategy, and specific bibliographic tools (Dubin *et al.*, 1978).

C. Externally Stimulated and Self-Regulated Instruction

Externally stimulated bibliographic instruction is facilitated by a teacher or librarian, whereas self-regulated instruction is largely controlled by the learner. Studies of various instructional stimuli, conventional and self-contained, have not yielded definitive findings. Two groups of Earlham College biology students were exposed to a lecture–demonstration form of instruction and to a performance-oriented guided exercise (Kirk, 1971). Although neither strategy proved superior, students taught by a librarian sought more assistance from librarians than those who used the guided exercise. In another study 400 Alabama elementary school pupils were divided into two groups, one receiving integrated instruction from the classroom teacher and the other traditional instruction from the librarian (Smith, 1978). Statistically significant differences between treatments were not evident. Similarly inconclusive results were reported for a class of California high school students (Reveal, 1976).

Time constraints, staff limitations, and logistical problems have forced librarians to consider alternative strategies for the delivery of bibliographic instruction. These strategies have included programmed instruction, mediated presentations, and computer-assisted instruction. Programmed instruction is a particularly attractive alternative to personalized teaching in those cases where discrete knowledges and skills predominate. Advantages claimed for programmed learning modules include self-pacing, logical ordering of information, immediate reinforcement, improved self-image, and modest cost following development of the material. Numerous studies involving many disciplines have addressed the comparative merits of programmed instruction and conventional teaching, and it must be noted that the balance sheet of these studies indicates no clear advantage for programmed instruction (Hardison, 1977; Mayhew, 1977; Roth, 1978; Sellmer, 1973; Wendt, 1963; Wilbert, 1976). However, the proved effectiveness of this form of instruction makes it an important strategy for large, introductory applications.

D. Mediated and Computer-Assisted Learning

That we live in a multimedia environment has become an overworked, but nevertheless accurate cliche. Nonprint presentations have been used extensively in support of bibliographic instruction, and there is some research evidence that audiovisual instruction is at least equal in effectiveness to the more conventional approaches (Evans, 1969; Fjällbrant, 1976; Kuo, 1973; Wassom, 1967). Slide/tape programs, perhaps the most commonly employed media, offer several advantages over films and videotapes: low cost, ease of updating, flexibility, and speed of presentation. Despite these significant advantages, there are some equally important caveats. Media presentations are often expensive; may deprive the learner of a personalized, interactive experience with a teacher; and tend to be overly detailed (Hardesty, 1976). The impersonal nature of self-instructional and mediated strategies may reduce the extent and quality of subsequent interaction with the library staff. The expertise required to produce a polished multimedia program and the lack of transferability to another setting should also be weighed when various approaches are considered.

Although many library operations are now routinely executed by computer, the application of computer technology to bibliographic instruction is limited (Axeen, 1967; Culkin, 1972; Genung, 1967; Hansen, 1972). High developmental costs and the lack of computer literacy in the library profession probably account for the limited advances in this area. A major experiment at the University of Denver, known as the Query Analysis System, was initiated to increase library utilization by sociology students. The Denver system employs computer-aided instruction that is designed to link the language of the student, the terminology of sociology, and the descriptors used by librarians and indexers. Students may enter search terms in a conversational, interactive mode. Terms are subsequently refined and related to appropriate bibliographic sources. User input of new terms for future manipulation is a novel feature (Drabek *et al.*, 1978). Perhaps future experimentation will incorporate linkages between vocabularies, bibliographic sources, and citations from commercially available data bases.

VII. REFLECTIONS

Bibliographic instruction, in spite of its many converts and applications, is nevertheless vulnerable on a number of fronts: lack of conceptual definition, spotty research, uneven financial support, and insufficient endorsement outside of the library community. If history may be counted upon to distill lessons for the future, it is just such emerging services and outreach programs as bibliographic instruction that are the first to feel the budgetary knife. Sustaining and enlarging upon the progress to date will require commitment, flexibility, better research, and some new directions.

Conceptual clarification is needed to transcend the artificial dichotomy of instruction or information. Bibliographic instruction covers those enabling skills and knowledges which allow library clients to acquire varying degrees of self-sufficiency. Instruction should be relevant, voluntary, and never considered as a substitute for the direct provision of information. More energy and imagination ought to be focused on the marketing and delivery of bibliographic instruction programs. Creative and aggressive advertising is too often a missing ingredient in the planning phase of instructional services (Graef and Greenwood, 1979). The predominant influence of the teacher suggests that bibliographic instruction, perhaps under the rubric of bibliographic update sessions, should be considered for this group (Lipow, 1979). Students in the humanities and social sciences have been the chief recipients of instruction. With the recent proliferation of vocational programs and professional schools, students in these programs should be increasingly "targeted" for instructional programs which meet their nontraditional informational needs.

The present research agenda is rather static and somewhat skewed. It is doubtful, for example, that future research should continue to concentrate on studies of media differentiation and the value of self-instructional approaches. The extant literature already suggests that various mediated and self-learning strategies are effective when they are appropriately applied and executed. Significant topics that have received little or no attention include the longitudinal impact of instruction; cost studies; the relationship of instruction to catalog use, reference inquiries, on-line services, and circulation patterns; and the content of instructional presentations. Ultimately, it is the quality of the questions that are asked and the care with which answers are sought that will determine the vitality and acceptance of bibliographic instruction.

REFERENCES

Abt, C. C. (1976). "The Evaluation of Social Programs." Sage, Beverly Hills, California.

Adams, M. (1979). Letter to the Editor. *Journal of Academic Librarianship* 5, 93-94.

Andrew, A. (1975). Getting started: Designing a program, proposal writing, funding: A conversation. *In* "Planning and Developing a Library Orientation Program." (Proceedings of the Third Annual Conference on Library Orientation for Academic Libraries, Eastern Michigan University, May 3-4, 1973.) (M. Bolner, ed.), pp. 1-11. Pierian Press, Ann Arbor, Michigan.

Association of College and Research Libraries. American Library Association (1975). Toward guidelines for bibliographic instruction in academic libraries. *College & Research Library News* 36, 137-139.

Association of College and Research Libraries. American Library Association (1977).

Guidelines for bibliographic instruction in academic libraries. *College & Research Library News* **38**, 92.

Atkin, P. (1971). "Bibliography of Use Surveys of Public and Academic Libraries, 1950–Nov. 1970." Library Association, London.

Axeen, M. E. (1967). "Teaching the Use of the Library to Undergraduates: An Experimental Comparison of Computer-Based Instruction and the Conventional Lecture Method." Unpublished dissertation, University of Illinois.

Benson, J. (1979). "Bibliographic Instruction: A Radical Assessment." (Paper presented at the Second Annual Southeastern Conference on Approaches to Bibliographic Instruction, College of Charleston, Charleston, South Carolina, March 22–23.)

Blazek, R. D. (1971). The influence of the teacher on pupil use of nonrequired library materials in mathematics—an experimental study. *Illinois Libraries* **53**, 528–544.

Bloomfield, M. (1974). Testing for library-use competence. *In* "Educating the Library User" (J. Lubans, ed.), pp. 221–231. Bowker, New York.

Bollier, J. A. (1979). Bibliographic instruction in the graduate professional theological school. *In* "New Horizons for Academic Libraries" (R. D. Stueart and R. D. Johnson, eds.), pp. 205–211. K. G. Saur, New York.

Bonn, G. S. (1960). "Training Laymen in the Use of the Library." (The State of the Library Art, Vol. 2, Part 1, R. Shaw, ed.) Graduate School of Library Service, Rutgers University, New Brunswick, New Jersey.

Breivik, P. S. (1977). "Open Admissions and the Academic Library." American Library Association, Chicago, Illinois.

Butler, H. L. (1942). The library in education. *Review of Educational Research* **12**, 323–335.

Cole, J. B. (1977). "Library Skills Instruction and Retention: A Report on a Skills Program for Fourth, Fifth, and Sixth Grades with a Note on Its Relationship to Use of the High School Library." Unpublished thesis, University of Chicago.

Corlett, D. (1974). Library skills, study habits and attitudes, and sex as related to academic achievement. *Educational and Psychological Measurement* **34**, 967–969.

Crossley, C. A., and Clews, J. P. (1974). "Evolution of the Educational Technology in Information Handling Instruction: A Literature Review and Bibliography." Research and Development Department, British Library, London. (OSTI Report 5220.)

Culkin, P. B. (1972). Computer-assisted instruction in library use. *Drexel Library Quarterly* **8**, 301–311.

Davis, E. (1970). The unchanging profile—a review of the literature. *Library-College Journal* **3**, 11–19.

Davis, R. A., and Bailey, C. A. (1964). "Bibliography of Use Studies." Graduate School of Library Science, Drexel Institute of Technology, Philadelphia, Pennsylvania. (Drexel Library School Series No. 18.)

DeWeese, L. C. (1967). A bibliography of library use studies. *In* "Report on a Statistical Study of Book Use" (A. K. Jain) pp. 45. Purdue University, Lafayette, Indiana.

Drabek, T. E., Shaw, W., and Culkin, P. B. (1978). The query analysis system: A new

tool for increasing the effectiveness of library utilization by sociology students. *Teaching Sociology* **6**, 47-68.
Dubin, E., Hurych, J., and McMillan, P. (1978). An in depth analysis of a term paper clinic. *Illinois Libraries* **60**, 324-333.
Dyer, E. (1978). Formal library science courses on library instruction. *Journal of Education for Librarianship* **18**, 359-361.
Dyson, A. J. (1975). Organizing undergraduate library instruction: The English and American experience. *Journal of Academic Librarianship* **1**, 9-13.
el-Hagrasy, S. M. (1962). The teacher's role in library service: An investigation and its devices. *Journal of Experimental Education* **30**, 347-354.
Evans, R. W. (1969). Using slides for library orientation. *Illinois Libraries* **51**, 300-303.
Fjällbrant, N. (1976). Teaching methods for the education of the library-user. *Libri* **26**, 252-267.
Ford, G. (1973). Research in user behavior in university libraries. *Journal of Documentation* **29**, 85-106.
Fox, P. K. (1979). "User Education in the Humanities in U.S. Academic Libraries." Research and Development Department, British Library, London. (British Library Research & Development Report No. 5474.)
Genung, H. (1967). Can machines teach the use of the library? *College & Research Libraries* **28**, 25-30.
Givens, J. (1974). The use of resources in the learning experience. *In* "Advances in Librarianship" (M. J. Voigt, ed.), Vol. 4, pp. 149-174. Academic Press, New York.
Graef, J. L., and Greenwood, L. (1979). Marketing library services: A case study in providing bibliographic instruction in an academic library. *In* "New Horizons for Academic Libraries" (R. D. Stueart and R. D. Johnson, eds.), pp. 212-228. K. G. Saur, New York.
Hacker, B. L., and Rutstein, J. S. (1978). Educating large numbers of users in university libraries: An analysis and a case study. *In* "Progress in Educating the Library User" (J. Lubans, ed.), pp. 105-123. Bowker, New York.
Hale, I. W. (1969). "The Influence of Library Services Upon the Academic Achievement of Twelfth Grade Students at Crestwood Senior High School, Chesapeake, Virginia." Department of Library Education, University of Georgia, Athens. (ERIC Document 047 694.)
Hansen, L. N. (1972). Computer-assisted instruction in library use: An evaluation. *Drexel Library Quarterly* **8**, 345-355.
Hardesty, L. (1976). "Survey of the Use of Slide/Tape Presentations for Orientation and Instruction Purposes in Academic Libraries." (ERIC Document 116 711.)
Hardesty, L., Lovrich, N. P., and Mannon, J. (1979). Evaluating library-use instruction. *College & Research Libraries* **40**, 309-317.
Hardison, D. D. (1977). "Library Instruction in a Community College: A Study to Determine the Comparative Effectiveness of Classroom Teaching and a Video Self-Instruction Unit for Developmental and Degree-Program Students." Unpublished dissertation, Virginia Polytechnic Institute and State University.
Harkin, W. D. (1971). "Analysis of Secondary School Library Media Programs in Re-

lation to Academic Success of Ball State University Students in their Freshman and Sophomore Years." Unpublished dissertation, Ball State University.

Harris, C. (1977). Illuminative evaluation of user education programs. *Aslib Proceedings* **29**, 348–362.

Henne, F. (1966). Instruction in the use of the library and library use by students. *In* "Conference on the Use of Printed and Audio-Visual Materials for Instructional Purposes" (M. Tauber and I. R. Stephens, eds.), pp. 164–190. School of Library Service, Columbia University, New York.

Hostrop, R. W. (1968). "Teaching and the Community College Library." Shoe String Press, Hamden, Connecticut.

Hyland, A. M. (1978). "Development and Administration of *The Ohio School Library/Media Test*: An Instrument for Assessing a Student's Library/Media Ability." Unpublished dissertation, University of Toledo.

Jennerich, E. Z., and Smith, B. H. (1979). A bibliographic instruction program in music. *College & Research Libraries* **40**, 226–233.

Joyce, W. D. (1961). A study of academic achievement and performance on a test of library understandings. *Journal of Educational Research* **54**, 198–199.

Katz, W. A. (1974). "Introduction to Reference Work, Vol. 2: Reference Services and Reference Processes," 2d ed. McGraw-Hill, New York.

Katz, W. A. (1978). "Introduction to Reference Work, Vol. 2: Reference Services and Reference Processes," 3d ed. McGraw-Hill, New York.

Keever, E. H., and Raymond, J. C. (1976). Integrated library instruction on the university campus: Experiment at the University of Alabama. *Journal of Academic Librarianship* **2**, 185–187.

Kennedy, J. T. (1970). Integrated library instruction. *Library Journal* **95**, 1450–1453.

Kirk, T. G. (1971). A comparison of two methods of library instruction for students in introductory biology. *College & Research Libraries* **32**, 465–474.

Kirk, T. G. (1975). Bibliographic instruction—a review of research. *In* "Evaluating Library Use Instruction." (Papers Presented at the University of Denver Conference on the Evaluation of Library Instruction, December 13–14, 1973.) (R. J. Beeler, ed.), pp. 1–29. Pierian Press, Ann Arbor, Michigan.

Kirkendall, C. A., ed. (1978). "Putting Library Instruction in Its Place: In the Library and In the Library School." (Papers presented at the Seventh Annual Conference on Library Orientation for Academic Libraries, Eastern Michigan University, May 12–13, 1977.) Pierian Press, Ann Arbor, Michigan.

Knapp, P. B. (1959). "College Teaching and the College Library." American Library Association, Chicago, Illinois. (ACRL Monograph No. 23.)

Knapp, P. B. (1964). The methodology and results of the Monteith Pilot Project. *Library Trends* **13**, 84–102.

Knapp, P. B. (1966). "The Monteith College Library Experiment." Scarecrow Press, New York.

Krier, M. (1976). Bibliographic instruction: A checklist of the literature, 1931–1975. *Reference Services Review* **4**, 7–31.

Kuo, F. F. (1973). A comparison of six versions of science library instruction. *College & Research Libraries* **34**, 287–290.

Ladner, M. M. (1966). "The Relationship Between Available Pre-College Library Ser-

vice and Ability to Use the College Library." Unpublished thesis, Emory University.
Lee, C. H. (1971). "The Library Skills of Prospective Teachers at the University of Georgia." Unpublished thesis, University of Georgia.
Lindgren, J. (1978). Seeking a useful tradition for library user instruction in the college library. *In* "Progress in Educating the Library User" (J. Lubans, ed.), pp. 71–91. Bowker, New York.
Lipow, A. G. (1979). Teaching the faculty to use the library: A successful program of in-depth seminars for University of California, Berkeley, faculty. *In* "New Horizons for Academic Libraries" (R. D. Stueart and R. D. Johnson, eds.), pp. 262–267. K. G. Saur, New York.
Lockwood, D. L. (1979). "Library Instruction: A Bibliography." Greenwood Press, Westport, Connecticut.
Lolley, J. (1978). Instruction in junior and community colleges. *In* "Progress in Educating the Library User" (J. Lubans, ed.), pp. 57–69. Bowker, New York.
Louttit, C. M., and Patrick, J. R. (1932). A study of students' knowledge in the use of the library. *Journal of Applied Psychology* **16**, 475–483.
Lubans, J. (1970). On non-use of an academic library: A report of findings. *In* "Use, Misuse and Non-use of Academic Libraries," pp. 47–70 College and University Libraries Section, New York Library Association, Woodside, New York.
Lubans, J. (1972). "Report to the Council on Library Resources on a Fellowship Awarded for 1971/72." University of Colorado Library, Boulder. (Mimeograph copy.)
Lubans, J., ed. (1974). "Educating the Library User." Bowker, New York.
Lubans, J., ed. (1978). "Progress in Educating the Library User." Bowker, New York.
McClure, C. R. (1974). Reference theory of specific information retrieval. *RQ* **13**, 207–212.
McDowell, S. (1977). "A Study of the Library Skills of Selected College Freshmen as Related to High School Library Orientation." Unpublished dissertation, University of Michigan.
McGregor, J., and McInnis, R. G. (1977). Integrating classroom instruction and library research: The cognitive functions of bibliographic network functions. *Journal of Higher Education* **48**, 17–38.
Mayhew, L. B. (1977). "Legacy of the Seventies: Experiment, Economy, Equality, and Expediency in American Higher Education." Jossey-Bass, San Francisco, California.
Miller, S. W. (1978). "Library Use Instruction in Selected American Colleges." Graduate School of Library Science, University of Illinois, Urbana. (*Occasional Papers*, No. 134.)
Mitchell, R. (1973). "Academic Achievement and Use of the Secondary School Library." Unpublished thesis, Tasmanian School of Education, Australia.
Moore, J. E. (1940). The relationships between library information and elementary school attainment. *Peabody Journal of Education* **18**, 27–31.
Oakley, A. D. (1978). "Content Analysis of Student Responses in Topic-Centered Library Orientation." Unpublished dissertation, Boston University.

Olevnik, P. O. (1978). Non-formalized point-of-use library instruction: A survey. *Catholic Library World* **50**, 218–220.

Perkins, R. (1965). "The Prospective Teacher's Knowledge of Library Fundamentals." Scarecrow Press, New York.

Phillips, L. L., and Raup, E. A. (1979). Comparing methods for teaching use of periodical indexes. *Journal of Academic Librarianship* **4**, 420–423.

Reveal, A. H. (1976). "Library Instruction and Team Teaching." (ERIC Document 144 604.)

Riecken, H. W. (1972). Memorandum on program evaluation. *In* "Evaluating Action Programs: Readings in Social Action and Education" (C. H. Weiss, ed.), pp. 85–104. Allyn & Bacon, Boston, Massachusetts.

Riley, L. E. (1962). "A Study of the Performance on a Library Orientation Test in Relation to the Academic Achievement and Scholastic Aptitude of a Selected Group of Freshmen College Students at Tuskegee Institute." Unpublished thesis, Atlanta University.

Roberts, A. (1978). "A Study of Ten SUNY Campuses Offering an Undergraduate Credit Course in Library Instruction." (ERIC Document 157 529.)

Roth, E. C. (1978). "Locus of Control and The Teaching of Library Instruction: A Comparative Study." Unpublished dissertation, University of Maryland.

Schiller, A. R. (1965). Reference service: Instruction or information. *Library Quarterly* **35**, 52–60.

Scrivener, J. E. (1972). Instruction in library use: The persisting problem. *Australian Academic and Research Libraries* **3**, 87–119.

Sellmer, D. F. (1973). "Teaching Fourth Grade Children to Use a Library Catalog: A Programmed Approach." Unpublished dissertation, Ball State University.

Smith, J. B. (1978). "An Exploratory Study of the Effectiveness of an Innovative Process Designed to Integrate Library Skills into the Curriculum." Unpublished dissertation, George Peabody College for Teachers.

Snider, F. E. (1965). "The Relationships of Library Ability to Performance in College." Unpublished dissertation, University of Illinois.

Stanton, V. (1978). The library school: Its role in teaching the use of the library. *In* "Progress in Educating the Library User" (J. Lubans, ed.), pp. 139–146. Bowker, New York.

Stevenson, M. (1977). Education of users of libraries and information services. *Journal of Documentation* **33**, 53–78.

Stoffle, C. J. (1978). Writing objectives for bibliographic instruction. *In* "Proceedings of the Southeastern Conference on Approaches to Bibliographic Instruction, March 16–17" (C. Oberman-Soroka, ed.), pp. 7–32. College of Charleston, Charleston, South Carolina.

Stoffle, C. J., and Bonn, G. (1973). An inventory of library orientation and instructional methods. *RQ* **13**, 129–133.

Stueart, R. D. (1971). "The Area Specialist Bibliographer: An Inquiry into His Role." Unpublished dissertation, University of Pittsburgh.

Surprenant, T. (1978). A comparison of lecture and programmed instruction in the teaching of basic catalog card and bibliographic information—results of a pretest. *In* "Proceedings of the Southeastern Conference on Approaches to Bibliographic

Instruction, March 16–17" (C. Oberman-Soroka, ed.), pp. 54–66. College of Charleston, Charleston, South Carolina.
Taylor, P. J. (1978). User education and the role of evaluation. *Unesco Bulletin for Libraries* **32**, 252–258.
Terwilliger, G. H. P. (1975). "The Library-College: A Movement for Experimental and Innovative Learning Concepts; Applications and Implications for Higher Education." Unpublished dissertation, University of Maryland.
Thompson, R. I., and Nicholson, J. B. (1941). Significant influences on general circulation in a small college library. *Library Quarterly* **11**, 142–185.
Tidmarsh, M. N. (1968). Instruction in the use of academic libraries. *In* "University and Research Library Studies" (W. L. Saunders, ed.), pp. 39–83. Pergamon, Oxford.
Tucker, J. M. (1979). The origins of bibliographic instruction in academic libraries, 1876–1914. *In* "New Horizons for Academic Libraries" (R. D. Stueart and R. D. Johnson, eds.), pp. 268–276. K. G. Saur, New York.
Vogel, J. T. (1972). A critical overview of the evaluation of library instruction. *Drexel Library Quarterly* **8**, 315–323.
Wagers, R. (1978). American reference theory and the information dogma. *Journal of Library History* **13**, 265–281.
Walker, R. D. (1963). "The Availability of Library Service and Academic Achievement." Illinois State Library, Springfield. (Research Series No. 4.)
Ward, J. E. (1976). Library and bibliographic instruction in southeastern academic libraries. *Southeastern Librarian* **26**, 148–159.
Wassom, E. E. (1967). "A Study of the Effects of Multimedia Instructional Techniques on a College Freshman Library Orientation Program." Unpublished dissertation, Oklahoma State University.
Weiss, C. H., ed. (1972). "Evaluating Action Programs: Readings in Social Action and Education." Allyn & Bacon, Boston, Massachusetts.
Wendt, P. (1963). "A Study to Determine the Extent to Which Instruction to University Freshmen in the Use of the University Library Can be Turned Over to Teaching Machines." Southern Illinois University, Carbondale, Illinois.
Wendt, P. (1967). New library materials and technology for instruction and research. *Library Trends* **16**, 199–210.
Werking, R. H. (1978). The place of evaluation in bibliographic education. *In* "Proceedings of the Southeastern Conference on Approaches to Bibliographic Instruction, March 16–17" (C. Oberman-Soroka, ed.), pp. 100–118. College of Charleston, Charleston, South Carolina.
Whitworth, T. A. (1970). The centrality of the librarian's role in the English technical college. *Research in Librarianship* **3**, 7–36.
Wiggins, M. E., and Low, D. S. (1972). Use of an instructional psychology model for development of library-use instructional programs. *Drexel Library Quarterly* **8**, 269–279.
Wilbert, S. S. (1976). "A Study of Competency-Based Instruction to Determine Its Viability as a Technique to Teaching Basic Library Skills to a Selected Sample of Seventh Grade Students." Unpublished dissertation, Wayne State University.

Wilson, P. (1979). Librarians as teachers: The study of an organization fiction. *Library Quarterly* **49**, 146–162.
Woodington, C. J. C. (1978). "The Effects of Elementary School Accreditation on the Development of Selected Library-Related Skills." Unpublished dissertation, University of Mississippi.
Young, A. P. (1974). Research on library-user education. *In* "Educating the Library User" (J. Lubans, ed.), pp. 1–15. Bowker, New York.
Young, A. P., and Brennan, E. B. (1978). Bibliographic instruction: A review of research and applications. *In* "Progress in Educating the Library User" (J. Lubans, ed.), pp. 13–28. Bowker, New York.

Library Materials Budgeting in the Private University Library: Austerity and Action

FREDERICK C. LYNDEN

Brown University

I.	Introduction	90
II.	The Library Materials Budgeting Literature	91
III.	Environment and the Budgeting Process	96
	A. University Budgeting Constraints	97
	B. Library Materials Budgeting Constraints	98
	C. How the Environment Affects Materials Budgeting	100
IV.	Budget Formulation and Presentation	101
	A. Budgeting Cycle	101
	B. Participants	102
	C. Budget Format	102
	D. Communication Process	103
	E. Documentation	104
	F. Sources of Funding	105
	G. Uses of Automated Data	107
	H. Use of National Indexes and Local Data	108
	I. Staff Participation	110
	J. Budget Presentation	110
	K. Meeting University Guidelines	111
	L. The Library as a Funding Priority	112
	M. Faculty Participation	112
	N. 1978–1979 Materials Budgets	113
	O. Arguments for Increasing Materials Funding	113
	P. Rationale for Modifying a Request	114

V. Collection Development and the Materials Budget............. 116
   A. Effects of Limited Budgets on Collection Development 116
   B. Priority of the Materials Budget 117
   C. Economic Conditions Causing Increased Materials Budgets 118
   D. Responses to these Economic Conditions 118
   E. Increases in the Twelve Libraries 119
   F. Allocations... 120
   G. Procedural and Administrative Methods for Reducing Expenditures 123
   H. Duplication 123
   I. Serials Review 124
   J. Selectivity and Patterns of Purchasing 124
   K. Serials... 125
   L. Microforms 126
   M. Foreign Materials..................................... 126
   N. Blanket Order Arrangements 127
   O. Mechanics of Spending Materials Funds 128
   P. Conclusions 129
VI. Interlibrary Cooperation and the Materials Budget.............. 131
   A. Rationale for Cooperation 132
   B. Cost Reductions 133
   C. Mechanics 133
   D. Political Implications 135
   E. Financial Considerations.............................. 137
   F. Other Cooperative Measures 138
   G. Interlibrary Loans and the Materials Budget 138
VII. Conclusion 139
   Appendix A 145
   Appendix B 146
   Appendix C 146
   Appendix D 147
   Appendix E 147
   Appendix F 148
   Appendix G 149
   Appendix H 150
   References 151

I. INTRODUCTION

Budgetary restraints remain in 1980 one of the most serious, if not the most serious, of problems facing academic libraries in America. The shrinking dollar value in the face of inflation and the stabilization of library budgets has had a particularly significant impact on collection development. As a result the question of acquisitions in austere times has once again garnered intense attention (see, e.g., Lynden, 1978b, 1979; Magrill and East, 1978). Librarians are being forced to pay much closer attention to all aspects of the library materials question, but of increasing pertinence is the area of budgeting for the acquisitions program. This essay is intended to address the aspect in several ways.

First, a concise overview of the literature on the budgeting process for library materials is presented. This review highlights articles that cover some of the practical aspects of how acquisition funds are raised, spent, or saved. Until recently, library literature on the subject has focused primarily on techniques for allocating collection development funds to subject areas and has largely ignored the process of building, justifying, and expending the collection budget. Interest in the fiscal, political, and administrative facets of materials budgeting is growing as librarians contend with the new economic realities.

Second, in hopes of contributing some concrete help in this vital area, a detailed analysis of the library materials budgeting process in 12 large private libraries is summarized.* This analysis focuses on three aspects of the materials budgeting: the formation of the budget itself, the relationship between the materials budget and collection development, and the influence of interlibrary cooperation on materials budgets. By focusing on the budgetary process, this study tries to illustrate how the 12 libraries are coping with the rising costs of library materials and institutional pressures to reduce expenditures.

II. THE LIBRARY MATERIALS BUDGETING LITERATURE

There are very few reviews or articles that specifically describe the budgeting process for materials because it is normally only one part of the entire sequence of financial negotiations with the university administration. However, because inflation rates for materials are unusually high and materials costs are one of the largest segments of a library's budget, acquisition budgets are ordinarily discussed separately

---

*This essay represents a shortened and up-dated version of a report resulting from a fellowship from the Council on Library Resources (Lynden, 1978a). The 12 institutions covered are Brown, Chicago, Cornell, Harvard, Johns Hopkins, Northwestern, Pennsylvania, Princeton, Rice, Stanford, University of Southern California, and Yale. Cited on list as new 1978a ''Librarian Materials Budgeting in Twelve Private University Libraries.'' Providence, RI.

from the rest of the budget, and general treatises on budgeting often single out special facets of budgeting for materials. Rogers and Weber (1971) in their chapter "Budgeting and Fiscal Management" mention the problems resulting from foreign purchasing, the expansion of publishing, collection "programs," the composition of collections, and the impact of processing, and Martin (1978) examines materials budgeting as part of the process of setting up an academic library budget, monitoring it, and closing it out. He also presents a case study that illustrates the budgeting process over 4 years, and he includes materials funding in his example. Lee's (1977) proceedings of a conference on no-growth budgets, held at Indiana State University in October 1976, describe various aspects of budgeting, including aspects of materials budgeting, whereas Kiley's (1977) bibliography of articles and books on library budgeting from 1970 to mid-1976 is useful and lists many articles directly concerned with materials budgeting. The Association of Research Libraries (1979) SPEC (Systems and Procedures Exchange Center) Kit *Cost Studies and Fiscal Planning* (March) includes cost studies on materials budgeting at Massachusetts Institute of Technology, Michigan, and Purdue. These documents illustrate the arguments used by libraries to convince university administrators of the need for larger materials budgets. The resources literature of 1977 and 1978 indicates a renewed interest in the budgeting process, particularly acquisition budgets (Lynden, 1978b, 1979).

Presentation of the materials budget is an important aspect of the budgeting process, particularly the preparation and justification. The Association of Research Libraries (1977c) SPEC Kit *Preparation and Presentation of the Library Budget* (April) includes presentations justifying the materials expenditures at Emory and Princeton, and the Association of Research Libraries (1977b), SPEC Kit *Allocation of Resources* (March) contains documentation for justifying material budgets at Dartmouth, Pennsylvania State, and Arizona State. Heyeck (1976b) discusses a number of planning strategies for requesting collection funds, including a local cost study, an analysis of the impact of devaluation on the acquisitions budget, a faculty survey, and the library's own fund raiser. Bacchetti (1976), looking at budgets from the university administrative viewpoint, suggests that librarians do more "budget modelling, trade-off analysis, and planning" as well as "search for other intra- and interlibrary productivity increasing measures." Munn (1968), in an article that has stood the test of time, notes that university administrators view the library as a "bottomless pit" and admonishes librarians about their lack of political clout. Webster (1977) also suggests there is "inadequate involvement in the university planning process."

The documentation of the costs of library materials is an important aspect of the preparation and presentation of the acquisitions budget. Lynden (1977) describes sources of information on the costs of library materials, indicating where libraries can obtain data on the costs of materials. Local cost studies are done by a number of institutions and the Association of Research Libraries (ARL) (1980) did a SPEC Kit on cost studies carried out in ARL libraries (January). Halstead (1975) began his *Higher Education Prices and Price Index* in 1975 and has published an annual supplement since. His data relate directly to academic libraries and include a separate table for average prices for United States hardcover books and periodicals and foreign monographs. The *American National Standard Criteria for Price Indexes for Library Materials* (American National Standards Institute, 1974) indicates how libraries can construct price indexes. An example of special indexes constructed to indicate the rise in prices of journals in a particular subject field is Clasquin and Cohen's (1979) index *Physics and Chemistry Journal Prices*. Downes (1977) recommends that federal agencies and professional associations collect and publish comparative data on such indicators as "acquisition expenditures per FTE [full time equivalent] student."

Although the allocation of acquisition funds is usually done after the materials budgeting process is completed, this apportionment can be an important consideration in the negotiations. Allocations can serve a political function in encouraging communications with the faculty and as a basis for determining future needs for support. The amount of literature on allocations is large, but much of the literature has considered methodology rather than the value of allocations to the budgetary process. Schad (1978) emphasizes how the allocation process can lead to the posing of important questions about the institution and its collections. The ALA (1979) *Guidelines for the Allocation of Library Materials Budgets* assumes that allocations will "enable the library to demonstrate to both fiscal authorities and patrons how money is being allocated and spent" and "provide a method for fulfilling collection goals and needs, as well as institutional goals." The *Guidelines* incorporate a short bibliography of articles on the subject. The ARL (1977a) SPEC Kit on the *Allocation of Materials Funds in Academic Libraries* (September) notes that "while the incentive for the examination of traditional methods of decision-making regarding the allocation of funds for collection development often has been economic, the result frequently has been to relate current acquisitions more closely to the university's goals and objectives." Johnson and Rutstein (1979) conclude that "allocation of the book budgets is one of the most political problems libraries have within the university setting."

An important consideration in the budgeting process is the source of funding. According to a study by Cohen and Leeson (1979), "academic libraries, particularly public ones, depend on their universities for the bulk of their financial support," and federal grants to academic libraries, on a direct basis, are of minor importance. The funding situation concerns academic librarians because many observers forsee an extremely austere future. The report of the National Enquiry into Scholarly Communication (1979) notes: "Research library budgets, which in the majority of cases depend on university budgets, are unlikely to increase significantly in constant dollars over the next decade." Some libraries have made a strong effort to raise outside funds. One method has been to hire an internal staff member to do fund raising. This approach was described in an early article by Eaton (1971), which recommends a library consider having its own development officer. A chapter from this Council on Library Resources (CLR) case study (Lynden, 1978a), examining the fundraising procedures at the 12 privately supported universities was published in an ARL (1978) SPEC Kit, *External Fund Raising in ARL Libraries* (October).

This CLR study also addresses the effects of limited budgets on collection development. Some conclusions Fry and White (1976) reach in their study of scholarly and research journals are supported in this study. Libraries continue to make shifts toward serials in their expenditures. Material cost increases continue to exceed the rate of funding received for materials, and the allocation for other expenditures, such as equipment and supplies, continues to rise (computer costs are one factor). Baatz (1978), in his CLR study on collection development, concludes that retrospective purchasing has been seriously curtailed because of a lack of funds, and use studies are receiving more emphasis now as libraries attempt to cut back on purchasing. Cooperation seems to "be much more complex than most librarians had thought" and requires funds to succeed. The study presented here confirms his findings. Machlup and Leeson's (1978) discouraging attempts to obtain documentation on library expenditures as documented in *Information through the Printed Word* are verified in this study by the lack of annual report statistics on purchasing, information on the source of funding, etc. Their observations on the cuts that libraries made are also corroborated by the actions taken in this study, e.g., reductions in serial subscriptions. They foresee better data through computerized statistics, such as those gathered by Evans (1978) at the State University of New York (SUNY). The Collection Analysis Project (CAP) (Gardner, 1978, 1979) is one signal that libraries are becoming more concerned about the management of the collection process during periods of limited funding. Another study, the Cline-Sinott study (1979), is symptomatic of the attention now being paid to the collection process. Cline and Sinott report that fund allocations for materials are largely historically based. Both CAP and the Cline-Sinott study urge a budgeting process for materials that takes account of all the forces affecting libraries: financial, political, environmental, economic, and historical.

The papers that follow also examine the effects of resource sharing on the materials budget. Cost avoidance has been the major result of resource sharing. Savings cannot be realized immediately, as Dunlap (1977), speaking at a national conference on resource sharing, points out: "The problem here may be that we tend to look for immediate results and for visible savings to justify expenditures. The real benefits of cooperative action cannot be realized in the short run." Other ingredients for effective resource sharing seem to be formalized structures and administrative participation. The Research Libraries Group (RLG), which expanded in 1979 beyond its membership of Yale, Columbia, New York Public, and Harvard after Harvard dropped out, has active participation of university administrators on its governing board. (Its expanded membership includes, among other universities, Cornell, Michigan, Princeton, University of Pennsylvania, and Stanford, all institutions ranking in the top twenty for size of collections) The RLG (1979) relies upon a series of formal programs for sharing resources. Since its inception RLG member libraries have canceled more than 3000 serial subscriptions and avoided placing more than 2600 new serial subscriptions. Regional and local efforts are only part of the solution to the fiscal crisis in building research library collections. Three recent studies: the report of the National Enquiry into Scholarly Communication (1979), the Council on Library Resources (1978) study on a National Periodicals Center, and Osburn's (1979) *Academic Research and Library Resources,* examine the crisis from a national perspective. The National Enquiry recommends a national bibliographic system, a national periodicals center, a national library agency, urgent attention to preservation, federal support for research collections, and better bibliographic instruction. The Council on Library Resources outlines a detailed plan for a national periodicals center that would relieve research libraries of the burden of maintaining extensive local periodical collections. Osburn suggests that the federal government has a responsibility for financial support to research libraries for maintaining the research system that the government created. He also urges librarians to be more aware of trends in research and scholarship; to participate actively in the university communications and planning process; and to "approach their work in a more academic manner than they have in the past" by gathering management information.

III. ENVIRONMENT AND THE BUDGETING PROCESS

The library budgeting environment at private university libraries is strongly influenced by the economic conditions at the parent institution. An analysis of ARL Statistics shows that 1976–1977 was one of the worst years in 15 years for library materials expenditures in the academic libraries in this study (see Appendix A); 1977–78 was equally bad. Four of the 12 libraries showed a drop in materials expenditures during both years. The worst previous year was 1971–1972, when six of these libraries had a decrease in expenditures. Because private libraries are very dependent upon the financial situation at their own institutions, it is important to understand the local fiscal constraints when the budget is being prepared. The university's financial annual report, university budget documents, the university bulletin or newsletter, the alumni magazine, development literature, and other official university reports can provide the background for the librarian's understanding of the local budgeting environment. The need for greater selectivity, cooperation with other libraries, cooperative storage, and other cost-saving measures will become more apparent when librarians comprehend the conditions that dictate the budgeted amounts. Likewise, as conditions improve librarians can be aware of the opportunities for extending library services. Reading the official literature of the university, however, cannot substitute for the personal contacts with faculty and administration in a university, and in these times of financial stringency librarians must be cognizant of the competing interests. Budgeting is very much a political process, and each librarian must interact with other campus staff with these factors in mind.

A. University Budgeting Constraints

Two institutions that have made university budgeting a campuswide concern are Yale and Stanford. The description of the conditions prior to 1976–1977 come primarily from their documents, but other financial annual reports and library annual reports help to create a composite picture of the conditions resulting in the decreased expenditures for materials during 1976–1977 and 1977–1978. The following factors were operative:

1. The inflationary spiral (Although the double-digit inflation of 1974 had begun to subside by 1975, there has been a steady increase in the CPI since then, and 1979 was expected to again show a double-digit percentage increase.)
2. Dollar devaluation (The decline of the dollar, which began in 1972, worsened again in 1978.)
3. The uneven performance of the stock market (Although there was a surge in 1976, the market declined during most of 1977 and had not recovered by the end of 1978.)
4. Federal policies imposing additional costs (The examples of higher social security taxes; new safety, health, and pollution standards, new approaches to pensions; and compliance with affirmative action programs indicate a few of the additional costs.)
5. Oil price increases and their effect on fuel and energy costs
6. Increases in the numbers of faculty in the two highest ranks
7. A decline in federal research and development funding (From 1967 to 1976, research and development funding showed a general decline in real dollars.)
8. Pressures to keep the tuition steady

9. Maintenance of major buildings erected in the boom of the 1960s
10. Maintenance of the programs initiated in the boom of the 1960s

These are some of the major economic factors with which institutions of higher education must contend. Individual institutions are affected at different times by these economic pressures depending on their investment policies, their salary levels, their funding drives, their location, etc. Among the institutions whose material expenditures declined, different conditions led to each library's decreasing materials expenditures in 1976–1977 and 1977–1978. One easily identifiable common factor for the four institutions whose material expenditure declined is their location in the East and Midwest, both areas hard hit by the energy crisis. However, one has to look at the individual circumstances of the institutions (and the library) to understand the reasons for the decreases. If one refers again to the chart on material expenditures at the 12 libraries, (Appendix A) one can see that during the first 10 years of the 15-year period, there were 20 decreases. In the last 5 years there were 15 decreases, indicating the economic factors above were having their effects.

B. Library Materials Budgeting Constraints

The library budgeting environment is also affected by publishing trends and the collecting practices of libraries. Following is a summary of the major trends since 1970:

1. Inflation in book prices (From 1970 to 1978 there was a 65.6% increase in the prices of United States hardcover books, based upon the *Weekly Record* 18th month final figure for 1978. During the same period, the CPI increased by 68.0%. Although the level of increase for books is less than the CPI increase, university libraries buy heavily abroad, where increases are greater.)
2. American book title output steady (The American book title output of both new titles and new editions has remained remarkably steady for the past 5 years, 1974–1978, remaining at a level of approximately 40,000–41,000 titles.)
3. Increase in world book production (According to the latest estimates of UNESCO, world book production is up. In 1970 the

estimated world book production was at a level of 521,000 titles, and by 1976 the total was 591,000. Research libraries must buy a large share of foreign titles.)

4. Foreign purchases ranging from 25 to 60% of total (Foreign purchases in the 12 libraries range from 25 to 60%, and the dollar devaluation and a high level of inflation in the prices of foreign publications continue to affect purchasing.)
5. Inflation in periodical prices (From 1970 to 1978, there was a 164.9% increase in the prices of United States periodicals. During the same period, the CPI increased by 68.0%. The overall level of increases is alarming.)
6. Inflation in scientific periodical prices (From 1970 to 1978, there was a 223.6% increase in the prices of chemistry and physics journals in the United States. These fields appear to be sustaining an astronomical level of inflation.)
7. High level of material dollars spent for serials (The 12 libraries spent a median of 41.5% in 1972–73 and by 1977–1978 they were spending 55% or a rise of 2.25% per year. The rise has been slow but steady, although some libraries in 1977–1978 noticeably cut back on the proportion.)
8. Decline in retrospective purchasing (This is a trend reported by Magrill and East (1978) and confirmed by the visits to the 12 libraries.)
9. Reduction of blanket orders (This is a trend reported by Magrill and East and also confirmed by the visits to the 12 libraries.)
10. Cancellation of serial titles (This is a trend reported by Magrill and East and also confirmed by the visits to the 12 libraries.)

These factors have resulted in a phenomenon widely described in the literature: an increasing rate of expenditures coupled with a decreasing rate of acquisitions. The rate of increase (decrease) of added volumes in the last 15 years was compared for the 12 libraries. The added volume rate was averaged during three 5-year periods, and the overall increase (decrease) was computed. There was an increase in the average rate of volumes added for the 12 libraries of 19.47% between 1962–1963 to 1966–1967 and 1967–1968 to 1971–1972. In contrast, there was a 15.85% decrease in volumes added between 1967–1968 to 1971–1972 and 1972–1973 to 1976–1977 (see Appendix B).

C. How the Environment Affects Materials Funding

The materials budgeting environment of private university libraries for the 1970s has been marked by economic hardships for the parent institutions, including decreased support from the federal government for research and development and graduate fellowships, poor performance of capital markets, increasing personnel costs, and general inflationary trends for goods and services, particularly fuel and energy. Universities have responded by increasing tuition, reducing utility usage, cutting staffing levels, and drawing down reserves. Libraries have been directly affected by these measures. Because universities cannot take these steps indefinately, they eventually must institute wide-ranging cost reductions. Most institutions have already established programs to reduce operating expenditures, and libraries—and library budgets—are now under close scrutiny. University administrators are concerned about exceeding present levels of library expenditures, but they are also worried about what financial stringency will do to the quality of the library.

University attention has focused on library costs in particular because their inflationary rise has been greater than other areas of university expenditures. Materials costs, in particular, are rising faster than university income and officials are concerned about how they can continue to maintain first-rate research collections and still keep their budget in balance. Two universities are very concerned about the increasing proportion of the operating budget that the library is consuming. In one case, the library proportion of operating expenditures has *steadily* increased from 8.94% (1972–1973) to 10.35% (1976–1977). This must end or the other university programs will be affected. In the other case, library expenditures have hovered around 10% but have reached 11.1%. Again, the university was concerned about the *steady* increases from 9.4% (1971–1972) to 10.7% (1976–1977).

Every university visited has had at least one period of deficit spending during the past 15 years. Despite these monetary setbacks, universities have continued to maintain diversified academic programs. In fact, universities consider their educational resources as a major asset:

> First of all, for universities, as with other nonprofit organizations, the "bottom-line" is how well the institution is achieving its basic purposes—i.e., the status of its academic programs rather than the status of its funds. Consequently, higher education has trailed profit-oriented firms in the development of fiscal standards of measurement (Cornell University, 1977).

Universities continue to change their curriculum and offer innovative programs in order to maintain their leadership and excellence. The health of an institution depends upon its ability to attract staff and students and to carry on research. As a result, despite the shortage of funds, there is continuous growth and development in curricular programs and research. The library must react to these changes by providing the resources for teaching and research even in these difficult financial circumstances.

Some librarians have argued that materials costs are relatively insignificant in comparison to personnel costs. As Richard DeGennaro (1977) has said: "in the end, any significant savings in library expenditures must come from eliminating positions, because that is where the money goes." However, he and other librarians have pointed out that there are limits to the personnel cuts that libraries can absorb. Once these limits have been reached, the next most important segment of the library budget is the materials segment. (Despite soaring energy and fuel costs because of oil shortages, large library buildings do not receive special attention from university administrators because these costs are usually absorbed in general university overhead, with the exception of two libraries, Harvard and Yale, which now include heating, lighting, and maintenance in their central library budget.) University administrators also have focused great attention on the costs of collection building because they receive the greatest faculty pressure in this area. Therefore, it is important to look at the materials budgeting process to see how librarians measure the costs of materials and justify their expenditures.

IV. BUDGET FORMULATION AND PRESENTATION

A. Budgeting Cycle

At all of the institutions studied, the formal university budgeting cycle now occupies most of the academic year, beginning from 6 to 9 months before the budget becomes effective. The informal budgeting process lasts most of the calendar year. As Rogers and Weber (1971, p. 89) have stated: "the procedure of preparing, presenting, and negotiating the budget is rapidly becoming a continuum that is likely to begin over a year in advance of the fiscal year to which the budget applies." The materials budget is, without exception, incorporated into this regular budget process and considered within the context of the entire library budget. This time frame means that the director of libraries, who presents the budget in every library studied, usually calls upon his staff during the fall for information relating to the collection needs of the faculty (or library) and the costs of materials and does not put the budget to bed until the spring.

B. Participants

In nine libraries, the collection development librarian is a participant with the director in the budgeting process. In the three remaining libraries, the technical services assistant director is responsible for coming up with a statement of needs, after consulting with the acquisition librarian or collection development personnel, about funding requirements. In half of the libraries a business manager is also an active partner in the process. Three of the six business managers have MBAs (one is a combination MBA/Library Degree from Chicago), and two have a business background. The other business manager has an accounting degree. Those libraries without a business manager rely for financial information upon an administrative assistant or an accountant who reports to an assistant director. Two libraries, Cornell and Northwestern, had a business manager and this position was not replaced after the incumbent's departure (Heyeck, 1976b, p. 168). Four of the large libraries (among the top 20 ARL institutions in collection size) have a business manager and four do not. Two of the smaller libraries have a business manager and two do not.

C. Budget Format

All of the institutions do incremental budgeting. There is no institution among the 12 that prepares a formula budget or uses the Planning Programming Budgeting System (PPBS). Some of the budgetary documents, however, do have elements of what might be termed a program approach, i.e., an explanation of the objectives to be achieved and the consequent costs. For example, the Princeton budget for 1976–1977 submitted to the Priorities Committee, a committee of faculty, students, and staff that reviews the budget and establishes 4-year provisional plans, recommends the addition of several positions, stating the objectives to be achieved and the salary per position. [See the ARL (1977c) SPEC Kit No. 32, *Preparation and Presentation of the Library Budget* (April), for a sample of the Princeton budget.] Stanford's budgetary document also has a program approach. The items for addition to the budget are listed by priority under such headings as "Collection Development Staffing Needs," or "Collection Surveys," or "Computer Terminal," giving the cost and the rationale for each increment.

D. Communications Process

The communication process ranges from formal to informal, but at almost every institution there is a fiscal document, usually in a line by line format, and an analytical piece that explains the line items. The analytical piece ranges from some notations on the line item budget to a 200 or 300 page document. As noted above, the analytical document often describes program objectives and relates budgeted amounts to short analyses of library needs. Brevity, according to some administrators, is much appreciated in a budget document. The document can and frequently does have appendices or supporting reports but a succinct summary statement of essential needs is most desirable. The librarians interviewed sometimes prepare a separate document for budget base increases or special one-time projects (e.g., installation of a circulation system).

The university administration has usually been prepared in advance for special requests through direct contact with the university budget officer, both formal and informal; communications to other university officials, such as the president or development officers, and contact with the faculty, both formal and informal; presentations to the faculty library committee or visiting committee; and articles in university publications, such as the alumni bulletin, university newsletter, or student newspaper. The last approach is usually preceded by more direct discussions with appropriate officials, but sometimes an "orchestrated" campaign is felt helpful. Regular communication with appropriate staff is essential to the budgeting process.

A key to the budgetary process is a relationship of trust between the university administration and the library. Over and over again, directors of the libraries visited used the terms "honesty," "forthrightness," "integrity" when describing the approach taken with university officials. Another aspect of this type of communication is a certain style, which can be called "calm," "unemotional," and "low key." If the university administration is confident that it is dealing with a thoroughly competent and honest library administration, then, given adequate revenues, budget recommendations are more likely to be acceptable. In two cases, university librarians said that they had called errors in their own presentation to the attention of the administration. One librarian emphasized the importance of consistently presenting carefully researched and documented budgets. The university administration at this institution has commended the library for its thoughtful and well-organized presentations. In the dialog between the library and the administration, there is a common recognition that there is a finite amount of money available. For the most part, there is also a basic understanding that inflation is the prevailing condition and the university wants to do what it can. In two documented cases, Stanford and Yale, the library has been given favored status in budget-cutting programs. Such recognition of the library's needs has obviously been preceded by much groundwork on the part of the library.

E. Documentation

Documentation is an important part of the library's budget presentation. It can vary from the library's budget document, to a newspaper article on the closing of catalogs, to the annual report, and the timing, when such documentation is forwarded to the administration, can vary depending on the special circumstances. For example, many libraries have already alerted university administrations about the closing of the Library of Congress' (LC) catalog and the adoption of the Anglo-American Cataloguing Rules (AACR 2) because these factors will affect their budgets in 2 or 3 years. Annual reports often discuss future library projects that will affect the budgeting process. (It was startling to learn that 4 of the 12 libraries included in this study had no annual report.) Some libraries have begun to forego preparing support documentation of the library's material funding needs because of the circumstances at their institution. Until recently they have faithfully presented elaborate information on price increases and publishing trends, but this has had little apparent effect because their institution cannot afford to support the library's requests at the required level. Other libraries feel such documentation is important because persistent and consistent reporting of facts on the costs of materials will ultimately make university administrations aware of the ground being lost by the library through inflation.

F. Sources of Funding

General university funds remain the primary source of monies for material expenditures in the libraries studied (see Appendix D). In 1976–1977, 9 of the 12 libraries received 70% or more of their materials income from general funds. The next largest source of income was gifts, grants, and fees. Endowments constituted the smallest group among income categories. Half of the libraries received under 12% of their income from endowment during 1976–1977. This situation has caused great concern on the part of both library and university administrators, who are hard pressed to come up with university dollars for acquisitions. Half of the university administrators interviewed felt that endowments were an essential source of future funding for acquisitions, although most agreed that it is difficult to obtain endowment funding for acquisitions. (See the ARL SPEC Kit *External Funding in ARL Libraries* for a more complete discussion of this topic.) Gifts, grants, and fees make up an important share of the acquisitions dollars, and they come from a variety of sources. One university library, which has its own development office and fund raiser, supports almost all of the annual increases through "outside" funding rather than university funds. University alumni, local foundations, and friends' groups provide significant revenues for the libraries. Many libraries also plow back funds from duplicate sales of books, lost books, and fines. Outside users fees have also been used for purchasing materials. Fees and fines can be a significant source of income. In 1976–1977, one library reported that 8.6% of its material expenditures was derived from fees and fines. Federal grants still play an important role in some of the institutions that were visited. Another source of federal monies is the National Endowment for the Humanities, which provides funds for resources on a challenge basis. Many of the libraries also received Office of Education basic grants of $3,855. Some libraries mentioned additional internal sources. Harvard University Library uses dollars made available by the faculty from the endowment of several chairs. Another library supports its material funds through sales of microforms. Salary savings are used at year's end for supplementary acquisitions by at least two libraries, and departments in two institutions make transfers to the library for purchase of materials.

Before he submits the annual request, the business officer or the accountant usually has added the special funds, many of which are restricted, into the materials budget in order to estimate the materials income available to the library. Once these regular sources of income are plugged into the budget, then the special requirements of the selectors and inflationary rates are considered. It is then possible to make estimates of the level of funding from university sources that is required. Sometimes the budget letter will break down unrestricted, restricted, gift, and government funds that support materials purchases.

Librarians and university administrators of the institutions studied here are convinced that it is essential to secure external funding for library materials. Some elements of their efforts to obtain outside monies merit attention:

1. Some libraries have prepared a historical record of expenditures grouped by major sources of income to define their funding needs; to project annual budgetary support for materials; to aid in presentation of the annual budget request; and to provide data for raising additional monies from foundations or friends.
2. Six of the libraries visited have appointed staff members whose specific duties are to seek funds from outside sources. Some of these staff members have full-time positions and others combine related duties.
3. Six of the libraries have been included in the capital fund campaign of their institution, and funds for collections constituted 50% or more of the library campaign targets.
4. Some library administrators believe national foundation support is drying up as a source of materials funding and recommend alumni, corporations, or local foundations as possible contributors.
5. Some novel techniques for advertising the needs of libraries have been used by these libraries, including a specially printed annual report for friends of the library; a shopping list of titles and their prices in a library newsletter for friends, book plates sent with annual fund literature, and leaflets to describe what contributions can do.

G. Uses of Automated Data

One of the original purposes of this study was to determine to what extent budget calculations are based upon scientific management or automated data, and whether national price indices are used in preparing budget recommendations or local cost studies are constructed. The following statistics show that the emphasis has been placed on automating the ordering systems in the 12 libraries rather than the accounting systems:

Library Accounting Systems	Library Ordering Systems
Automated 5	Automated 8
Manual 7	Manual 4

To date, library automated accounting systems have developed slowly because most universities already have an automated financial system which is too costly for the library to duplicate. However, a library-based machine system has the advantage of the capacity for providing library management data. One of the most promising systems, combining ordering and accounting with management data, is the Computer Assisted Processing System (CAPS), recently developed at Harvard University Libraries (1977). The Office for Systems Planning and Research describes its features as follows:

> Through the use of several pre-designated coding schemes (REVIEWCODE [for serials], SUBJECT CODE, LANGUAGE CODE, FORMCODE) combinations of financial, bibliographic, and other specially coded data can be compiled into reports and made available for further analysis (p. 2).

This information will allow Harvard to track materials expenditures (book, serial, and nonbook) using combinations of factors, such as language, subject, and vendor, and to produce management reports for such activities as vendor evaluation, donor solicitation, and materials budgeting. The Yale automated ordering system can generate receipt statistics by vendor showing average cost per title, and it also has the capability of printing a list of accessions by LC class, giving number of titles and cost. The majority of the automated accounting systems currently have a limited management information capacity, but libraries with automated accounting systems are attempting to improve their report-generating capabilities.

H. Use of National Indexes and Local Data

Almost none of the libraries studied relies primarily on the national price indexes for predicting increases for materials. Instead, the libraries studied depend upon cost data from their local acquisitions and use the national figures for comparability, to help get local figures in sharper focus. Local figures have the advantage of reflecting the special "mix" of scholarly books purchased by an academic research library and showing the cost of materials after discount rather than list price. They can also incorporate foreign materials that currently are not well covered by indexes. Administrators are less convinced by national rankings and national price data and are only interested in learning about what it costs to obtain materials for research and teaching needs at their own institutions.

Stanford University Libraries has prepared a local study on the average costs of domestic monographs, foreign monographs, periodicals, and government documents at Stanford since 1971–1972. Relying upon a combination of sampling and manually recorded invoice statistics, the study shows cost trends since 1968–1969 and is used to project the expenditures needed to maintain the current level of collecting in an inflationary period. A separate calculation is made to determine the number of titles Stanford will need to acquire to maintain its share of world book production. The foreign cost figures are given in United States dollars so they already reflect the costs of devaluation of the American dollar against foreign currencies. Other libraries routinely calculate their local rate of inflation and use it for budgetary purposes. The Acquisition Department of the University of Chicago annually prepares a sample of United States, British, and German journal and monograph costs and computes an index figure for Chicago, comparing its figures to the *Higher Education Prices and Price Indexes* by D. Kent Halstead. The University of Southern California (USC) library has calculated its average cost per monographic volume and per serial subscription and uses these data in its annual budget request. Cornell University Libraries has prepared extensive documentation for its Library Board. This documentation includes tables showing the movement of book and periodical price indexes as compared to movement of a local index figure for total expenditures for library materials and appropriated budget amounts; appropriated funds, endowments, and other income as a percentage of total acquisitions income; changes in expenditures for books and library materials as a percentage of total library expenditures; and total library expenditures as a percentage of university total expenditures for educational and general purposes. Rice University Library has compiled figures for its University Committee on the Library showing the unit cost per title added at Rice and illustrating the decline in new titles added as expenditures rise. They have also compiled figures on the increments that will be required to allow the library to stand still in terms of purchasing power as well as the restoration increment required to improve the library's collection position. Princeton University Library (1977) has compiled an extensive report in response to a mandate from a Presidential Committee, the Special Committee on Library Acquisitions and Losses. This committee was formed because of a dramatic erosion in the rate of acquisition between 1974–1975 and 1975–1976. The study concluded that the "main burden of decline in purchasing since 1974 has fallen on the Social Sciences and the Humanities." It recommended that the university attempt to maintain a rate of 68,000 monograph titles a year (based upon the levels of purchases of United States and United Kingdom publications by Princeton in the late 1960s and early 1970s and calculated as a proportion of the total output of United States and United Kingdom publications) and they established an amount required to restore the previous rate of book expenditures (calculated on the basis of the shortfall in History, English, and other fields for book expenditures— $230,000 in 1977–1978 and rising to nearly $300,000 in 1980–1981). With respect to losses, which were estimated at 4.35% of the Firestone Library's open stacks and 10% of the branch libraries volumes (in all, some 150,000 volumes with a replacement cost of approximately $3 million), the committee recommended that the library continue to spend its annual replacement budget of $50,000, adjusted for inflation and establish appropriate security measures.

The documentation of library acquisition costs is improving, but most of it comes without the benefit of the computer and is compiled at the behest of outside authorities. It is essential for librarians to assume the responsibility for keeping regular cost statistics that will be useful for budget presentation and to begin to improve the capacity of their computerized systems for management purposes.

I. Staff Participation

Not all of the building of the documentation for materials increases takes as formal an approach as the special studies mentioned in the last paragraph. The budget request usually takes into account requirements beyond inflationary increases, which sometimes will need to be built into the budget base. For example, new programs may be called to the attention of the collection development librarian by a selector, or a branch librarian may be aware of a new professor with unique research interests which will require special support. At one library studied, the management council, consisting of major department and division heads, and the director are involved in arriving at the materials budget figure. Input from staff in these situations is very important, and at most institutions there is feedback on library needs from librarians responsible for collections which is channeled to appropriate directors. (Unfortunately, there is very little knowledge among library staff about how the budgetary process works.) There is input from such staff members prior to the budget presentation, and the staff member then receives a figure when the budget has been approved.

This situation is changing. For instance, at Stanford everyone on the staff is given detailed information about the budgetary process through the University staff bulletin, the *Campus Report*. The University of Chicago also publishes a budget report in *The University of Chicago Record*. These universities make the assumption that a completely open budget process promotes a better understanding of how university resources are utilized and gives more opportunity for widespread input. Within the libraries at Stanford, the Assistant Director for Administrative Services also meets with the staff members from each department to discuss the budget before it is submitted, and after it has been approved there is a staffwide discussion of its implications.

J. Budget Presentation

The library director reports to the following university officials about budget matters:

Provost, 7
Executive vice president, 1

Associate or vice provost, 2
Dean of Faculty and Academic Affairs, 1
Dean of the Faculty of Arts and Sciences, 1

In most of the libraries, therefore, the director of libraries reports on budgetary matters to the top academic administrator (the Dean of Faculty and Academic Affairs and the Dean of the Faculty of Arts and Sciences are the top administrators in the group cited above). The library director is at a level of a department head in the reporting relationship to the university administration, and the library follows the same procedures as other academic departments. The libraries are generally asked to submit their budget requests for the following fiscal year by a certain date. The initial university request for budget figures from departments may be couched in such terms as: What would be the budget required to maintain the status quo? or "We think we can give you only $X." At one institution, the administration announces a percentage guideline for increases and asks departments to make a case for deviation from it. At another institution, the administration gives the library a target based upon enrollment and tuition projections and asks the library to describe how the money will be allocated and the deficiencies that would exist under such an allocation.

K. Meeting University Guidelines

When the library is given monetary guidelines or expenditure targets, how are they reconciled with materials inflationary increases and dollar devaluation? The library has to set internal priorities. In one institution the librarian was given a mandate for an overall increase of 3% (salary increases were excluded from the 3% target), and by adjusting most other expenditure categories to zero increases the librarian was able to boost the materials budget to a 5% increase. The librarians at each institution were questioned about the priority of the materials budget in relation to other library costs, and some had made reductions in personnel in order to preserve the materials budget. Reduction of supplies, hours, student assistants, and binding budgets were mentioned as other areas of cuts. Salaries were considered as another variable. One librarian noted that he saw two areas as equal: salaries and materials budgets. He commented: "Librarians are zealous in supporting salaries, and faculty are more interested in the materials budget." At the University of Pennsylvania, the library book budget base was permanently enlarged in 1972–1973 through staff cuts.

L.   The Library as a Funding Priority

After the library has made its internal decisions on the budget and prepared an initial request, a conference is usually scheduled with the provost or appropriate administrator. It is here that a selling job must be done if the library wishes to exceed the established guidelines. The university's priorities are also made clear here. When asked about the kind of priority library funding has in the unversity's budget, the administrators generally replied that they felt the library was holding its place near the top of the priority scale.

M.   Faculty Participation

The negotiations with the university administration may require more than one meeting, and the materials budget may not always be at issue. (Some librarians have also pointed out that the university guidelines may be so rigid there may be nothing to negotiate, and the term "discussions" may be more appropriate.) Once the discussions are complete, customarily the budget must be approved by the president and board of trustees before it becomes final. Some librarians must also interact with faculty budget committees, such as the Priorities Committee at Princeton, before the budget is finalized. The librarian at Princeton must present written and oral arguments to the Priorities Committee, a faculty committee that operates intensively during the fall semester and makes overall policy recommendations to the President. Most university librarians keep their own faculty library committee up to date on budgetary matters, but several indicated a reluctance to involve the faculty to a great extent. They prefer the freedom to manage their budgets independently and expressed concern about local responsibilities being assigned to a central bureaucracy. However, support from special faculty committees has been an important stimulus for increasing materials funds at some of these institutions.

N. 1978-1979 Materials Budgets

At all of the libraries studied, the materials budget had been set for 1978-1979 and the average percentage increase was 8%, ranging from a low of −3% to a high of 15%. The median percentage increase was 9.5%. In view of the rate of inflation in the costs of materials, the budgeted increases, both average and median, fall below what is required to maintain collections at previous levels. According to Theodore Samore (1978, p. 243) in his analysis of college and university library statistics in the 1978 *Bowker Annual:* "due to stubborn inflation most academic libraries appear to be stagnating with respect to collections, staff, and services."

O. Arguments for Increasing Materials Funding

One question that the study hoped to answer was what are convincing arguments for increasing funds for materials expenditures. This question was asked both of the university librarians and the university administrators.

The university librarians interviewed emphasized five basic approaches they considered to be successful in obtaining funds for materials expenditures. First, there has to be a completely honest approach in order to maintain credibility with the university administration. The relationship with the administration is very important. The university needs to be aware of all the factors contributing to a library program. If the budget preparation is thorough and attempts are being made to make the operation more efficient, then a trust can be built up. Once the administration has confidence the library knows what it is doing and is playing within the rules, then it is easier to make a case for a particular sum. Second, it is important to have allies, particularly the faculty and the deans. Third, maintaining buying power is an important argument because everyone recognizes that inflation and devaluation have hurt collections. Fourth, relating arguments directly to collections and the teaching and research of the university is also very important. This can be done by allocation systems, collection evaluations, and working closely with deans and faculty. Fifth, external evidence, such as rankings, seems to have less impact, but where external evidence can be related directly to the local situation it can be effective; e.g., accreditation reports assisted one library in convincing the administration that it needed an improved materials budget.

The university administrators also stated what they considered to be the most convincing arguments for increasing materials funding. First, trust between the administrators and the librarian is an essential element in convincing the administration. Second, there needs to be more awareness of library needs on the part of the faculty who use the collections. The faculty then can convince the university administration of the library's needs. Third, the inflationary increase required to maintain current purchasing levels is also an important argument. Fourth, what it costs to develop collections and how these collections support research and teaching can be a convincing argument. There need to be reasonable and satisfactory arguments showing how the reduction of books and journals is eroding the ability of the faculty to teach and do research. Universities would like to give libraries more money for collections, but they require more specific information on the strength of collections and undergraduate/graduate usage. Feedback from faculty and deans on what is required to do research is a primary factor. Fifth, pure ranking among ARL libraries is not as convincing as the ARL ranking in relation to another factor, such as the university's ranking in receipt of federal research and development funding. In other words, ARL rankings are helpful if there are supporting data to show how any slippage will hurt a university's research or teaching program.

P. Rationale for Modifying a Request

When one compares the independent replies from university librarians and university administrators, it is striking how much agreement there is on what it is librarians need to do to make a case for more materials funds. However, in spite of the best arguments, the university if often unable or unwilling to meet the funding needs of the library. The discrepancy lies in the forces previously described in Section III on environment.

Administrators made frequent reference to the burden on general university funds and the issue of materials costs rising at a higher rate than other nonpersonnel costs in the university. One administrator dramatized the inflation issue on his campus by speaking of: "lots of buildings well lighted and full of books, but no money for staff, student funds, or faculties." Another administrator lamented: "in the absence of large gifts it is not likely the university can simultaneously fund inflationary increases on books and periodicals and mechanization equipment purchases." The library is clearly in competition with other segments of the university for a finite amount of resources. Although the growth rate of libraries is slowing, the growth rate of university revenues is also slowing. Libraries also need more funds for technology. In the 12 libraries, the category "other costs" rose while salaries declined, as a proportion of total library expenditures from 1970/1971 to 1977/1978. "Other costs" averaged 9.58% of the total expenditures of the 12 libraries in 1970/1971 and by 1977/1978 "other costs" averaged 12.02% of the total expenditures (see Appendix F).

The administrators who see declining university revenues, competing campus departments, and inflated library costs as the forces causing tighter materials budgets have numerous recommendations for library economies. To close the gap between expenditures and revenue, they recommended reducing personnel, cutting hours of service, selective collection development, developing cost models, weeding, exploiting technology to achieve greater efficiencies, and more cooperation. These suggestions are all too familiar to research librarians, with the possible exception of cost models (although there is material in the library literature on the topic). They also recommended some revenue-raising approaches, such as increasing endowment funds, getting the federal government to recognize national collections worthy of support, and greater commitment to the library in annual fund-raising drives. Again, these are acknowledged means in the library field of attaining a better financial position for libraries. Perhaps, in the past, librarians have neglected to keep administrators adequately informed about crucial library issues and their costs. If administrators are to anticipate the future directions of research libraries, then libraries will need to provide budget planning documents. Magrill and East (1978) note that:

> Some libraries have moved to long-range planning because of the necessity of budget planning. *Without a clear plan of future priorities, a library's budgeting process is at the mercy of strong and probably conflicting pressures, both internal and external. Careful budgetary planning is long-range planning of a very important kind.* . . . *(p. 17).*

If the chart on materials expenditures is examined, it can be seen that the library with the least number of decreases is Harvard University Library. Although much of its success will undoubtedly be attributed to the wealth of the institution, certainly one factor that has contributed to the library's financial success is that university administrators were prepared 10 years in advance for the massive expenditures that would be required in 1976–1977 and 1977–1978 by a planning study completed in 1966. This study analyzed future library growth and made projections of library costs. Not only did it call for greater efforts in securing endowments, but it also predicted a greater reliance on computer processing, increased use of microforms, and additional space needs. The predictions of budgeted amounts for particular areas were in some cases too high and in some too low, but the overall University Library expenditures figure was low by only 0.3%. The specific predictions are not really an important issue. What is significant is that university administrators were prepared 10 years in advance for the massive expenditures that would occur in the future, and they were made aware of some of the critical issues to be faced. Other libraries should seriously consider this approach to financial planning. This kind of budgetary planning can also be applied in the area of collections, as is noted in the next section of this contribution.

V. COLLECTION DEVELOPMENT AND THE MATERIALS BUDGET

A. Effects of Limited Budgets on Collection Development

One of the major questions the CLR study (Lynden, 1978a) attempted to address was the degree to which limited funds have hurt collection development in the 12 research libraries. There was general agreement that two areas have suffered greatly—retrospective buying and serials purchasing. Otherwise, there was little agreement among the directors of the libraries who were queried. In the area of retrospective purchases, one librarian now planning a large-scale collection evaluation stated his conviction that numerous retrospective gaps would be uncovered in the collections because of limited funding.

Several directors expressed a concern about the lack of direct evidence of unsatisfied needs. They both indicated that faculty were not complaining, and suggestion boxes were not full. Another director emphasized that his library had not satisfied the "unrequested" needs. One library survived the cutbacks with a minimum of pain by using deliberate and constructive collecting strategies, which eliminated duplicate titles and low-priority serials titles, and steadily increased the acquisitions budget. Another library, which has managed to keep pace with inflation, suggested a strategy of avoiding new collecting areas and strengthening already distinguished collections. At one library, the decline in the number of titles has resulted in an alliance of library and faculty, which will in the long run benefit the library. Limited funding therefore has had both positive and negative effects on collection development. The beneficial influences of reduced materials budgets have been improved collection practices, e.g., elimination of duplicates, more selective collecting, evaluation of collections, heightened awareness of need for user input, and political alliances. However, limited materials funding has created collection gaps, frustrated users, and produced uniformly standard collections.

B. Priority of the Materials Budget

Each librarian was also asked about the priority of the materials budget in his institution. Every library considers the materials budget a high priority. This is indicated by remarks in their annual reports as well as in their interviews.

The interviews showed that libraries had increased their materials budgets at the expense of other areas. For example, one director indicated that bindery expenditures had been cut to enhance the materials budget. He had also cut his personnel budget. When his university was implementing an austerity program, another director did not fill positions in order to strengthen his arguments for a higher materials budget. A third director transferred budgeted personnel to the book budget. A fourth director reduced his expenses in three areas—personnel, binding, and supply budget—in order to preserve his materials budget. A fifth director said that he is considering a reduction of service hours or positions if the materials budget is threatened. A sixth director has made his cuts in personnel to soften the reductions in the materials area. Exactly half of the librarians made special efforts to preserve the materials budget at the expense of other areas.

There appears to be a definite relationship between personnel costs and the materials budget. In one institution studied, the university increased the library's budget for 1978–1979 by 2%. At the same time, the university mandated a 7% overall increase in salaries. This meant that the library had to find the additional funds by cuts in its programs. The library eliminated six positions without layoffs and made some increases in the outside user's fees and contractual services. There were still insufficient funds to cover the salary payments, therefore, the materials budget had to be reduced. The *Higher Education Prices and Price Index Supplement* for 1977 indicates that in the past few years universities and colleges have restricted salary increases to minimize the effects of inflation in their overall operations. These "savings" have been realized by holding professional salaries below the rate of the consumer price index. Ultimately, library materials budgets will be affected as faculty intensify efforts to make up for salary deprivation.

C. Economic Conditions Causing Decreased Materials Budgets

In the pattern of decreases in materials expenditures of the 12 libraries over the past 15 years, there is a cluster of decreases in 1970–1971 and 1971–1972. These decreases were preceded by (and concurrent with) an inflationary recession which occurred in the United States from 1969 to 1971. Many of these conditions have prevailed throughout the 1970s. Another indicator of the conditions that caused a decrease in the materials expenditures in 1970–1971 and 1971–1972 was a large operating deficit in each of the universities prior to or during the same period.

In some institutions there had been deficits prior to 1969–1970 but not of the magnitude of these years. (It is interesting to note that frequently when there is a decrease in materials expenditures there is also a deficit in the university operating expenditures in the preceding year.) Another factor contributing to the decline was the leveling off of government funding, which began in 1968–1969 but was not yet fully effective in 1969–1970 because of the carryover of grants and contracts awarded in previous years. These economic conditions continue to affect the ability of the universities to respond to library requests for funds.

D. Responses to These Economic Conditions

The universities coped with these fiscal emergencies by spending reserves of income accumulated during better times. They also began a program of systematically reducing expenditures, eliminating nonessential academic and nonacademic programs, developing new sources of income, and increasing returns on their investments. Some universities also began to rely more upon financial forecasting.

At the same time, libraries began to formulate strategies for responding to these harsh economic realities. The Yale librarian Rutherford D. Rogers (1973) suggested in his annual report that libraries begin to adopt new methodologies and attitudes:

> The directors of the major libraries perceive with a clarity never heretofore approached that only through cooperative enterprises can the escalation in library costs be brought under control. In a period of stationary or shrinking budgets, there must be fresh approaches to sharing resources and to cooperation that usher in a new way of operating libraries and of providing access to publications of research significance . . . The fundamental reality is that each library can expect to have a smaller percentage of world publishing output and libraries are going to have to build collections cooperatively and share what is available (p. 5).

Mr. Rogers announced that Yale was joining the Center for Research Libraries; was beginning a cooperative cataloging program with Divinity Schools from Harvard, Yale, Princeton, and Union Theological Seminary; and was initiating exploratory discussions in relation to what was to become the Research Libraries Group. In the previous year, Stanford University Library Director David C. Weber had released in his annual report a "Book Selection Strategy During Increased Austerity" which defined some specific internal responses to the new economic conditions. Section V discusses the latter approach, and Section VI takes up the cooperative response, which is intimately related to the collection strategies.

E. Increases in the Twelve Libraries

Although most of the 12 libraries have had an increase in their materials expenditures in all but 1 or 2 years, the increases which they have received have not kept pace with inflationary rates for library materials as recorded in the published indexes. From 1970–1971 to 1976–1977, the median percentage increase in materials expenditures for the 12 libraries was 62.8, or about the same level as the increase for books listed in *Publisher's Weekly,* 64.9 from 1970 to 1977 (see Appendix G), while the average percentage increase in materials expenditures for the period was 72–73%. However, the national periodical price increase during this period was 136.2%. Because most of the libraries spend 50% or more of their materials funds on serials, the clear implication is that more than half of their purchasing power has been eroded by inflation. The Higher Education Price Index (HEPI) shows the combined prices of books, periodicals, and foreign monographs rose by 97.8% from fiscal 1971 to fiscal 1978. From this vantage point, the loss in purchasing power for the median library is still 35%. Halstead weights his index toward monographic purchases, giving serials a weight of only 30%. He gives foreign monographs a weight of 15%, when this increase should be spread over the types of materials. One must assume foreign serials are rising faster in price than foreign monographs. Whichever measure is used, the general trend has been a major loss in purchasing power, and it is most likely greater than shown by the indexes. Collection development librarians have coped with reduced acquisition funds through allocations, procedural and administrative changes, and greater selectivity.

F. Allocations

Allocations are an important means of monitoring and controlling expenditures on collections. The methodology of allocation should be mentioned briefly. In no case did a library use a formula to determine current allocations. Librarians prepared allocations using information from historical expenditure patterns, current expenditure patterns (particularly overspending and underspending), expected expenses for new programs, changes in faculty research or programs, published indexes, and dollars available. Most libraries begin allocating by removing the expenditures for standing commitments, such as serials, blanket orders, publisher standing orders, and gifts and exchanges. They usually increase these based on local inflation factors, tempered by published information. Then, the expenditures for each department area or subject are allocated using some or all of the above factors with the heaviest weight on historical patterns. Sometimes the allocation base has been established by formula. For example, Princeton uses a formula for its base (see the ARL SPEC Kit No. 36, *Allocation of Materials Funds*). Princeton's base allocations are derived from a 3-year average of expenditures for each department as well as factors for sponsored research, expansion or contraction of programs, and a formula of intensity based upon publication and enrollment patterns. Some libraries have found their collection development policies useful for indicating clear strengths so they can "put their money where their policy is." Stanford's collection evaluation program has been helpful in the allocation process by providing new and more precise information on the adequacy of collections. Libraries do not consider their allocations rigid once established and modify them according to changing circumstances.

Allocations can help collection development librarians cope with limited budgets in several ways. First allocations are of major importance in making selectors aware of budget limitations. Every library had an internal accounting report showing library allocations, commitments, and expenditures which was forwarded to selectors. Seven of the libraries have a monthly expenditure statement, three have a weekly statement, and the remaining two report on a biweekly and quarterly basis. Selectors receive these reports on a regular basis, but for convenience sake they often receive reports relevant only to their selection areas. Two of the collection librarians said that they do not dwell upon the allocations but expect that selection will be based upon need and should have no relation to the money available.

Second, allocations can serve to focus the needs of the selector. At Chicago, before allocations are made, each selector is sent a questionnaire that is a prelude to discussions on the selector's area of responsibility. The selector is asked about changes in enrollment, faculty, curriculum research activities, rate of scholarly publication, and costs of books and journals. They are also asked about areas or types of material that have been eliminated or reduced and about any anticipated large expenditures. They are also requested to identify areas that are underfunded.

Third, allocations can serve a political function in communications with the faculty. (This of course, can, be a two-edged sword.) Allocations can help to inform faculty members on the level of support the library is giving to their disciplines. One director said that reports to the faculty members on expenditures in each department had stirred a strong reaction to maximize the amount of funding in the materials budget. When asked about the problem of proprietary attitudes, the director pointed out that allocation targets are worded very carefully to state that the library has "set aside in its budget" certain amounts. In his library, the allocations are by department because he believes the utility of a book depends upon how it supports a department, not on its subject. The faculty at Princeton were unhappy with the allocation system there, but in the report of the Special Committee on Library Acquisitions and Losses (Princeton University Library, 1977), they made several interesting recommendations. They suggested there be a central pool for the purpose of purchasing items too broad in scope to allocate to a particular field, to relieve concern about historical aberrations in funding, and to satisfy major unanticipated needs. They also requested notification prior to major increases or decreases in funding for particular departments and recommended establishment of record keeping and reporting, which could be used for long-range planning. The central pool or contingency fund concept is already used in at least three other institutions.

Fourth, allocations can be valuable as a collection management tool for the purpose, as the Princeton report suggests, of long-range prediction and planning. Indeed the purpose of a budget is planning, management, and control. Libraries have a combination of allocations which include departments, subjects, branches, type of materials (serials—sometimes broken down by periodicals and monographic series, documents, microforms, maps, rare books), procurement type (gift and exchange, standing order, blanket order, university press order, reserves, replacement), and miscellaneous accounts (preservation, insurance, postage). Some internal accounting systems include figures on the number of titles or copies purchased. The categories above can be used to analyze expenditures on a historical basis. The breakdown by type of material is particularly significant in view of cost differentials. Many libraries now have the capacity to separate data for serials into periodicals and monographic series. Northwestern University has automated serial statistics broken down by periodicals and monographic series for the last 7 years. At Northwestern, the addage that it is not possible to buy books because of heavy serial expenditures has been laid to rest. Despite serial expenditures greater than 50%, the figures at Northwestern show that the library is buying more books, i.e., monographs and monographic series, than periodicals, and the number of books purchased had not fallen below 50% by 1977–1978. It may be best for librarians to speak about "standing commitments" which are cutting into their book budgets. At Stanford University Library, all expenditures are coded by type of material: books, subscriptions, subscription backsets, government document serials, and government document nonserials. In addition to subject or branch breakdown, therefore, it is possible to break out expenditures by type of material. No library was able to use its automated system to show foreign expenditures by country. Foreign expenditure data would be helpful in measuring the cost rise and in recovering funding lost because of currency fluctuations. Cornell University and Stanford have data on expenditures by country, but these data were obtained manually (see Section V, M, on foreign materials). The Harvard University Library CAPS system will be able to produce this kind of expenditure data.

G. Procedural and Administrative Methods for Reducing Expenditures

At each institution a question was asked about formal procedures for reviewing expensive purchases, duplicates, and serials. Slightly over half of the libraries had specific instructions on expensive purchases. Seven libraries have established a dollar amount which, if exceeded, requires permission from the chief collection development officer before purchase. Only two of the seven have written regulations and the remainder have informal systems. Of the two libraries that have formal regulations, Stanford University Library has two administrative regulations, "Purchase, Sale, and Acceptance of Gifts of Library Materials" and "Policy and Regulations for Monitoring Book Funds," which require approval for materials expenditures exceeding certain specific amounts. Northwestern University Library has a special fund for expensive purchases ($200 or more), and there is an authorization form for requesting monies from this fund. The authorization form requires a description of the materials, a comparison with similar materials held by the library, a check on availability in other area libraries and other formats, the name of a department or departments that could benefit from the material, and signatures from three faculty members (which are optional). The form also suggests that promotional materials or reviews be attached. (A form similar to this is used at Stanford University.) Six librarians and the Assistant University Librarian for Collection Development meet to discuss and approve these recommendations. Although three of the remaining libraries have no specific dollar amount or written regulations, it is their practice to send all requests through the collection development officer.

H. Duplication

The general practice of the 12 libraries with reference to duplication is standard; i.e., avoid duplication except where it is required for teaching or research. Brown and Princeton have incorporated a written statement on duplication into their collection development policies, and the University of Chicago has issued a *Collection Development Policy Announcement* on duplication. There is now some concern about blanket policies on duplication because use studies have shown that a small proportion of the collection is used very heavily. At one library the chief of collection development said that his library was increasingly working with a sensitive loan policy, giving branch libraries and circulation a right to make decisions on duplication. In circulation, a queue will determine whether or not a second or third copy is needed.

I. Serials Review

There were six libraries with systems for controlling the growth of serial subscriptions. Two other libraries have established procedures for the review of serial requests and four libraries have no systematic way of checking on serial purchase recommendations. It is surprising that one-third of the libraries have no established procedures for review of serial recommendations in view of the high cost of serials.

J. Selectivity and Patterns of Purchasing

Limited funds and the buying power crisis have directly affected the purchasing patterns of the 12 libraries. Serials have taken a larger and larger portion of the budget at these libraries at the expense in some cases of the humanities and social sciences. (A considerable number of the libraries reported a decrease in several areas in 1978, but it is too early to see whether such a development will become a trend.) Foreign purchasing seems to be holding steady at between 30 and 60% of purchases for the 12 libraries. (The percentage is difficult to determine because so few libraries keep adequate statistics.) However, as an economy measure several libraries are considering dropping some foreign blanket orders, and another library is deemphasizing its foreign purchases. Retrospective buying has been severely limited or almost eliminated by the lack of adequate funding. Any retrospective buying has been very selective, for new programs or in response to faculty requests. In special programs, such as area studies where special funding is available, libraries still do retrospective buying. Ten of the 12 libraries have some kind of blanket or approval plan, but 4 of these libraries are tightening up some plans and eliminating others.

In spite of potential savings from converting to microforms, there is no evidence of large-scale conversion to microforms. Libraries are still very much aware of user resistance. However, three of the libraries, Northwestern, Princeton, and Yale, are just completing major microform studies exploring the potentials of microform use in their libraries (see Section V, L).

As a result of reduced materials funding and the loss in purchasing power, gifts are taking on a greater significance at some of the libraries studied. In 1977–1978, more books were received as gifts (and blanket orders) at the University of Chicago than in any other way. Yale reported that in 1977 "the decline in purchases has been offset to some extent by an increase in materials acquired through gifts and exchanges." These changes have all been taking place gradually over the past decade as libraries have attempted to stretch their materials budget dollars.

K. Serials

The impact of the inflationary spiral has been most obvious in the area of serials acquisitions (see Appendix H). Almost all of the libraries have implemented a serials cancelation project during the past decade. All report that such projects are difficult and time consuming and have found the results to be disappointing in comparison to the effort. An equally strenuous effort has to be made in avoiding the purchase of new subscriptions. James Skipper, former president of the Research Libraries Group, estimated that during the average 15-year life of a serial, $975 is spent on paying the subscription, staff costs, shelf space, and binding and preservation. Some librarians have suggested the need to set a ceiling on the number of subscriptions or to keep the serial expenditures at the same percentage level of the budget. According to statistics from the 12 libraries, the majority of libraries reached expenditure levels of 50% or more for serials in 1974–1975. The effects of the serial expenditure growth rate can be severe. Because of the different inflation rates of monographs and serials, if there are no changes in the numbers of subscriptions the percentage of materials budgets expended on serials will continue to rise. Murray S. Martin (1978) provides a dramatic example of this problem, assuming a 15% per annum rise in cost of serials and a 10% rise for books with a static budget for materials:

> It is even more sobering to consider the quantities of units such an expenditure distribution represents. In the base year, assuming a cost of $10 per book and $20

per subscription, 45,000 books and 25,000 subscriptions were purchased. In the fifth year, 25,000 subscriptions are still being purchased, but only 1,742 books (p. 84).

L. Microforms

There seems to be a general reluctance to purchase microforms as substitutes for books and the purchase of large sets has become very selective. Sometimes large microform sets are purchased because of a year-end windfall that has to be spent within a limited time. This is not to deny the value of the original source material, which is very often available only in microform. However, librarians are looking more frequently to the Center for Research Libraries or to regional cooperatives for these materials. There still appears to be very little purchasing of microforms as substitutes for the hard copy, e.g., in lieu of binding, but a change may occur when the results of the microform studies referred to earlier are available. At one institution, a member of the microform committee has pointed out that theft and mutilation of periodical volumes (a University of Iowa study shows that thousands of pages of heavily used journals are missing from single issues) is a horrendous problem which can be alleviated by the purchase of microforms instead of binding serials. Another member of the committee suggested that by purchasing microform of journals published simultaneously in hard copy and microform that as much as $33,000 a year can be saved from one publisher. However, the savings from microform are still being debated. Some librarians feel that savings in acquisition costs are offset by increased processing and bibliographic control costs. Through improved facilities, staffing, equipment, and user orientation, Princeton has overcome negative attitudes toward the use of film. Although there has been no large-scale conversion to microforms, they are playing a more important role in libraries. According to Robert Grey Cole (1978), ARL research library collections contained one unit of microforms for every six volumes in 1967–1968, and by 1976–1977 the figure was slightly under one unit per every two volumes.

M. Foreign Materials

It is difficult to measure the effects of reduced budgets on the purchase of foreign materials in the 12 libraries studied because of the paucity of hard data on foreign materials. Librarians recognize the need for these data, and some with automated ordering systems fully intend to include parameters that will reveal the actual foreign expenditure data necessary to make calculations on losses from currency revaluations. The University of Chicago asks its comptroller to provide it with cumulative totals of payments to various foreign vendors in order to calculate the loss in purchasing power of its acquisition dollars. Some libraries have asked for a special subsidy from the university administration to offset the buying power lost through foreign currency changes. Two libraries, Stanford and Cornell, have released data on their foreign expenditures. Cornell actually has expenditure totals from each country. Stanford relies on a sample of cataloging done in 1971 and again in 1976. These data may be skewed by cataloging patterns as well as gift receipts. It appears obvious that this is an area where documentation needs to be improved.

Three libraries expressed skepticism about the level of foreign acquisitions. In one library, the medical faculty expressed no interest in non-English materials. In another library, there has been what was termed a "great demise" in foreign language buying, particularly Slavic materials. Two other libraries specifically mentioned cuts in Slavic materials, which are expensive to obtain because they frequently require time-consuming exchange arrangements. Except where special funding is available, foreign language materials are one area where libraries are cutting expenditures.

N. Blanket Order Arrangements

Libraries have become much more selective in their blanket order arrangements. Four of the universities with blanket order plans are canceling arrangements with publishers and interpreting their profiles with dealers in a stricter fashion. At one university the library has dropped a number of publishers from its university press plan and has eliminated two large scientific publishers from its standing order list. At another university, the approval plan profile has been further restricted, and more titles are being returned. Two foreign blanket order plans have also been phased out at this university. At a third university the library has only a limited university press plan and they are considering giving up a foreign blanket order plan. Another library has only one approval plan, and it is diminishing in importance as selectors are purchasing more individual titles using an automated ordering system that is securing titles faster than the gathering plan. Two libraries of the 12 rely entirely on individual selection for acquiring materials. Five libraries still depend upon gathering plans for reducing individual selection of standard trade items.

O. **Mechanics of Spending Materials Funds**

Frequently a library will have more funds to spend than were originally budgeted at the beginning of the year. Additional gifts may be received, extra departmental monies may be transferred to the library, salary savings may supplement the budget, or a portion of a governmental or foundation grant may be given to the library for materials expenditures. No library mentioned losing acquisition monies during a fiscal year, but one university library budgets anticipated gifts into its materials fund and these funds are not always received. All libraries carry over their endowment funds, and gifts are treated the same way. Seven of the 12 university libraries can now carry over unexpended materials funds coming from the university. University administrations do not want libraries to be forced to spend their money before the end of the budget year. However, a few universities will carry over only funds committed to purchases. Three universities do not allow libraries to carry over university appropriations. One of these libraries has a deposit system with dealers in order to spend unspent university appropriations prior to the end of the fiscal year. This system has proved to be a great help in billing as well, and the library argues that any amount lost in interest is more than made up for by improved processing. The vendor sends the library a statement and the university is not flooded with invoices to process. Selection decisions are not affected by university funds being returned at the end of the fiscal year because libraries with this provision usually spend their university appropriations first. If funds are remaining, it is possible to transfer expense from endowments to spend out the general appropriation, or a library can use a deposit account as noted above.

Ten of the libraries studied use a commitment system for materials expenditures. The commitment systems are internal, because university accounting offices cannot cope with keeping track of literally thousands of small expenditures for libraries. These thousands of small expenditures are also a real problem for libraries. Many purchase orders are never acknowledged or filled, and libraries are left at year end with a commitment rather than an expense. Half of the libraries allow their selectors to overcommit, depending upon the fund. For example, if the fund is for foreign materials, then overcommitment is frequently desirable because of delivery problems. Two libraries try to spend their monies as evenly as possible by using projections and alerting the selectors if the expenditure rate is off target. One of the two libraries uses a mathematical model of expenditure rates to monitor expenditure rates. It remains difficult to persuade administrators of the complexities of spending materials budgets.

The patterns of purchasing do not appear greatly affected by the source of funds. Federal grants, until Title IIC, have been general and have helped support general collection development. In instances where there have been specialized grants, these grants have supplanted general monies that could then be used elsewhere, having the same effect. Many libraries benefited from large federal Title IIA grants in 1969–1970, but by 1971–1972 these grants had been phased out.

National Defense Education Act (NDEA) Grants for area studies have been helpful to five institutions (Chicago, Cornell, Harvard, Princeton, and Yale) in supporting their specialized collections on South East Asia, South Asia, Korea, and the Near East, but these grants have supported already strong collections. It also appears that Title IIC grants in 1978 and 1979 concentrated more on access than on acquisition. The National Endowment for the Humanities (NEH) program has also supported access as well as acquisitions. Two libraries reported that efforts to seek funding for specific collections (an undergraduate core collection and a medieval studies collection) have not met with success. Some directors also spoke pessimistically about the possibilities of obtaining collection development funding in the future. One said that the money from foundations is going to projects that will contribute to national solutions. It is therefore getting harder and harder for an institution to obtain funds for its own program.

P. Conclusions

Collecting patterns, allocation systems, and procedural and administrative changes have evolved in the 12 libraries in response to inflationary pressures and decreased funding. Some specific measures taken by these libraries to respond to inflation and reduced budgets merit special attention:

1. Allocations need to respond more to the local priorities of teaching and research. The University of Chicago questionnaire on allocations is an example of a method for encouraging selectors to consider local factors in apportioning the funds. Allocations are not only useful for setting aside monies for programs but can make selectors aware of budget limitations, give focus to selectors' responsibilities, communicate budgetary needs to the faculty, and serve as a collection management tool.
2. Some libraries now have formal systems for reviewing expensive purchases, duplicates, and serials. Every library should adopt formal, written regulations that will ensure that purchase decisions are made prudently. By ensuring that a purchase decision is reviewed by several persons, that faculty are brought into the process, and that availability in other area libraries is considered, formal procedures can result in more systematic building of collections.
3. Serial purchases constitute a major element in the cost of building collections. Libraries need to have better data on serial purchases. Northwestern's automated statistics on serials are an example of the type of data which is needed on the "standing commitments" that libraries have. The University of Chicago system for balancing serial purchases against monographic budgets is another illustration of a means of requiring examination of each serial purchase.
4. The de-emphasis of retrospective buying is a serious problem for research libraries. Murray Martin makes an appropriate analogy for libraries when he speaks of deferred maintenance in railroads. Universities need to be aware that deferring purchase of retrospective materials will affect the long-term quality of the collections. Consideration needs to be given to cooperative means of obtaining specialized materials.
5. Libraries need to give more emphasis to utilizing their current collections. Northwestern's scholar-librarian concept (which concentrates on exploiting its current collections by well-trained staff with advanced credentials who can work with the faculty to make better use of collections already there) can be used by other libraries to exploit their resources. Libraries need to build upon current strengths and avoid expanding into new fields. Three libraries of the 12 have just completed major studies of microform

applications at their libraries, and it seems that the full potential of microforms as substitutes for binding, as replacements for lost and mutilated journals, and for little-used monographic collections has not yet been realized.

Other means of reducing materials expenditures have been enumerated in other subsections of Section V. Cooperative purchases of serials and cooperative serial cancellation programs appear to be a promising means of limiting the "standing commitments" that diminish funds available for the purchase of books and other materials. The RLG programs for serial purchase and cancellation are model programs for reducing these commitments. This section has been devoted to reductions; and Section VI will cover cooperation and its effect on the materials budget.

VI. INTERLIBRARY COOPERATION AND THE MATERIALS BUDGET

One of the principal motivations for interlibrary cooperation is monetary, i.e., extending services at lower costs. The ability of libraries to grow and expand their services is directly determined by personnel, operating, and materials costs. This study, focusing as it does on materials budgets, has concentrated on examining the relationship between interlibrary cooperation and library materials funding. Three major cooperative programs concerned primarily with collections—the Center for Research Libraries, the Research Library Group, and the UCB (the University of California at Berkeley) Stanford Research Library Cooperative Program—are discussed in detail because most of the libraries studied have participated in at least one of these enterprises. Librarians at each institution were asked to evaluate the degree to which materials costs were a factor in forcing libraries into networks, common storage facilities, or other forms of interlibrary cooperation. Librarians were also asked whether they had cost figures that showed the tradeoffs between the cost of cooperation and acquisition savings and whether or not they were actually citing in their budget requests the savings to be gained through sharing with other libraries. One assumption was that if a major motivation of cooperation were economy, then any measure of the effectiveness of cooperation would include cost figures. There was an attempt to ascertain whether or not librarians and administrators viewed cooperation as a means of reducing costs. Librarians were also questioned about the kinds of collection cooperation that were occurring on their institutions and the direct effects of these arrangements on their budgets for materials. Each question was directed at discovering the possible connections between interlibrary cooperation and materials funds. This study was seeking hard data, that is, statistical quantification of the benefits of cooperative arrangements in the 12 university libraries that were visited.

A. Rationale for Cooperation

In reply to the question about the degree to which materials costs were a factor in forcing libraries into interlibrary cooperation, a majority of the librarians first responded that the rising costs of materials had not compelled them to join cooperative ventures. However, one librarian modified his response by indicating that shared access was encouraged by limited funds, and another indicated that rising materials costs might very well force libraries into greater cooperation in the future. One librarian noted that cooperation was still in the formative years and had not reached its full potential. Other librarians stated very definite cost factors as influences on their participation in cooperative enterprises.

Annual reports and proposals for cooperation also show cost considerations are paramount. A principal objective of the Midwest Interlibrary Center, now the Center for Research Libraries, was to save funds:

> First, libraries are now approaching the point where there are not enough copies of research materials to be in every library where research in that subject is being carried on. As a result, libraries are placed in the position of having to bid against each other for scarce materials with unfortunate results for the limited budgets under which they operate (Williams, 1972, p. 265).

The first problem to be cited in the 1973 program statement for a consortium of research libraries (Yale, New York Public, Harvard, and Columbia) was clearly financial. This consortium is rapidly expanding and in early 1980 includes 17 members of the Association of Research Libraries. Similarly, the aim of the UCB/Stanford Research Library Cooperative Program, established in 1977, is to inhibit the exploding costs of library collection growth while insuring quality library service.

B. Cost Reductions

When librarians were asked whether they felt that cooperative programs reduced costs, there was unanimity. None saw cooperation as reducing costs but all viewed it as a means of avoiding increased expenditures. They emphasized this conclusion by expressing cost avoidance as "slowing down costs," "decreasing their magnitude," "retarding them," or "softening the blow." One librarian argued that cooperation could not be viewed only in a defensive fashion because it was also designed to improve services, increase access, and extend bibliographic control. Most agreed that sharing resources offered some control over rising costs although some increases were considered inevitable. Most also concurred that journal subscriptions could be reduced through cooperation. One librarian suggested that cooperation could be used internally in a political sense as a justification for cutting costs. Although there was consensus about cooperation extending a library's capabilities, one librarian questioned whether the faculty would agree. "In the macroworld they agree, but in the microworld there is resistance."

Administrators, when questioned, raised three important considerations central to any large-scale investment in a cooperative venture. First, a major issue is the mechanics of a cooperative program—can material be delivered in a timely fashion? Second, a related issue is political. Large storage centers, such as the Center for Research Libraries, purchase little-used materials for research use of the membership. Can the faculty be persuaded of the need for an insurance policy where benefits are not immediate? Third, a final issue is financial. The libraries must be able to justify cooperation costs in relation to benefits received. They must be able to show how their money is spent for shared resources, and where it has helped them avoid costs.

C. Mechanics

At some libraries there were expressions of doubt about the high cost of the Center for Research Libraries (CRL), relative to its benefits. The high membership cost and the small traffic was mentioned as contributing to these concerns. It appears that higher traffic is inhibited by the lack of bibliographical guides to the CRL's purchase of collections. This was a uniform criticism of the CRL. A specific criticism relates to the method of reporting the CRL's large microfilm projects. These projects are reported to members by a newsletter with several titles per sheet rather than by card with one title per card. Frequently the newsletter is circulated and then filed. Most universities rely upon the memory of the individual who reviews large purchases to determine whether the CRL has a title. There are other deficiencies of a bibliographic nature which are being remedied. The University of Chicago, Northwestern, and the CRL are compiling a complete bibliography of current newspapers received by these two libraries and the CRL. To augment the CRL's catalogues and supplements, a union list of currently received science serials is also being prepared by the University of Chicago, the John Crear Library, and the CRL with Title IIC funding. Another criticism leveled at the CRL related to its cancellation program. Five years ago, the CRL received a Carnegie grant for coordination of serial cancellations. According to some, this program has not been well publicized, and there is confusion on how it works. As a result, some libraries have not participated.

Despite these drawbacks, libraries generally praised the CRL for its contributions in making available little-used materials that might otherwise have had to be purchased by participating libraries. Three libraries from this study recommended that the Center for Research Libraries be used as the core library for a national periodicals library. In this connection, the Journal Access Service initiated by CRL was mentioned specifically as a model program. One library, Cornell University, advertises the Journal Access Service at its public service points with a flyer. The CRL attempts to expedite delivery for this program by using the British Library Lending Division for items that the CRL does not hold and by sending requests via computer network. The Research Libraries Group (RLG) has also emphasized delivery in its system. A flyer at the Yale Library reference desk advertises the special features of RLG, including undergraduate privileges, delivery by United Parcel Service, and the RLG Bibliographic Center, which does searches for materials needed by users. The Stanford/Berkeley cooperative system has expedited delivery through the appointment of coordinators, advertisements in flyers and newsletters, and regular bus service for books and users, leaving four times a day. The mechanics of cooperation both at the Center and in other cooperative programs are elements in their cost effectiveness.

The expensive monographic order and new serial purchase program at RLG are excellent models for effective resource sharing. Information on purchases is sent to the RLG Bibliographic Center, which coordinates decisions with other member libraries through entry of purchase decisions into an on-line Cooperative Purchase File in the RLG automated cataloging system, RLIN. The RLG also compiled a machine-readable union list of RLG serials that was distributed on microfiche. Members were thus made aware of current serial purchases by RLG libraries.

D. Political Implications

The success of cooperative ventures often depends on timely access. In other words, the faculty are easily discouraged by delays or nondelivery. They also need to be persuaded of the need for using institutional funds for titles that are not of immediate benefit for the local institution. The Center for Research Libraries may already be a special case, because it uses institutional funds for a national collection, purchasing materials that some members will never use. As early as 1964, Paul Buck (1964) expressed his concern about the financing of the Midwest Interlibrary Center, now the Center for Research Libraries:

> Collections of highly specialized material need not be duplicated on the shelves of many individual libraries if they can be housed and maintained cooperatively. As in the case of specialization, it seems clear that national projects of this kind will have to be supported nationally; they cannot be financed adequately if they must depend on voluntary self-assessment by research libraries (p. 157).

Several years later the Committee on Research Libraries of the American Council of Learned Societies (1969) recommended that a National Commission on Libraries and Archives:

> incorporate into the National Library System the facilities of the Center for Research Libraries and other cooperative programs that serve the national research interest, and that Federal support be provided to such agencies (p. 12).

The Center for Research Libraries is an acknowledged necessity for research, purchasing materials that individual libraries cannot support alone. However, as its costs rise, will the institutions be able to afford it? There were some doubts expressed by librarians interviewed about the value of belonging to the CRL as measured by the tangible returns. Some librarians interviewed expressed the hope that the CRL would become the national periodicals library and receive federal funds. Support from the federal government may be a long-term answer to these financial issues.

Each library visited was asked what effect they saw a national cooperative system, such as the national lending library or national periodicals library, would have on their budgets and acquisitions. All the libraries questioned were extremely positive about the effects of a national periodicals center. They felt that it could take away some cost pressures caused by journals, particularly scientific journals. There was skepticism about how soon such a program could be implemented, however, and about delivery capability. The libraries in the West were in favor of a national program that had a regional base. One librarian suggested there should be a tiered system with regional availability of heavily used journals. Another librarian expressed the opinion that there will be a reluctance to lean on a national center until it is reliable, until it has the materials and the delivery capability. The use or non-use of such a facility is often a local political question.

Faculty and administration support is crucial to the success of cooperative programs, particularly at the local and regional level, where costs must be borne by a smaller group of libraries. Cooperation requires sacrifices—immediate access is certainly one—and these sacrifices must be acceptable to the institution. This is where the political support of the administration and faculty is essential. Two university administrators suggested that consortia or resource sharing use the model of the Interuniversity Communications Council, Inc. (EDUCOM) program or the Committee on Interinstitutional Cooperation. In each of these groups top administrators are members of the policy-making boards. This kind of organizational structure gives the administrators a major decision-making role, and consequently a more complete understanding of the rationale for the group's activities. One administrator felt that Association of Research Libraries might have more impact if university administrators were included in its organization. The Research Library Group has included administrative vice presidents from the universities and the President of the New York Public Library in its Board of Directors. There are important political considerations when the structure of any cooperative program is established.

E. Financial Considerations

When study participants were asked "Are there demonstrable savings from participation in a cooperative group?" most librarians replied negatively. In the perspective of the Center for Research Libraries, the question is really moot. Libraries can keep statistics of interlibrary loan requests to the CRL and decisions made to avoid purchases, but there are many titles added to the CRL that are of no immediate interest to individual libraries. (This is not to say that libraries should not keep records of interlibrary loans and decisions to avoid purchases and assign costs to them. Cost–benefit analysis is important in managing any program, but it is not likely the balances will be in favor of the local institution in a program such as the CRL's.) In the case of the Research Library Group or the UCB/Stanford Research Library Cooperation Program, such cost data are important, if only to answer the question posed by one university administrator—"Much of it [cooperation] has been paid for by special grants, what will we do when the grants run out?" When questioned about keeping figures on the tradeoffs between the costs of cooperation and acquisition savings, only one library, Yale University, responded positively to this inquiry. Yale's Report of the University Librarian indicates the types of savings achieved:

> The Research Libraries Group continued to offer attractive options for Yale restraint in purchasing expensive items as well as serials. Seventy-five expensive items ranging in value from $200 to as much as $8,000 were petitioned through the RLG Bibliographic Center by all member libraries. In the absence of this one program, the Yale Library would have felt obliged to buy an additional $70,000 worth of books (Rogers, 1978, p. 6–7).

The Yale Associate Librarian for Collection Development has more detailed records in his annual report, and the *First Annual Report of the Research Libraries Group* also gives cost figures for the serial subscription review program and the subscription cancellation program. According to the Research Libraries Group (1976) *Annual Report,* after the annual program costs are calculated over a 5-year period, a cumulative balance saved is $638,675. This type of information is extremely useful for demonstrating the benefits of such a program (in this case the acquisition and deacquisition costs are emphasized, but service benefits can be derived from the borrowing statistics) as well as improving the program's efficiency.

F. Other Cooperative Measures

One by-product of the original RLG program was an RLG Union List on fiche, which contained new subscriptions of member libraries and was updated on a regular basis. A union list can be an invaluable tool within a library system for avoiding duplicates among branches and making informed decisions in collection development. It is an equally significant tool for cooperative systems for the same reasons. The UCB/Stanford Research Library Cooperation program has as one of its goals a joint union list of serials. It was surprising, therefore, to discover that six of the libraries in this study did not have a union list. Only one library had an on-line union list. Several of the libraries intend to prepare one and some had portions of their serial collections listed, but it was nonetheless striking that half of the libraries visited did not have a union list by June 1978.

There were several examples of informal cooperation where libraries had retarded costs. For example, one library is purchasing the Human Relations Area Files jointly with a state university library and housing the collection in its library. This arrangement includes access for students of the public institution to the private institution. These two libraries are also sharing information on $500 purchases and putting catalog cards for these titles in their catalogs indicating ownership. In another instance of cooperation, two private libraries are sharing the purchases of large microfilm projects that are not available through the CRL. Because of legal complications, the two libraries are not purchasing the projects jointly but have set aside funds and are alternating purchases of large sets. Another library cooperates with a major public library in the purchase of the Presidential Papers on film and participates in an informal citywide group of research and special libraries that has formed collection groups, including a Task Force on Newspapers. These examples indicate some of the possibilities for cooperative collection programs, which can decrease the magnitude of material expenditures.

G. Interlibrary Loans and the Materials Budget

It was originally the intention of this study to determine whether interlibrary borrowing increased during times of cutbacks in materials expenditures. There are several reasons that this appeared impossible. First, the interlibrary loan statistics in ARL statistical reports have been recorded for only 4 years and are not adequate to determine any trends because this time span (4 years) allows for only 3 years of budget comparisons. Second, the number of interlibrary requests to borrow is so infinitesimally small in comparison to the overall circulation of books that it is doubtful that any statistical comparison would be useful. As an example, in 1976–1977 Yale University circulated 1,233,313 volumes, while at the same time there were only 5779 requests to borrow items. The number of requests to borrow is less than 0.5% of the number of volumes circulated.

VII. CONCLUSION

Since the early 1970s libraries have lived with stringent budgets, and university financial trends seem to indicate continuing austerity for the foreseeable future. The growth rates of libraries and publications are slowing somewhat, but the sources of revenue for universities have also slackened. For example, in "1967 the government provided approximately 24% of the educational and general revenue of the average private institution. In 1976, the corresponding figure is 20%" and "nationally inflation has grown annually by 6.7% while private giving has increased less than 4%" (Harvard University, 1977, pp. 74–75). With the prospects of a tax revolt, poor stock market performance, and persistent inflation, universities are under great pressure to reduce their costs. At the same time, they are faced with equally strong pressures to meet the salary demands of their faculty and staff, and the nonlabor costs of higher education, particularly energy, have continued to rise. Because libraries are labor intensive and are also confronted by rising publication costs, it is likely university cost pressures will continue to adversely affect the operations of libraries. The university administrators consulted during the study agreed that universities cannot continue to give libraries increases consistent with or higher than inflationary rates. Richard DeGennaro (1977) has suggested that:

> Libraries are experiencing a substantial loss in their standard of living as a result of inflation, increasing energy costs, and changing priorities in our society. We can rail against it and search for scapegoats, but it would be better if we came to terms with this painful reality, and begin to reduce our excessive commitments and expectations to match our declining resources (p. 435).

The experiences of the 12 libraries in this study have provided examples of successful responses to these adverse economic conditions as well as fresh insights into means of controlling costs in the future.

Libraries are making progress in defining more precisely the various elements of materials costs. The ARL now requires all libraries to report serials costs, and some libraries are able to distinguish between the costs of monographic series and periodicals. Other libraries have built features into their automated ordering systems for reporting the costs of materials by subject, format, language, and country. Despite these advances, some of the questions asked by William Dix in a speech on budget reductions in 1971 still cannot be answered by the libraries studied:

1. Of the monographs we bought last year, how many were new, how many old, and how were the expenditures distributed between old and new?
2. How much did we spend for serials?
3. How many of our serial titles are duplicated, in how many copies, in what locations, and why?
4. How much did we spend on acquisitions for each of the last five years in each field of knowledge, broken down roughly to the level of teaching departments, and programs?
5. How many universities have an acquisition policy statement which identifies the ten or twenty sub-fields within each discipline and indicates for each of these sub-fields the level of completeness to which the library aspires? (Dix, 1972, pp. 9–10).

None of the libraries can answer question 1, although the Princeton study by the Special Committee on Acquisitions and Losses produced estimates on retrospective purchases in making its arguments for increased retrospective support for the Princeton History and English departments. Most libraries have satisfactorily answered questions 2 and 3, in responding to ARL questionnaires and in the process of reducing library duplication. Many libraries can answer question 4. Princeton University Library did prepare expenditure data for university departments for the past 8 years for the Special Committee. Other libraries keep their allocations by department, branch, or subject so it is possible to estimate departmental support by using allocations. Such estimates are naturally imprecise because of contingency funds, standing order funds, or gift and exchange funds that cannot be assigned easily to departments. With reference to question 5, 10 of the 12 libraries now have or have begun collection policy statements. Unfortunately, the statements lack uniformity because libraries have either modified the ALA guidelines or not used them at all.

Libraries need to keep more precise records of materials expenditures in order to show how they are supporting the academic programs of their university. Further questions, such as how much is spent on foreign materials, how much is spent for microforms, or how much of the materials budget comes from endowment, gifts, or grants, cannot be easily answered by many libraries. Annual reports are not published by 4 of the 12 libraries, and, as a result, there is no official record of management data for these libraries. Annual reports that are published vary in quality. For example, some do not record the number of serial titles held by the library, the number of interlibrary loans, serial expenditures, etc. Although these data are available in *ARL Statistics* it would be helpful to confirm it in annual reports with the narrative that interpreted atypical increases or decreases in library figures reported to ARL, especially since university administrators are increasingly expecting libraries to give them hard data on funding needs, relating library materials costs to the teaching and research programs of the university. Past expenditure data are very important for future priority setting and planning.

Three of the libraries in this study, Harvard, Princeton, and the University of Southern California, developed long-range studies in the late 1960s designed to alert their university administrations to the magnitude of future library costs in specific areas. Similar efforts would appear to be in order as we enter the 1980s, but few libraries are currently working on such studies. One promising attempt has been made at Stanford University, which has established a faculty committee, chaired by the Provost, to study "the nature of Stanford Library Services over the period 1980–2000" and to develop "a practical conceptual model of the Stanford Library system suitable in structure and detail for decades to come."

These planning efforts result in a continuing dialogue between library and administration which is very desirable. There needs to be more structure to the communication process by which libraries find out about curriculum changes, program developments, and new research studies. Although each library has informal contacts to discover the directions of the university curriculum there are few examples of formal systems to include the library in the process of curriculum development. At Cornell the Provost, before he approves any new program, must check a box on a form that asks the question about consideration of the library. Although most collection development staffs are very alert to the indications of new curriculum directions and have excellent contacts, the library is still frequently not included in academic decision making in a formal sense when new university programs are considered. Participation in university planning is an essential element in budget preparation and there are administrators who see communication between the library and themselves as an area for reexamination. If librarians can be included in deliberations on new curricula, they can be of great assistance to the university as well as to the library.

In addition to more precise expenditure data, long-range planning, and improved communication with the administration, libraries need to do their own fund raising or give special assistance to their development office. By using friends' groups and library visiting committees, the library can make its needs known in the community from which universities derive a great part of their support. Libraries can appoint their own development officers and enlist support from the entire staff in advertising the resources of the library. The library also should be mentioned in all the promotional literature that is distributed by the university.

Changing the service expectations of the library will be another contribution toward reducing costs and maintaining adequate funds for acquisitions in future years. Almost without exception, the administrators interviewed are expecting libraries to achieve more efficiencies administratively through automation and technological advances. Librarians, in contrast, doubt that much more reduction of staff is possible.

Librarians must consider reducing their service commitments to the academic community. As a librarian in England has stated the problem:

> In particular, it is important to establish what is absolutely necessary for teaching and research, and for academic staff to be aware of financial realities, to be prepared to modify their demands on their library, and to be willing to accept a policy of planned insufficiency, the impact of which can be counteracted by sensible area planning, and some degree of reliance on local cooperation and use of national resources (Cowley, 1977, p. 92).

Although it may not be possible to obtain materials locally, it will be possible to procure them cooperatively from within a system.

Most libraries examined here have participated or are participating in some form of cooperative activity. The success of these cooperative ventures depends heavily upon the commitment of the university administration and faculty because pressures to obtain materials locally are usually strong. Hence the enlistment of university administrators and faculty in the planning process helps to ensure the success of cooperative programs. Sometimes the method of cooperation can reduce university anxieties about the reduction of local funding or materials resulting from cooperation. For example, one library in the study intends to cooperate with another institution on the purchase of materials neither library was able to obtain through its own materials budget. Each library will compile a list of materials desired and the materials common to both lists will be purchased and shared. In this way, administration and faculty cannot complain of sacrifices because all purchases will be an enhancement to the collections. Such a scheme will require outside funding and cooperative priority setting of needs. Even this kind of effort can be more productive if faculty and administration are included in the early deliberations. In any cooperative venture, once support is gained from faculty and administration, it is also essential to set up mechanisms for publicity, bibliographic control, and delivery. The Research Library Group (RLG) has provided examples of procedures and administration which are distinctive. The RLG's Bibliographic Center and its new serial purchase program, expensive item program, and preservation program are models for other libraries wishing to begin cooperative undertakings.

Cooperation seems essential if libraries are to extend their resources in the face of financial constraints. Many of the librarians in the study believe that national cooperation would have a significant impact in reducing the magnitude of materials costs. Regional specialization, cooperation, and document delivery are key elements in any national scheme to relieve some of the pressures on individual research library budgets. Regional specialization might take the form of a new Farmington Plan, which would consist of subject and area specialization on a regional basis. Certain libraries would be designated as national resource collections and would be required to loan items from these collections either as originals or in facsimilies. Such a program would tend to cover fringe materials not heavily in demand on a local basis. Document delivery might use telefacsimile transmission or possibly include stipends for researchers to travel to collections of national prominence. Planning for national cooperation requires participation from university administrators in order to ensure that the participating institutions are willing to forego collecting in areas assigned to other libraries. In the long run this might require specialization by universities. Such specialization has been proposed by Steven Muller (1978), President of Johns Hopkins University, in an article on the future of American universities:

> The new American university will seek to receive federal support for research on the basis of substantial long term funding. An effort will be made to designate selected universities as major research centers and to obtain endowment for them as such. In order to include the largest possible number of universities, this effort may take the form of suggesting that major research centers be designated by area of research rather than on a universal basis; so as to make it possible, for instance, for one institution to be endowed as a major research center in one area, such as cellular biology, whereas another university might be endowed for quite a different area, such as environmental engineering (p. 33).

In order to avoid the pitfalls of one-sided research, there might be more than one institution designated as a center for cellular biology, thus ensuring competition and higher quality research. Specialization among universities might also match library specialization, instead of vice versa, because library resources would be a key criterion in deciding on the area of specialization.

In the future it is not likely that local materials budgets will grow by quantum leaps, and the incremental increases received will be insufficient. Libraries will need to adjust their commitments to the amount of funding available locally, while at the same time providing access to external collections. Libraries will also need to create more realistic expectations of service from their clientele. For instance, patrons may have to wait longer for some materials because they are not available locally. If librarians continue to make advances in computerized access to collections while at the same time costs for the technology decrease, it may be possible for libraries to maintain access to larger and larger collections without local materials costs rising as fast. Low-cost storage centers will also provide an answer to the dilemma of little-used materials occupying expensive campus library space. Computerized data on expenditure and circulation patterns will enable libraries to match their collecting with the instructional and research programs of their local university. Specialized research collections will be maintained with the help of the federal government, with a national periodicals library, a national lending library, or regional depositories as backup. Libraries will raise more endowment for book funds, but despite this support they will depend more heavily upon shared resources to see them through the austere days ahead.

APPENDIX A:
Decreases in Material Expenditures—ARL Statistics

Fiscal Year	Brown	Chicago	Cornell	Harvard	Johns Hopkins	Northwestern	Penn	Princeton	Rice	Stanford	USC	Yale
1977–1978		X		X		X	X					
1976–1977	X	X				X		X				
1975–1976						X						
1974–1975			X				X					X
1973–1974	X	X									X	
1972–1973												
1971–1972	X		X					X	X	X		X
1970–1971	X		X				X		X		X	X
1969–1970									X			
1968–1969					X			X				
1967–1968						X						
1966–1967												
1965–1966												
1964–1965					X		X					X
1963–1964	X											

APPENDIX B:
Average Volumes Added During 5-Year Periods

	1962–1963 to 1966–1967	1967–1968 to 1971–1972	1972–1973 to 1976–1977
Brown	31,008	49,194	36,038
Chicago	148,769	152,199	108,141
Cornell	127,388	174,857	162,343
Harvard	225,106	255,503	225,838
Johns Hopkins	99,790	83,081	47,025
Northwestern	65,890	82,060	83,996
Penn	76,736	96,239	95,036
Princeton	104,358	99,092	89,495
Rice	28,247	36,051	38,792
Stanford	154,596	199,430	152,104
USC	50,427	64,698	60,782
Yale	135,596	198,501	155,074
Total	1,249,911	1,490,905	1,254,664
Average volumes added:	103,993	124,242	104,555
	19.47% increase	15.85% decrease	

APPENDIX C:
Total Library Expenditures as Percentage of University Operating Expenditures

	1977	1976	1975	1974	1973	1972	1971	1970
Brown	4.74	5.27	4.82	4.74	5.04	4.88	4.69	5.45
Chicago	2.48	2.44	2.50	2.42	2.52	2.53	2.48	2.51
Cornell	3.02	3.05	3.25	3.14	3.26	3.25	3.43	3.37
Harvard	5.64	5.69	5.50	5.61	5.43	NA[a]	NA[a]	NA[a]
Johns Hopkins	2.49	2.52	2.47	2.38	2.14	2.06	2.40	2.41
Northwestern	3.63	3.82	4.08	4.12	4.11	4.14	4.16	3.49
Penn	2.09	1.98	2.03	2.14	2.07	1.89	1.78	1.66
Princeton	4.11	4.94	4.99	5.09	5.06	4.90	4.86	4.32
Rice	5.56	5.53	5.47	5.09	5.73	5.02	5.06	NA[a]
Stanford	3.64	3.47	3.32	3.50	3.41	4.49	4.50	4.60
USC	1.60	1.63	1.65	1.79	1.75	1.88	2.07	1.79
Yale	5.46	5.37	5.78	5.74	5.52	5.10	5.34	NA[a]

[a]NA, not available.

APPENDIX D:
Sources of Materials Funds, 1976–1977

Institution[a]	University and department funds (%)	Endowed (%)	Gifts, grants, and fees (%)
Library A	51.0	32.0	17.0
Library B	36.4	42.0	21.6
Library C	87.4	11.9	.7
Library D	52.1	31.5	16.4
Library E	76.6	14.53	8.86
Library F	71.4	8.4	20.2
Library G	94.3	.7	5.0
Library H	85.75	7.125[b]	7.125[a]
Library I	86.0	12.6	1.4
Library J	74.8	7.1	16.8
Library K	86.6	8.2	4.2
Library L	83.12	9.01	7.85

[a]A, Source is the business manager; B, source is the annual report; C, source is the business manager; D, source is budget documents; E, source is budget documents; F, source is business manager; G, source is business manager; H, source is assistant director for technical services; I, source is business manager; J, source is budget documents; K, source is financial report; L, source is acquisition librarian.

[b]Divided in half because the library was not able to divide its special funds into endowment, gift, and grant as requested.

APPENDIX E:
Average Material Expenditures During 5-Year Periods, Twelve Institutions

	1967–1968 to 1971–1972		1972–1973 to 1976–1977
Brown	541,200		713,126
Chicago	1,039,909		1,280,225
Cornell	1,440,368		1,848,708
Harvard	1,717,432		3,084,009
Johns Hopkins	459,188		948,219
Northwestern	835,212		1,379,109
Penn	901,127		1,179,917
Princeton	1,088,675		1,600,415
Rice	455,764		578,240
Stanford	1,221,871		2,239,792
USC	656,054		1,018,311
Yale	1,828,391		2,329,020
Total	$12,185,191		$18,199,091
Average materials expense:	$1,015,433	49.36% increase	$1,516,590

APPENDIX F:
Percentage of Library Expenditures[a] for Personnel, Materials, and Operating

	1970–1971			1977–1978		
	Personnel	Materials	Operating	Personnel	Materials	Operating
Brown	66.28	24.14	6.57	60.06	30.92	5.62
Chicago	61.07	26.82	7.34	62.58	25.53	9.11
Cornell	62.99	25.63	8.20	59.27	27.73	10.81
Harvard	63.72	20.32	12.13	58.83	24.50	13.71
Johns Hopkins	60.88	24.48	11.28	52.64	28.70	17.37
Northwestern	58.10	32.30	6.36	54.96	20.21	22.99
Penn	64.54	25.22	6.13	64.36	23.99	8.50
Princeton	58.84	34.75	4.95	60.15	32.83	5.11
Rice	54.34	37.46	5.65	46.76	38.53	12.40
Stanford	61.88	24.53	10.26	53.98	30.74	12.30
USC	59.55	32.40	5.73	56.67	33.44	7.69
Yale	55.24	26.29	16.12	59.74	26.33	11.95
Weighted average	60.90	26.31	9.58	58.07	27.46	12.02

[a]Does not include binding.

APPENDIX G:
Materials Budget Increases

	1970–1971	1977–1978	Percentage change
Brown	$ 446,222	$ 837,880	87.77
Chicago	$1,032,555	$1,357,048	31.43
Cornell	$1,443,734	$2,337,368	61.90
Harvard	$1,771,858	$3,569,946	101.48
Johns Hopkins	$ 484,704	$1,234,078	154.60
Northwestern	$ 949,720	$1,368,909	44.14
Penn	$ 913,171	$1,298,623	42.21
Princeton	$1,274,128	$1,978,637	55.29
Rice	$ 447,636	$ 732,998	63.70
Stanford	$1,539,780	$3,144,636	104.23
USC	$ 812,231	$1,624,934	100.06
Yale	$1,835,534	$2,821,033	53.69
Totals	$12,951,273	$22,306,090	72.23 (weighted average)

APPENDIX H:
Serials/Monograph Ratio[a]

Library	1972–1973	1973–1974	1974–1975	1975–1976	1976–1977	1977–1978
Brown	32	51	54	50 (45)	61 (59)	58 (42)
Chicago	48	51	53	48 (35)	50 (50)	55 (55)
Cornell	43	46	50	52 (NA)	53 (NA)	NA (NA)
Harvard	NA	NA	NA	44 (44)	44 (44)	44 (44)
Johns Hopkins	59	59	57	57 (57)	60 (60)	63 (63)
Northwestern	39	41	45	50 (45)	52 (52)	56 (63)
Penn	45	48	55	54 (54)	50 (50)	57 (57)
Princeton	32	34	35	46 (46)	56 (56)	49 (49)
Rice	51	57	54	58 (58)	57 (57)	57 (57)
Stanford	40	40	40	41 (44)	43 (51)	39 (43)
USC	NA	52	55	56 (63)	56 (61)	45 (53)
Yale	30	31	34	37 (41)	36 (40)	38 (38)
Total	419	510	532	593 (532)	618 (570)	561 (564)
Median	41.5	48	53	50 (45)	52.5 (52)	55 (53)

[a] Percentages rounded to next whole number if 0.6 or more. Prior to 1975–1976 the figures are internal. After 1975–1976, if figures are identical to figures in parenthesis, they are from ARL. The internal figures include medical, except Johns Hopkins, Northwestern, Stanford, U.S.C., and Yale. Princeton and Rice do not have medical schools. It appears the larger libraries have a smaller proportion of serial expenditures. The median library passed the 50% serial expenditures in 1974–1975 and the average library passed it in 1976–1977.

REFERENCES

American Council of Learned Societies. Committee on Research Libraries (1969). "On Research Libraries." MIT Press, Cambridge, Massachusetts.
American Library Association. RTSD, Resources Section (1979). Guidelines for the allocation of library materials budgets. *In* "Guidelines for Collection Development" (D. Perkins, ed.), pp. 30–40, 51–52, & 73. American Library Association, Chicago, Illinois.
American National Standards Institute (1974). "American National Standard Criteria for Price Indexes for Library Materials." American National Standards Institute, New York.
Association of Research Libraries, Systems and Procedures Exchange Center (1977a). "Allocation of Materials Funds in Academic Libraries." Association of Research Libraries, Office of University Library Management Studies, Washington, D.C.
Association of Research Libraries, Systems and Procedures Exchange Center (1977b). "Allocation of Resources." Association of Research Libraries, Office of University Library Management Studies, Washington, D.C.
Association of Research Libraries, Systems and Procedures Exchange Center (1977c). "Preparation and Presentation of the Library Budget." Association of Research Libraries, Office of University Library Management Studies, Washington, D.C.
Association of Research Libraries, Systems and Procedures Exchange Center (1978). "External Fund Raising in ARL Libraries." Association of Research Libraries, Office of University Library Management Studies, Washington, D.C.
Association of Research Libraries, Systems and Procedures Exchange Center (1979). "Cost Studies and Fiscal Planning." Association of Research Libraries, Office of University Library Management Studies, Washington, D.C.
Association of Research Libraries, Systems and Procedures Exchange Center (1980). "Library Materials Cost Studies." Association of Research Libraries, Office of University Library Management Studies, Washington, D.C.
Baatz, W. H. (1978). Collection development in 19 libraries of the Association of Research Libraries. *Library Acquisitions: Practice and Theory* **2**, 85–121.
Bacchetti, R. F. (1976). Funding for libraries: a five year projection, the institutional scene. *In* "Managing Under Austerity: Summary Proceedings," pp. 17–28. Stanford University Library, Stanford, California.
Buck, P. (1964). "Libraries and Universities: Addresses and Reports." Harvard University Press, Cambridge, Massachusetts.
Clasquin, F. F., and Cohen, J. B. (1979). Physics and chemistry journal prices in 1977–78. *Serials Librarian* **3**, 381–386.
Cline, H. F. and Sinnott, L. T. (1980) "Building Library Collections." Lexington Books, Lexington, Massachusetts.
Cohen, J., and Leeson, K. W. (1979). Sources and uses of funds in academic libraries. *Library Trends* **28**, 35–46.
Cole, R. G. (1978). "Organizational Document, Planning Meeting on Establishing a Strategy on Bibliographic Control of Microforms, April 7, 1978." n.p.
Cornell University (1977). "Financial Report for the Fiscal Year Ended, June 30, 1977." Cornell University, Ithaca, New York.

Council on Library Resources (1978). "A National Periodicals Center: Technical Development Plan." Council on Library Resources, Washington, D.C.

Cowley, J. (1977). Balancing the library budget. In "Proceedings of the 2nd Blackwells Periodical Conference, Trinity College, Oxford, 23-24 March 1977." Serials Group, School of Librarianship, The Technical College, Loughborough.

DeGennaro, R. (1977). Copyright, resource sharing, and hard times: A view from the field. *American Libraries* **8**, 430-435.

Dix, W. S. (1972). Reflections in adversity; or, how do you cut a library budget? *Louisiana State University Library Lectures* No. 17-20, 8-18.

Downes, R. N. (1977). Critical challenges in steady-state financing: a perspective. In "Library Budgeting: Critical Challenges for the Future," pp. 1-14. Pierian Press, Ann Arbor, Michigan.

Dunlap, C. R. (1977). Resources sharing goals: comments. In "Library Resources Sharing: Proceedings of the 1976 Conference on Resource Sharing in Libraries, Pittsburgh, Pennsylvania" (A. Kent and T. J. Galvin, eds.), pp. 39-45. Dekker, New York.

Eaton, A. J. (1971). Fund raising for university libraries. *College & Research Libraries* **32**, 351-361.

Evans, G. T. (1978). The cost of information about library acquisition budgets. *Collection Management* **2**, 3-23.

Fry, B. M., and White, H. S. (1976). "Publishers and Libraries: a study of scholarly and research journals." Lexington Books, Heath, Lexington, Massachusetts.

Gardner, J. J. (1978). Issues encountered in the Collection Analysis Project. In "Collection Analysis in Research Libraries: An Interim Report on a Self-Study Process" (D. E. Webster, ed.), pp. 1-4. Association of Research Libraries, Office of University Library Management Studies, Washington, D.C.

Gardner, J. J. (1979) CAP: a project for the analysis of the collection development process in large academic libraries in "New Horizons for Academic Libraries (Papers presented at the First National Conference of the Association of College and Research Libraries, Boston, Massachusetts, November 8-11, 1978), pp. 456-459. K. G. Saur, New York.

Halstead, D. K. (1975). "Higher Education Prices and Price Indexes." U.S. Government Printing Office, Washington, D.C.

Harvard University (1977). "Financial Report to the Board of Overseers of Harvard College, 1976-1977." Coopers & Lybrand, Boston, Massachusetts.

Harvard University Library (1977). "Computer Assisted Processing System." Harvard University Library, Office for Systems Planning and Research, Cambridge, Massachusetts.

Heyeck, J. C., ed. (1976a). "Managing Under Austerity: A Conference for Privately Supported Academic Libraries: Summary Proceedings." Stanford University Library, Stanford, California.

Heyeck, J. C. (1976b). Planning strategies for austere times: administrative services. In "Managing Under Austerity, Summary Proceedings" (J. C. Heyeck, ed.), pp. 163-178. Stanford University Library, Stanford, California.

Johnson, K. S., and Rutstein, J. S. (1979). The politics of book fund allocations: a case study. In "New Horizons for Academic Libraries" (Papers presented at the First

National Conference of the Association of College and Research Libraries, Boston, Massachusetts, November 8–11, 1978), pp. 330–340. K. G. Saur, New York.

Kiley, G. D. (1977). Bibliography. *In* "Library Budgeting: Critical Challenges for the Future" (S. H. Lee, ed.), pp. 97–111. Pierian Press, Ann Arbor, Michigan.

Lee, S. H. (1977). "Library Budgeting: Critical Challenges for the Future." Pierian Press, Ann Arbor, Michigan.

Lynden, F. C. (1977). Sources of information on the costs of library materials. *Library Acquisitions: Practice and Theory* **1**, 105–116.

Lynden, F. C. (1978a). "Library Materials Budgeting in Twelve Private University Libraries," Providence, RI.

Lynden, F. C. (1978b). Resources in 1977. *Library Resources and Technical Services* **22**, 310–334.

Lynden, F. C. (1979). Resources in 1978. *Library Resources and Technical Services* **23**, 213–245.

Machlup, F., and Leeson, K. (1978). "Information Through the Printed Word. The Dissemination of Scholarly, Scientific, and Intellectual Knowledge. Vol. 3: Libraries." Praeger, New York.

Magrill, R. M., and East, M. (1978). Collection development in large university libraries. *Advances in Librarianship* **8**, 1–54.

Martin, M. S. (1978). "Budgetary Control in Academic Libraries." JAI Press, Greenwich, Connecticut.

Muller, S. (1978). A new American university? *Daedulus* **107**, 31–45.

Munn, R. F. (1968). The bottomless pit, or the academic library as viewed from the administration building. *College & Research Libraries* **29**, 51–54.

National Enquiry into Scholarly Communication (1979). "Scholarly Communication: Report of the National Enquiry." Johns Hopkins Press, Baltimore, Maryland.

Osburn, C. B. (1979). "Academic Research and Library Resources: Changing patterns in America." Greenwood Press, Westport, Connecticut.

Princeton University Library (1977). "Report of the Special Committee on Library Acquisitions and Losses, 27 May 1977." Princeton, New Jersey.

Research Libraries Group (1976). "Annual Report, 1975–1976." Research Libraries Group, Branford, Connecticut.

Research Libraries Group (1979). "Progress Report," June 1979. Stanford University, Stanford, California.

Rogers, R. D. (1973). Report of the University librarian, July 1971–June 1972. *Bulletin of Yale University* **69**, 5–7.

Rogers, R. D. (1978). Report of the University librarian, July 1976–June 1977. *Bulletin of Yale University* **74**, 6–7.

Rogers, R. D., and Weber, D. C. (1971). "University Library Administration," pp. 89–111. H. W. Wilson Co., New York.

Samore, T. (1978). College and university library statistics: analysis of NCES survey. *In* "Bowker Annual of Library and Book Trade Information." pp. 243–248. Bowker, New York.

Schad, J. G. (1978). Allocating materials budgets in institutions of higher education. *Journal of Academic Librarianship* **3**, 328–332.

Webster, D. E. (1977). Choices facing academic libraries in allocating scarce resources. *In* "Library Budgeting: Critical Challenges for the Future" (S. H. Lee, ed.), pp. 97–111. Pierian Press, Ann Arbor, Michigan.

Williams, G. (1972). Center for research libraries, its origin, policies and programs. *In* "University and Research Libraries in Japan and the United States." pp. 264–274. American Library Association, Chicago, Illinois.

Individual Decision Theory: An Overview

James D. Sodt

University of Kentucky

I.	Introduction	155
II.	Background: Individual Decision Literature	156
III.	Optimism	156
IV.	The Subjective Expected Utility (SEU) Model	163
V.	Bayesian Models	174
VI.	Conclusion	182
	Selected Bibliography	183

I. INTRODUCTION

Library-use studies have ranged from library circulation analysis to national population samples of adult reading and media preferences. One direction that seems to be evident is that researchers are focusing on the individual as he copes with his problems and then noting the institutions, persons, and aids he selects to assist himself as he makes his way through each situation. As librarians look more and more at man as information gatherer and processor, so it is that the decision becomes a more and more significant element in that view.

This contribution presents an overview of the individual decision literature which deals with attempts to model and explain individuals' behaviors in simplified laboratory-based decision situations. Factors such as the values assigned to alternatives and the estimated likelihood that an outcome will actually occur are central concepts in decision theory. Variables such as the amount of information selected prior to making a decision, the cost of that information, the benefit derived from a correct decision, the reliability of the sources, and the pace at which predecision data are presented are some examples of those explored.

It is hoped that as librarians model their services upon findings from behavioral research, reviews such as this one will help them avoid reinventing the wheel or repeating past mistakes and dead ends.

II. BACKGROUND: INDIVIDUAL DECISION LITERATURE

Research in decision making is a fairly recent development. Abraham Wald's work during World War II was classified as secret material, and the field did not coalesce into a research area until after Ward Edward's review of the literature (Edwards, 1954). In the beginning, decision research was formed from economics and psychology. At the center of the research stood the economists' working metaphor for purposive humans—the economic man. This creature was highly rational, and decision research ever since has been the comparison of the decision-making behavior of this rational man with that of real persons.

This review follows three major themes through the literature. The first is the initial optimism researchers had regarding the match between rational models and actual human decision behavior. Dominant models make up the second and third themes. These are the subjective expected utilities model (SEU) and the Bayesian model, respectively.

III. OPTIMISM

The high point of optimism came in the late 1960s and is reflected in one of the two major reviews published in 1967. The review by Peterson and Beach (1967) examined studies in which descriptive, inferential, and predictive statistical models were compared to persons' judgments and estimates. Their review is summarized in some detail because it provides an excellent entry into the field.

These authors began by dividing the intuitive statistical literature into three parts: (1) that concerned with describing samples of data, i.e., intuitive descriptive statistics; (2) that concerned with the use of those data as a basis for inferences about populations, i.e., intuitive inferential statistics; and (3) that concerned with the use of those inferences as a basis for predicting the make up of future samples from their populations, i.e., intuitive prediction.

The first division of the literature, intuitive descriptive statistics, focused on two major problems: The judgment of proportions and the estimate of means and variances. In both cases, the subjects estimated population parameters on the basis of presented samples. The measure of accuracy was the correspondence between the estimates and the calculated statistics. In the case of estimating proportions, persons' abilities to make these estimates are extremely accurate. "The maximum deviation of the means estimate from the sample proportions is usually only 0.03–0.05, and the average deviations are very close to zero" (Peterson and Beach, 1967, p. 30). The biases were found to be least pronounced in cases of very high and very low proportions. No trend, e.g., underestimation, was established. For both simultaneous and sequential displays, greater exposure resulted in greater accuracy.

When the data were interval or ratio scaled, the subjects' accuracy in estimating means and variances was similarly high. Estimates of means varied slightly with increases in sample variance, sample size, and presentation pace. In the case of estimates of the variance, accuracy increased with sample size but declined with an increase of the means. Subjects seemed to estimate "the coefficient of variation (standard deviation/mean) rather than the variance" (Peterson and Beach, 1967, p. 30).

In addition to that bias, individuals tended to weight deviations of data from the sample means. When estimating variance, subjects operated as if they were raising the deviations to a power other than two. Small powers increased the weight of small deviations; large powers increased that of large deviations. Distributions that were normal prompted a model employing small powers to account for subjects behavior; large-tailed or saddle-shaped distributions were best reflected by large powers.

In the second major division of inferential statistical intuition, Peterson and Beach pointed out that "the theory of statistical inference specifies what kind of inferences should be made from the samples, and the experiments compare inferences made by men with optimal inferences" (Peterson and Beach, 1967, p. 32). Inferences about population parameters, the consistency of these inferences, and methods for determining the size of the sample were the focus of study in this area. The central difference between inferential and descriptive statistical intuition was the criterion of a good performance. In the descriptive case, it was the accuracy of the subjects' judgments; in the inferential case, it was the "degree to which intuitive inferences agree with optimal inferences given by the statistical model," i.e., optimality (Peterson and Beach, 1967, p. 32). Because in life situations the population parameters are generally not known, the best guess on the basis of the sample would seem to be a good strategy to employ. That is what optimality studies attempt to model.

As in the descriptive case, considerable interest in proportions has been shown by experimenters and some important theoretical questions have emerged. In many of these studies, the bookbag and chips experimental paradigm has been used. The subject is to estimate the likelihood that the mix of colored chips is a given proportion. He draws chips from the bookbag and revises his estimate on the basis of the information the sample mix provides him. Peterson and Beach report that when subjects' estimates are compared to Bayesian statistical inference models, the estimates are conservative. That is, the subjects undervalue the information the sample provides and consequently revise their estimates less than optimally. Peterson and Beach state that a revision from 0.50 upward to 0.75 is typical in cases in which the Bayesian model changes to near certainty.

Attempts to explain the fact of conservative information utilization have constituted a large proportion of the effort expended in this area. Procedural variables, such as incentives, sequential ordering, and sample size, all affect conservativism slightly; they do not eliminate the pattern. Instructional variables, interestingly enough, effected no change at all.

Two other approaches to the explanation have demonstrated a greater effect. One is the hypothesis that persons' subjective interpretations of sampling distributions are more flat than the samples indicate statistically. As Peterson and Beach put it, "The persistence of conservativism in spite of variations in procedure suggests that it has roots in the fundamental aspects of subjects' understanding and use of information" (Peterson and Beach, 1967, p. 33). Substituting flatter distributions into the Bayesian model results in improved predictions of subjects' estimates and tends to confirm this view.

The second approach suggests that subjects do not aggregate information well over trials. In studies where subjects revised their estimates after each datum was examined, the final probability estimates were far more conservative than the Bayesian model indicated they should be.

Conservatism continues to appear in estimates of means and variances. Here confidence estimates are substituted for probability estimates, as they are formal equivalents. Confidence rose with increased sample size, increased difference between population means, and increased population variance. For estimates of central tendency the conservatism has been simulated by treating deviations as if they were raised by powers less than two (but greater than one). There may be a connection between this finding and that of the flat sampling distributions, but it is not explicit in the literature.

Many of the studies reviewed by Peterson and Beach are analogous to signal detection theory studies in the structure of the subjects' task, i.e., deciding from which population a sample is taken. In the case of signal detection, the decision is whether the population confronted is one of random noise or of noise plus signal. Peterson and Beach conclude that there is considerable similarity between the findings of signal detection studies and those of intuitive statistics. Specifically, in both kinds of studies the subjects display conservativism and have trouble aggregating information across trials. The authors take this resemblance to indicate the generality of the intuitive statistical framework.

Because inaccuracy or nonoptimability would be of little interest if the effects were merely random, studies of consistency are of considerable importance in intuitive statistics. Consistency is defined in terms of "the degree to which relations among the subjects' inferences correspond to the constraints required of statistical theory" (Peterson and Beach, 1967, p. 35). For if responses are suboptimal but consistent, then the models can be adjusted to describe the behavior, and conjectures can be made as to the reasons for the differences. If the responses are not in some way consistent with the statistical models, then the models are inappropriate as means of understanding human inference behavior. The experimental strategy is to take advantage of the theoretical principle that consistency underlies accuracy. This strategy is implemented by creating inaccuracies for inferences about two or more aspects of a population and comparing the subjects' combination of these aspects with their treatment in the model.

One such aspect that has been studied is the principle that probability estimates of an exhaustive mutually exclusive set of events should sum to 1.00. Some subjects' estimates did this; many did not. The overall results were inconclusive in Peterson and Beach's view.

In other areas, adults were found to be quite consistent. Examples are where estimates for the unions of events are expected to equal the sums of estimates for compound events and when the estimates for joint occurrences are expected to equal the product of the estimates of the component events.

Peterson and Beach called these static judgments examples of structural consistency as opposed to process consistency, in which the subjects must change their probability estimates as they observe a sequence of data samples. Except for highly complex situations, the subjects showed a high level of consistency. In cases where subjects' flat, conservative sampling distributions were substituted for theoretical ones, the models reflected the subjects' responses with high accuracy. This finding was seen to be an indication that individuals' subjective estimation processes are very much like the process rules of formal statistics.

In the experimental paradigms discussed above the subjects generally played a passive role, receiving information in the form of samples without expending any effort or incurring any cost. While the thrust of the research based upon this experimental paradigm is of considerable importance, as Peterson and Beach point out, in life one assertively acquires information exerting control over one's information environment. The size of the sample is a key element one can generally control. The individual must trade off the greater accuracy associated with larger samples against the costs of acquiring them.

The studies are of two types. In one the subject determines in advance how large a sample he wishes; then, after observing the data, he takes an action indicating his decision. The second approach, called optional stopping, allows the subject to sample continuously in sequence. He may at any time conclude that he has enough information to make his decision. Most research has examined this second kind of study. The subject finds himself in a situation much like one finds oneself in everyday decision situations: Does he have enough information or should he get more? Variables such as the cost of the data and the payoff for accurate or correct decisions have been manipulated to determine their effect upon the amount of information purchased.

In experiments where subjects selected their sample sizes in advance, the payoff amount given for correct inferences produced no effect. In the optional stopping model, however, costs and payoffs did exert an influence on the number of information items purchased. The impact of the cost and payoff variables was less than what the Bayesian models predicted.

Another relevant finding has to do with the manipulation of prior probabilities. In Bayesian models prior probabilities are those assessed by the subject before further information is provided him; posterior probabilities are those assessed after the information has been examined. When the prior probabilities were reduced by increasing the number of alternative choices, the sample sizes were increased. "With just two hypotheses, the average amount of data purchased decreases as the prior probabilities become more extreme, that is, depart from .50-.50, but the rate of decrease is somewhat less than that called for by the optimal model" (Peterson and Beach, 1967, p. 38).

When the diagnostic value of the data was manipulated, it was found that an increase in diagnostic value was reflected in a decrease in the number of items purchased. Again, the amount of the effect is less than the optimal model prescribes.

Peterson and Beach conclude the results of optional stopping sample size experiments are similar to the results of other inference task studies. "Variables that would influence the behavior of statistical man also influence the subjects' behavior, but to a smaller degree. This effect may be summarized by the statement that subjects are only partially sensitive to the relevant variables. . . . The same kind of effect characterizes conservativism" (Peterson and Beach, 1967, p. 38).

According to Peterson and Beach, there are more studies in the area of probability learning than in any other area of study in behavior in uncertainty research. Probability learning involves making intuitive predictions about events to be sampled from populations in situations with feedback. The statistical problem solver would always choose the most frequent event, but human predictors do not. The authors reject the use of stochastic learning models as an unacceptable approach to the problem. The assumption in stochastic models is that the decision maker manifests random behavior. This view is antagonistic to that of the intuitive statistical approach, which is deterministic and which attempts to do more than merely reflect human decision behavior. The intuitive statistical approach describes behavior in a way that can lead to explanations that are as complete as possible of the existential aspects of the human decision process.

The challenge to researchers in probability learning is to account for the divergence of human behavior from that of statistical man. One hypothesis is that subjects do not understand the implications of sampling and sampling distributions. Studies indicate that subjects' assumptions about random sequences "admit sequential dependencies." Because information environments are multidimensional, experiments are employed in which:

> Each trial is a random sample from a population with correlated dimensions. The use of cue information is investigated by permitting subjects to observe the outcome of all but one of the dimensions in the sample. These observations, the cues, are used to predict the value of the observation on the remaining dimension, the criterion. Then the sampled value of the criterion is revealed to provide feedback and to permit learning of the relations between the various cue-dimensions and the criterion dimensions (Peterson and Beach, 1967, p. 39).

Essentially, this paradigm compares the subjects' prediction behavior to a regression model that optimally relates cues by weighting them to predict the criterion value. Early work found that subject performance was poor because of the complexity of the tasks.

> More recent studies have used simpler stimuli. The magnitudes of the subjective cue weights achieve the same rank order as the objective cue-weights and do so in relatively few trials, but the amount of separation among the subjective weights is sometimes less than the separation in statistical man's multiple regression equation. As in the experiments on conservativism and on information purchase, subjects are only partially sensitive to differences in relevant variables; they treat the cues as more equal in predictive value than they actually are (Peterson and Beach, 1967, p. 40).

Thus, Peterson and Beach (1967) conclude that overall when human inferences and those of statistical man are compared:

> the normative model provides a good first approximation for a psychological theory of inference. Inferences made by subjects are influenced by appropriate variables and in appropriate directions. But there are systematic discrepancies between normative and intuitive inferences. For example, the latter are usually too conservative; subjects apparently fail to extract all the information latent in samples of data. In addition, when intuitive inferences are sensitive to variables relevant to the normative model, the degree of sensitivity is often less that optimal (pp. 42–43).

For Peterson and Beach, there were problems that were unresolved, to be sure, but essentially the research was in the right channel. The problems were primarily in the fine tuning needed to eliminate conservatism. Their conclusion is sharply contrasted by these recent remarks by Slovic *et al.* (1977) who see an "increased scepticism" in researchers regarding the ability of the normative model to describe inferential behavior.

> The view of humans as good intuitive statisticians is no longer paramount. A psychological Rip Van Winkel who dozed off after reading Peterson and Beach and roused himself only recently would be startled by the widespread change of attitude exemplified by statements such as: "In his evaluation of evidence, man is apparently not a conservative Bayesian: he is not Bayesian at all," or "man's cognitive capacities are not adequate for the tasks which confront him," or "people systematically violate the principles of rational decision making when judging probabilities, making predictions, or otherwise attempting to cope with probabilistic tasks" (p. 3).

Becker and McClintock (1967) reviewed the decision literature at the same time as Peterson and Beach. They provide a definition of normative models in terms of five axioms; descriptive models differ only in the relaxation of one or more of these axioms. This definition is another indicator of the field's optimism and confidence in the normative model.

In sum, the optimism displayed in the late 1960s represented more than a mood. It buoyed up the normative approach to decision research. If the feeling that these models were not close approximations to actual decision behaviors, the course of research very likely would have been quite different. For example, the tremendous efforts that went into researching conservatism might never have been expended; or the subjective expected utility (SEU) model, to be considered next, might not have dominated interest for more than half the life of the discipline.

IV. THE SUBJECTIVE EXPECTED UTILITY (SEU) MODEL

The SEU model has its roots in the original problems undertaken by decision research. Its principal architect was Ward Edwards. It was Edwards who wrote the first two major reviews in the field and in so doing contributed much to drawing the field together. It is helpful to view the SEU model as a solution growing out of perspectives and problems of the early days of decision research. It is helpful, as well, to view this early literature in light of its connection to information studies.

Edwards' earlier paper was called "the first extensive review of the theory of decision making in the psychological literature" (Edwards and Tversky, 1967, p. 11). Edwards' approach starts with economic principles and moves the discussion toward psychological aspects. Grounded in interpretations of Bentham's utility theory the review examines five areas: "the theory of riskless choices, the application of the theory of riskless choices to welfare economics, the theory of risky choices, transitivity in decision making, and the theory of games and of statistical decision functions" (Edwards, 1954, p. 380).

The heavy accent on such economic notions as value and utility can be clearly seen in the theory of riskless choice. The area of study itself is presently in a state of transition, moving away from these original roots (Slovic et al., 1977, p. 7). The theory of riskless choices is based upon the metaphoric model of the economic man. This creature has three properties: He is completely informed; he is infinitely sensitive; and he is totally rational. While in the theory of risky choices and the theory of games the first assumption is relaxed, in the theory of riskless choices it is taken to mean that the decider knows all the possible actions available to him and all the related outcomes. The second assumption has been shown to be relatively unimportant; sensitivity is taken to mean that the environmental variables are continuous and the economic man reacts to minute changes in his environment.

The main assumption is rationality, which entails two things: "[Man] can weakly order the states into which he can get, and he makes his choices so as to maximize something" (Edwards, 1954, p. 381). Weak ordering, in turn, entails two assumptions. The first is that economic man can always tell whether he prefers one option to another or is indifferent. The second is that his choices are transitive. This means that if he prefers A to B and B to C, he will prefer A to C.

Additionally, rationality entails the principle of maximization. Utility is the construct maximized in riskless choices. In risky choices the maximized construct is expected utility which, roughly speaking, is the average value of the distributions of utilities one confronts in these choices. The maximization principle means that in addition to ordering the alternatives before him, the economic man always chooses the option which appears best to him. As trivial and obvious as this assumption seems, it does not universally obtain.

Edwards points out that many psychologists are distrustful of the assumptions that define economic man. He argues that because the assumptions are testable, the tests should be the criteria rather than a vague uneasiness. If the data match the theory, then it has heuristic value. For better or for worse, the economic–rational man and these tests of his reflections on the rest of the population have had considerable effect in setting the agenda for decision research.

Besides the set of assumptions that follow directly from economic man, another central principle in the theory of riskless choices is the principle of indifference. The notion of indifference is an aspect of rationality. The person always knows whether he prefers one thing to another, or knows whether he is indifferent. The indifference curve can be empirically constructed for a person by noting his choices between options and also noting the combinations where he is indifferent. For example, in the context of information objects, a person may be indifferent when presented a choice between two abstracts and a bibliography of 10 items, or between three abstracts and a 16-item bibliography, and so forth. From these data, a curve can be constructed on a graph where number of abstracts represents one axis and the number of bibliographic items the other. Any future combination of abstracts and items plotted above the curve will indicate a preference for that option.

Edwards discusses a controversy in the literature that arose over whether these curves could be constructed from ordinal level data, as opposed to cardinal or interval level data, which are harder to produce. It need only be noted here that ordinal data are sufficient to construct such curves, and that according to Edwards (1954) the indifference curve approach "has firmly established itself as the structure of the theory of riskless choice" (p. 386). Thurstone's work in psychophysics is an example of experimentation in this area.

Two psychological observations are made by Edwards. The first is that real human beings are neither perfectly consistent in terms of transitivity nor perfectly sensitive. The sensitivity aspect results in curves that appear to be bands or regions of indifference. Edwards contends that probabilistic decision theories can account for this problem over the long run, and that the precision of the curve can be maintained. The other observation is that graphic displays break down past the third dimension and so does our intuitive, nonmathematical grasp of the nature of these curves. Edwards despairs of being able to experiment in this N-dimensional realm but notes that psychologists are inclined to find this realm less important than economists do, since the latter are seeking to establish theories of general static equilibrium.

In summing up discussion of the theory of riskless choice, Edwards assesses the progress in that area. He makes two points, one negative, the other positive. The first is that the assumptions required by researchers in this area, such as Thurstone, are very numerous and no clear empirical meaning would remain if they were not made. The outlook on this point is no better 20 years later. Despite numerous technically brilliant studies, Krantz and his associates could sense no cumulation of knowledge in the form of laws of preferential choice behavior (Krantz *et al.*, 1974).

The second area Edwards considers briefly is the application of riskless choice to welfare economics. The inclusion of this area by Edwards follows from the economics base from which he is operating and extends into societal and policy issues that are of considerable importance to economists and political philosophers. If the outlook were brighter here, it could be a significant area for persons interested in national information policy, as well. The major pitfall in this area concerns what might be called naive utilitarianism, which can be summarized as follows: The best economic policy is the one that maximizes the total utility, summed over all members of the economy. "The greatest good to the greatest number" is often an equivalent remark.

The early economists assumed that utilities were interpersonally comparable and measured on a cardinal scale. Consequently, all societal utility problems were easily solved. Both principles, however, were subsequently abandoned; and the question remained: What would be the basis for economic policy?

Essentially the answer has not been an easy one to discover. Pareto achieved considerable early success using the principle of compensation, together with the idea that change was desirable only if everyone were left no worse and at least one person were better off. Pareto's approach succeeded in theory but not in application. John Rawls' *Theory of Justice* attempts to extend Pareto's work into a successful solution. Until a solution is achieved, information researchers would do well to approach questions of group decision making, information utilities, and national information policy with respect, if not with trepidation.

It is in the theory of risky choices that greater promise for information research is evident. First of all, for researchers used to dealing with the term "uncertainty" the distinction between this concept and risk is important. Edwards (1954) defines a first-order risk as "a proposition about the future to which a number can be attached, a number that represents the likelihood that the proposition is true" (p. 391). Saying a coin flip will result in heads is an example of the sort of proposition Edwards refers to. Second-order risks pertain to propositions that are based upon more than one probability distribution. For example, what is the likelihood of getting a head on the second coin flip if a tail on the first flip ends the game? Because the probability in question depends upon another probability, the risk is considered to be of a higher order.

Uncertainty also has to do with future events that have probabilities between zero and one, but for which it is much more difficult, if not impossible, to assign numbers. Edwards gives an example of assigning a number to the event that the reader will drink a glass of beer upon completing reading his article. The probability is in most cases neither zero nor one but some exceedingly difficult to determine number in between. This for Edwards is uncertainty. This concept does not enter into the theory of risky choices, which primarily involves first-order risks. Uncertainty is an important element in the theory of games, which is briefly discussed in a later section.

An important antecedent to the SEU model builds upon the notion of risk. It is the expected utility concept. Originally conceived as expected value, which is defined as the product of the monetary value of an outcome and its probability of occurrence, the concept was changed to reflect the observation that the utility of an amount of money is not always the same as its face value. The measure of expected utility rests on the principle of the indifference curve mentioned above in the section of riskless choices. If a person is indifferent between a 50% chance of winning $10.00 or of winning nothing, on the one hand, and an offer of $7.00, on the other, then for him the utility of $7.00 is equal to the expected value of the gamble, which is 5 units or utiles. The approach used here is to transform by using indifference curves expected value into expected utility.

Edwards (1954) notes three conclusions that can be drawn from the literature's treatment of expected utility: "First, . . . risky propositions can be ordered in desirability, just as riskless ones can. Second, . . . the concept of expected utility is behaviorally meaningful. Third, . . . choices among risky alternatives are made in such a way that they maximize expected utility" (pp. 392–393).

The "classical" formulation of expected utility was proposed by the economists von Neumann and Morgenstern. For them expected utility was the sum of the products of the subjective utilities and the objective probabilities. Eventually it was realized that subjective probabilities might not equal objective probabilities. It was also found that subjects had preferences for some probabilities over others; this tendency has proved to be a problem for other models, as well. Another troublesome offshoot of the shift to subjective probability is that the sums of subjects' estimates do not generally match the sums of the corresponding objective probabilities, even when it is obvious the sum should be 100%. Much work followed Edwards' early assessment of the difficulties. In the face of these difficulties, Edwards suggests that attempting to scale subjective probabilities may be a blind alley. He recommends the subjects' weighting objective probabilities as the best alternative apparent at the time.

Two other problems were noted at that early point. The first was the interrelation of subjective probabilities and utilities. Unless it was known how they were interrelated, only flawed predictions could result. The second problem was the observation that variances of the utility distributions also had an impact. For example, the opportunity to win $1 million with certainty might be preferred to a 50–50 chance of winning $4 million, even though the utility for the second choice exceeded 1 million utiles.

The last section of Edwards' review deals with the theory of games. The essence of game theory is the choice of strategies in the face of uncertainties concerning situations involving an opponent. A significant construct from this domain of study is the minimax loss strategy. In this strategy the individual attempts to choose a strategy that minimizes the negative consequences of the worst possible outcome. Whether in two-person or in N-person games, the guiding idea is to look for such strategies. When the structure of a game permits both players to accomplish this aim, a solution is found. Such solutions are called saddle points. In zero-sum games, where every gain for one player results in a similar loss for the opponent, solutions are more likely to be found than in nonzero games. As games become more complex, the likelihood of a single or a small number of solutions diminishes. In an overall principle related to utility theory, the theory of games dictates that if players minimize their maximum expected loss, then a saddle point exists, and consequently no reason exists for changes in strategies.

According to Edwards (1954), von Neumann and Morgenstern's seminal work assumes "utility to be linear with the physical value of money involved in a game and to be interpersonally comparable" (p. 408). It is interesting to note that the position adopted here avoids the difficulties encountered in the theory of risky choices and resembles the approach taken in welfare economics.

The games theory approach was adopted by Wald for use in statistical decision problems. Wald framed his analysis as a choice of strategies in a game against nature.

> The statistician must decide, on the basis of observations which cost something to make, between policies, each of which has a possible gain or loss. In some cases, all of the gains and losses and the cost of observing can be exactly calculated . . . . In other cases, as in theoretical research, it is necessary to make some assumption about the cost of being wrong and the gain of being right (Edwards, 1954, p. 409).

Alternatives to the minimax approach inherent in the theory of games include a maximax strategy where a maximization of maximum gain is employed; a combination of minimax and maximax strategies; the minimax of regret, "where regret is defined as the difference between the maximum which can be gained under the strategy adopted" (Edwards, 1954, p. 409). Another important alternative is to assume that nature is not a hostile opponent and that the key to solution is the maximization of expected utility. This approach is limited by the fact that nature does not provide an easy means of assigning a probability to each outcome. Knowing the probability of an outcome is essential to calculating its utility. This last alternative begins to resemble the expected value approach to statistical decision problems.

Summing up Edwards' overview, the importance of utility and the problems associated with that concept is apparent. Transitivity and maximization are central concerns with the rational treatment of utility. In the theory of riskless choice the introduction of indifference allowed the substitution of less rigid scales. This relaxation does not obtain successfully in the realm of welfare economics. The issue of proper scales carries over to the theory of risky choices, where the outcomes of the research were not entirely clear at the time Edwards wrote his review. Central to the controversies is the decision either to employ subjective utility scales or to assume that monetary scales are sufficiently acceptable substitutes. Furthermore, the problem of intransitive behavior has complicated matters, as well.

Edwards reviewed the decision-making literature again in 1961. This time he saw three large divisions in the literature: static models, dynamic decision making, and experimental games (Edwards, 1961). The last of these areas has evolved into a research field of its own. The topic of welfare economics discussed in his first review has dropped away. Only in Becker and McClintock (1967) does the topic of interpersonal comparison of utilities reappear in the major reviews of the literature. The focus narrows down to individual decision making and away from groups and games and opponents. The SEU model emerges at the theoretical center of the field.

The significant distinction is between static and dynamic decisions. By far the more active area in terms of research is static decision study. At the time, Edwards saw four models in static risky decision theory. The common elements in the four are the notion that a quantity can be obtained by taking for each possible outcome of a given course of action a number representing the value of the payoff and a number representing the probability of obtaining that payoff, multiplying the two, and then adding across all possible outcomes of the course of action. All four models assert that a decision maker behaves as though he compares these sums and chooses the course of action, from those available to him, for which the sum of probability-value products is largest. The models differ in that the measure of value can be objective (in dollars, or some similar physical measure) or subjective (subjective value is sometimes called utility); and the measure of probability can similarly be objective or subjective. Four combinations of these possibilities therefore exist.

According to Edwards, at the time no one asserted that the objective value and objective probability were the proper elements of utility. Furthermore, von Neumann's maximization of expected utility model had also fallen away, leaving only the two cells which call for the subjective assessment of probability component. Even the alternative of subjective probability and objective values had little, if any, support by 1960; consequently, Edwards focuses his entire attention on the SEU model, where both values and probabilities are subjective.

The research on utility is complicated by two factors: First, it is difficult to parcel out the effect of the monetary or objective values; and second, it is hard to control for the interaction between subjective probability and subjective value. The first problem can be illustrated by asking someone the value of half of $10.00. If the person responds with anything other than $5.00, the result has to be considered unusual. The point is that it is difficult for persons to think beyond the obvious monetary value to their own deeper and less accessible feelings of subjective value. Consequently, even though subjective value is the construct used in recent decision research, the measure actually employed is the monetary values. These values are thought to be an accurate approximation of the subjective ones.

The second issue is the lack of independence between utility and subjective probability. The latter construct has its difficulties independent of the independence issue, however. As Edwards notes, it is fortunate that subjective probabilities, in the sense of direct estimation, are quite close to objective probabilities. This optimistic conclusion is, of course, corroborated by Peterson and Beach (1967). There is some distortion at the ends of the scale. Edwards points to the problem of subjective probabilities of a set of mutually exclusive and exhaustive events not summing to zero. A look at subsequent research indicates this problem was never satisfactorily resolved and played a significant part in the demise of this line of research.

By 1960, difficulty with deterministic models had led to a greater interest in stochastic models. These models, however, even with their less ambitious aim of merely describing decision behavior instead of explaining it, encountered their own difficulties. The one element of compromise involved in these models was the introduction of the notion that persons were transitive in their preferences probabilistically. What was thought of as inconsistency when complete transitivity was assumed is now thought of as intransitive behavior in the stochastic models.

Stochastic models, Edwards (1961) puts it,

> may, depending on the strengths of their assumptions, predict either of two kinds of stochastic sensitivity. Weak stochastic sensitivity simply asserts that if the probabilities of preferring A to B and B to C are both equal to or greater than .5, then the probability of preferring A to C is also equal to or greater than .5. Strong stochastic transitivity asserts that if the probabilities of preferring A to B and B to C are both greater than .5, then the probability of preferring A to C is equal to or greater than the larger of the other two probabilities (p. 483).

When strong models were compared to the subjective expected utility maximization model, however, the SEU was clearly better than the stochastic model. Edwards also notes that up to that time the research tendency was to look for support for the stochastic models, rather than to subject them to rigorous falsification tests. He notes that if these models withstand such tests, the job of the experimenter will be to determine the conditions under which transitive and intransitive decision behaviors obtain.

In addition to problems with additivity and transitivity, the variances of the outcome distributions still were problematical. The argument is that variance of a wager is as important a factor as the SEU in determining attractiveness. Edwards cites himself in research indicating that variance is at best a secondary factor in choices. The real problem, however, is that variance and utility are confounded. Moreover, skewness is confounded with subjective probability. Consequently, in 1960 the role of variance in the framework of decision studies was not clear.

Edwards next looks briefly at static decision theory. He cites the signal detection work as being the most significant research in the area. Overall, Edwards (1961) draws the following conclusion:

> Other applications of static decision theories will probably occur, especially as the probabilistic nature of military information-processing and decision making systems becomes increasingly recognized and the probabilities and values which control the decisions are displayed and used explicitly, instead of being used implicitly as in the case now. But static decision theories have only a limited future. Human beings learn and probabilities and values change; these facts mean that the really applicable kinds of decision theories will be dynamic, not static (p.493).

From this basis the SEU model dominated both the normative and descriptive research, since the latter was seen as merely a relaxation of the normative axioms. These principles are given by Becker and McClintock (1967).

The first axiom is transitivity. Its meaning remains unchanged from the definition given by Edwards. Intuitively, the axiom is a strong one, for those who violate it could be victims of a money pump operation. A person who prefers diamonds to rubies and rubies to emeralds but emeralds to diamonds could after several rounds of trading end up unable to afford rhinestones.

The second axiom is comparability. It means that a rational person always can and does know he prefers one outcome to another or is indifferent between them. The principle was not under strong attack at the time of Becker's review.

Dominance is the third principle. If an action, such as investing in a portfolio of stocks, leads to outcomes that are under all circumstances at least as good as a second investment, then a rational person would choose the stock portfolio if at least one of its outcomes was better than the alternative investment. This principle is also called the sure-thing principle, because one is guaranteed to gain or break even with the first choice. In situations where a minimax strategy is appropriate and several other game theoretical principles apply, the axiom does not obtain. The sure-thing principle was under considerable fire at the time of Becker and McClintock's review.

The fourth principle is irrelevance: Rational decision makers do not attend to irrelevant outcomes. The fifth principle is that of independence: One's probability estimates are unaffected by whether or not an outcome is desirable. In other words, a rational person is realistic in assigning probabilities and does not wish the likelihood of an unpleasant event downward. Neither of these axioms was free of criticism, but together with the other three, they made up the crux of the decision theory at the time.

By the time of the review by Rapoport and Wallsten (1972), the SEU model was still the "most general and influential theory for single-stage decision making" (p. 134). The major efforts in the field were being aimed at testing its key assumptions. The tests were in nearly every case designed to falsify rather than to support the model. Under the strain SEU began to buckle. A test by Tversky (1969) found the majority of subjects violated transitivity. An experiment by MacCrimmon (1968) found nearly 40% of the subjects violated the sure-thing principle, and the majority failed to uphold the principle that subjective probabilities and utilities are independent. Duplex gambles where probabilities and utilities of both winning and losing are involved caused violations of the independence axiom. Response mode, which should have been irrelevant, affected choice, further damaging the SEU model. Even tests generally favoring the model seemed always to include room for doubt. Wallsten argued that SEU obtained only for simple gambles, leading to the following summation:

> Moreover, if correct, the argument severely restricts the applicability of SEU theory to a very narrow, unacceptable class of experimental tasks. It seems then that the con-

flicting evidence pertaining to SEU theory is presently irreconcilable. Consequently, the basic experimental question should not be whether to accept or reject SEU theory as a whole, but rather to systematically discover the conditions under which it is or is not valid (Rapoport and Wallsten, 1972, p. 141).

Slovic *et al.* (1977) saw the assaults on utility theory to be a trend. The SEU model is conceded to work satisfactorily with simple gambles, but after that the challenges are everywhere. They observe that critics by this time outnumber the proponents. Alternative models abound. Even expected value reappears in one model. Portfolio theory allows for preferences for moderate risks in opposition to the maximization principle of SEU. Past advocates of SEU now call for reevaluations. The paradigm status is slipping away from SEU without a clearly dominant alternative in view. For 20 years the dominant idea of SEU theory now ironically appears to be itself a risky choice for librarians and others who may wish to adopt it as a basis for understanding information needs in a decision context.

V. BAYESIAN MODELS

The third theme that has run through the decision literature is the influence of the Bayes theorem. The theme is closely related to the other two, for Bayes' theorem deals with probability estimation. This ability to estimate is the basis for the optimism described by Peterson and Beach and comprises an important half of the utility models.

Specifically, Bayes' theorem deals with probability revision in the face of new information. As an example, Howard Raiffa reports having presented the following problem to a small group of attorneys. Two urns are each filled with red and blue balls. One urn is 70% red, the other 70% blue. One urn is removed and the task is to guess which urn remains and state the probability of one's being correct. Since the contents are unseen, the probability at the outset for making a correct guess is 50%. Suppose, however, that a sample could be taken of 12 balls and it turned out to be comprised of 8 red and 4 blues. The attorneys felt that the correct urn was the red (the choice was not unanimous), but the probability was so slightly altered "that they would behave as if the odds were still 50-50" (Raiffa, 1968, p. 8). Peterson and Beach (1967) report the typical response is to shift the probabilities to a 75%

likelihood the urn is predominantly red (p. 32). Because the problem is a straight probability problem, one can easily calculate the revision dictated by the Bayes theorem. The "correct" revised probability is slightly greater than 96%. Both the attorneys and the typical subject were conservative in the sense that they revised their probability estimates less than was called for by the ideal or normative Bayesian model. Throughout the decision literature the use of Bayesian models has in nearly every case been accompanied by a concern for the subjects' conservativism. The model has been maintained because of the perceived close fit to actual behavior, but always there has been the perplexing and persistent problem of conservativism.

The Bayesian model itself is based upon the concept of conditional probabilities, for example, $P(D|H)$, the probability that a datum will be observed given that a hypothesis is true. Because $P(D|H)$ is more likely to be known than its converse $P(H|D)$, Bayes' theorem is a handy means of determining the latter from the former. The theorem is generally given in the following form:

$$P(H|D) = \frac{P(D|H)\,P(H)}{P(D)}$$

in which $P(H)$ is the prior probability, or the probability that H is the case based on information known up to the time in question; $P(D)$ is the probability of a particular datum or sample; and in which $P(H|D)$ is the posterior probability or the probability of H based upon the prior information and the new information gained from the sample. The key to the theorem is the $P(D|H)$ element, which is interpreted as the probability D would be observed if H were true or as the impact of each datum on the hypothesis. The $P(D|H)$ element is calculated as the ratio between the joint probability of D and H and the probability of H: $P(D \cap H)/P(H)$.

In the case of the ball and urn problems in which there were two possible choices and therefore two possible hypotheses, the choice between the hypotheses according to the normative use of the Bayesian model is based upon the higher posterior probability. An alternative form of the Bayesian model is called the odds-likelihood ratio form, Ω_1, $= L\Omega_0$. This form is often used in studies in which two hypotheses are possible, such as the ball and urn problems or bookbag and chips problems.

The odds-likelihood ratio form is obtained by dividing one Bayes formula by another. In the urn problem given above, for example, the two possible alternatives are H_R, the predominately red urn, and H_B, the predominately blue urn. The formulas are

$$P(H_R|D) = \frac{P(D|H_R)P(H_R)}{P(D)} \text{ and } P(H_B|D) = \frac{P(D|H_B)P(H_B)}{P(D)}$$

respectively. When one divides, the P(D) term drops away. One is then left with the following elements: $P(H_R/P(H_B)$ or Ω_1, the prior odds; $P(H_R|D)/P(H_B|D)$ or Ω_0, the posterior odds; and $P(D|H_R)/P(D)H_B)$ or L, the likelihood ratio. L may also be expressed as $p^r q^{n-r}/p'^r q'^{n-r}$ in cases in which $p = q'$ and $q = p'$. This complementarity is typical as in the urn example in which 70/30 proportions hold for both the predominately red and the predominately blue urns. In these cases L may be further reduced to the term $(P|q)^{2r-n}$ in which P is the probability of getting a red ball, q is the probability for getting a blue one, and n represents the total number of balls drawn.

In the urn example with the sample of eight reds and four blues, the difference between the number of reds and blues in the sample, $(p/q)^{2r-n}$ is 4. Consequently the likelihood ratio is 0.7 × 0.7 × 0.7 × 0.7/0.3 × 0.3 × 0.3 × 0.3 or 0.2401/0.0081. The prior odds are 0.50/0.50, or 1. The resulting posterior odds are 0.2401/0.0081. Because these probabilities are assumed to sum to 1.0, dividing the numerator by their sum yields the posterior probability of 0.96775.

The Bayesian model is applicable to situations in which the decision making is dynamic, in which new evidence is encountered by the subject and the impact of the evidence is assessed by him in changing his estimation of the likelihood of various hypotheses or interpretations concerning what is true in his environment.

In his early reviews Edwards does little more than mention the Bayes theorem. By 1965, however, Edwards had observed in his own studies that "men have been highly conservative information processors; the more complex the display, the more conservative the human performance" (Edwards *et al.*, 1965, p. 306).

Three possible explanations for the subjects' tendency to underestimate the value of new information in the revision of their opinions when contrasted to the revisions called for by the model are the effect of the scales used, the bias of the payoffs in the experiments and the survival benefit of persons' being slow to alter their interpretations of goings-on around them (Edwards *et al.*, 1965). The first two suggestions have led to considerable empirical study.

By 1967, Becker and McClintock noted numerous studies which had a Bayesian basis, and they noted also the controversy between its proponents and its detractors. Some semantic problems were also noted in the tendency to consider static models as prescriptive and for dynamic models to be considered as unrelated. The distinction between stationary and nonstationary environments was maintained. The Bayesian model does not apply to nonstationary cases. A further assumption was encountering some questioning by this time and that was that not only must the environment remain stationary but the subject's values must do so as well. To assume that as a subject's bankroll changes his utility assessments are unaffected is a dangerous premise.

The Bayesian model was seen as something different from the prescriptive mainstream (the SEU model) but closely allied in its basic outlook and shared rational assumptions. Comparison to actual behavior was the central part of the methodology. Findings tended to show that similar to the Edwards (1965) group study the subjects gained less from the information they sampled than the Bayesian model indicated could be gained.

The suggestion was made by Edwards to investigate the effect of scales on conservativism. The work at that time showed that subjects showed progressively less conservativism when the form of the estimate changed from probability to log of the probability to verbal odds estimates. Least conservative of all were the log odds estimates. However, regardless of the form, the more diagnostic the datum, that is, the greater the change in opinion the sample required, the more conservativism was displayed.

By 1967, studies of the payoff structures had just begun to appear. Linear, logarithmic, quadratic, and all-or-none payoff alternatives were studied. Up to this point, however, most studies observed by Becker and McClintock provided the subject with no explicit payoffs at all, making comparison of studies difficult.

Becker and McClintock (1967) summarized the state of understanding of persons' information-purchasing behavior:

> It is astonishing how much information most people ignore, and how much they tend to overestimate the value of information . . . . People are willing to pay much more for information than the information could possibly help them. This suggests a

paradox . . . people overvalue information and at the same time ignore most of the information they receive. They appear to use only the "key" facts, yet are willing to pay for all the facts, useful and useless. (p. 253).

Peterson and Beach (1967) reporting on the intuitive statistical literature the same year encountered conservativism as well. They noted the differences in the revised opinions of subjects and Bayesian revisions were large but systematic, that is, in the proper direction. Two approaches to the explanation were noted. The first attempted to show the problem was essentially the result of subjects' avoiding the bounds of the scales used. The second attempted to show the problem rose from flaws in the procedures the subjects used in processing the data. Various procedural variables, such as incentives, payoffs, sample size, or instructions, had little or no influence. Peterson and Beach concluded that subjects intuitively conceived sampling distributions to be too flat with the result that they misinterpreted the relationship between the sample and the population from which it came. The subjects also seemed to have a limited ability to aggregate data over several trials.

By 1972 much testing of the Bayesian model had been accomplished, and Rapoport and Wallsten gave a negative assessment of the model's utility. In creating a context for their discussion of the Bayesian model, Rapoport and Wallsten (1972) make a distinction between sequential and dynamic decision-making tasks. In both the subjects are assumed to maximize some criterion, such as utility. The difference is seen to depend upon the effect of previous decisions upon the state to state changes in the decision situations. Opinion revision and optional stopping problems are examples of sequential tasks. Bayesian models are fundamentally important to the investigations in the literature of these tasks.

An optional stopping problem illustrates the effect of prior decisions on the decision situations. Using the same urns described above in Raiffa's opinion-revision task, the subject's task is to guess correctly the kind of urn presented to him using an optimal number of samples to assist his decision. The subject initially faces a 50–50 choice. In some situations with low payoffs and high sample costs, he may optimize his utility by guessing immediately. However, he may instead exercise his option of purchasing samples. Depending on what combination of red and blue balls are drawn, the costs, and the payoffs, the Bayes theorem can prescribe the optimal point at which one should stop seeking further information and guess. Rapoport and Wallsten consider this task a sequential decision-making task because the overall situation remains structurally unchanged after each decision to guess or sample. A prior decision does not send the individual down a path that constrains future actions. A dynamic decision situation is one in which prior decisions do impact the future decisions as in chess or betting over a series of races with changing capital.

In the studies of sequential decision making, the subjects generally displayed conservativism when compared to the Bayesian model in opinion-revision tasks. A similarity to the flat distribution conjecture made by Peterson and Beach was noted. In the Bayesian formula the data seem to fit a model where the likelihood ratio is raised to a power less than one. The likelihood ratio is obtained by dividing the probability of drawing a particular sample given that one alternative is true by the probability of drawing the sample given the other alternative. To say the data fit such a model does not explain why they do, however; and three alternative hypotheses are offered. The first is that the subjects "misperceive the diagnosticity of the data" (Rapoport and Wallsten, 1972, p. 153). The second is that they do not aggregate the information properly; and the third is that they are merely exhibiting a response bias. These options have all been pursued in the literature.

Green (1968) posed three objections to research using the Bayesian model. The first is that although the model fits the data, it does not allow for any explanation for them. To say the subjects' behavior can be described by a Bayesian model with the likelihood ratio raised to a power less than one is unsatisfactory for Green. To build the three alternative explanations into the model seems the necessary course, but at the cost of some of the optimism sensed and reported by Peterson and Beach (1967).

The second criticism leveled by Green is that the model is extremely difficult to falsify. The accuracy ratio used in some of the more complex studies is created by comparing the likelihood ratio data obtained from the subjects to the Bayesian likelihood ratios. This ratio is considered by Green to be elusive because it depends upon various parameters of the task and defies comparison between studies that are only slightly different. The research approach suggested as a part of this criticism is to focus more effort on the difficult task of falsifying the Bayesian model by inventing and contrasting alternative models to it.

Green's third criticism is related to the first. The research must go deeper to establish connections between the responses and the psychological processes beneath them. Scaling by developing identities between these underlying processes and the responses is the necessary next step according to this view. This imperative split the field into those willing to explore these scaling problems (e.g., Edwards; Peterson and Beach) and those who are not (e.g., Pitz, Shanteau, and Walsten).

Wallsten approached this difficulty by substituting a less rigorous monotonic function of the subjective probability ratio for the identity required by Green (Wallsten, 1968). Shanteau (1972) had subjects report as they moved through the sequence. Their reports were numerical estimates of the likelihood of one of the alternatives' being the case. The weighted sum of these values is used to predict the response. These alternative models created the beginnings of an assault on the Bayesian model, which eventually led to its decline.

Reviewing the studies that attacked the problem of conservativism, Rapoport and Wallsten observe that the phenomenon is pervasive, but not universal. Highly trained subjects, persons making estimates after each datum was observed instead of in batches, and those dealing with highly reliable data sometimes displayed no conservativism. Analyses of previous studies occasionally showed design problems which allowed subjects to ignore aspects of the data that were theoretically important.

Rapoport and Wallsten (1972) conclude that "the emphasis on comparing human estimates with Bayesian values, although understandable, has been perhaps somewhat misplaced" (p. 158). They base their conclusion on the false psychophysical basis upon which these comparisons rest. They point out that in psychophysical studies the objective measures against which the human responses are tested are themselves well measured and well understood. In the present case identical samples can have different Bayesian values and different samples identical Bayesian values. Also the subject is not dealing with an event that is one dimensional, like tones or lines; the complexities of the data may include scope or diagnosticity, sequence, value, cost, probability, reliability, and more.

The authors sum up their position as follows:

> Thus we think now that although conservativism certainly exists, it is at least as much dependent on the measures we have been using as on the decision maker's behavior, and that our theoretical understanding of human inference requires closer attention to aspects of the system other than just Bayesian probabilities . . . .

> To summarize, the Bayesian model . . . clearly has been insufficient to explain the observed results. It is not yet possible to determine whether the model is wrong merely in assumptions about parameters or in more fundamental ways. But it does appear as if experiments should not be restricted to having decision makers test hypotheses consisting of two binomial distributions and should include more single-subject designs (Rapoport and Wallsten, 1972, pp. 158, 166).

The difficulties with the Bayesian model have not been resolved in the subsequent years. Slovic, Fischhoff, and Lichtenstein omit discussion on the model in their 1977 review. They cite remarks to the effect that man is not only not a conservative Bayesian, but not Bayesian. The optimism regarding the Bayes model Peterson and Beach reported had nearly vanished 10 years later.

The alternative described by Rapoport and Wallsten fared no better. Dynamic decision theory, which deals with nonindependent multistage decisions with feedback, studies situations in which the subject must plan and adjust as he goes along. In 1972 even its advocates were aware of certain obvious handicaps:

> Other more prosaic reasons for the relatively little research on dynamic decision making are the tremendous difficulties in characterizing "state," "stage," "transformation rule," and "criterion function," and in successfully delineating segments of the environment plus a sequence of decisions as a dynamic decision process. The mathematics rquired to derive the optimal policy is relatively new, unpleasantly complex, and yields numerical rather than analytical solutions in all but simple cases. Also, because of their complexity, dynamic decision experiments are difficult to design and implement without on-line computers (Rapoport and Wallsten, 1972, pp. 166–167).

By 1977, the reviewers can only note two studies that followed the Rapoport and Wallsten review and, "after that, relative silence" (Slovic et al., 1977, p. 14). They speculate that mathematical sophistication, startup time, creation of cover stories, sheer complexity, and even the assumption that behavior is optimal led to its mute condition. The collapse may have been foreshadowed by Rapoport and Wallsten (1972): "Dynamic decision theory may prove useful only if discrepancies between the optimal and actual decisions are small, systematic, and the constraints are psychologically interpretable" (p. 167). Because few models indeed could make that particular claim, the untimely end of the cumbersome dynamic model may not have been so surprising after all.

VI. CONCLUSION

Decision research is an area of considerable interest to librarians, especially the theoretical work that is focused on the individual and his information-seeking behavior. This work is certainly welcome as an added perspective supplementing the extensive research findings focusing on the demographic characteristics of library users. Indeed, one is particularly encouraged to find several tendencies emerging from amid all of the controversy surrounding personality research: that subjective value assessment and subjective probability estimations are two trait manifestations demonstrating consistency across varying situations (Mischel, 1973, pp. 269–273). This finding has special appeal to those skeptical of the value of antiseptic laboratory studies when projected into the real world of libraries.

At best, the two fundamental aspects of utility (and decision theory), subjective probability estimation and value assessment, have been shown to be consistent in moving from the laboratory setting to the real world. The immediate conclusion to be drawn from this congruence is that the deviations observed in actual information use are probably attributable to the differing situations in which the patron finds himself. Moreover, because the librarian is in control of a substantial portion of the information-seeking context of library users, these findings—intelligently applied—could result in improved service.

This conclusion must be cautiously drawn, however, for one is still uncertain about the factors responsible for these invariant use patterns. Clearly, as a review of the literature reveals, the decision theorists themselves remain unaware of the causes of this intriguing consistency. Thus the librarians' search for the key to information-seeking behavior remains elusive, even if closer than before.

Some results of the concerted effort to predict the characteristics of information-seeking behavior would appear to warrant emphasis, however. First, the rational model clearly fails to match actual information-seeking behavior. It seems that the guide of rationality is not particularly helpful in modeling decision behavior and must be expanded and rechanneled in order to more accurately reflect the real, if less predictable, world of actual information-seeking behavior.

Second, the research reviewed here does suggest that people do tend to underutilize the information they purchase (i.e., cost in time, money, and energy), at least in comparison with purely logical models such as those based upon Bayes' theorem. They also appear to overbuy when compared to the Bayes model. Whereas man seems not to be an intuitive statitician, he does exhibit these tendencies consistently. Acquisitions librarians will no doubt recognize the pattern. What the emergent model of information-seeking behavior will ultimately look like remains unclear, but the recurring patterns do indicate that a useful model is possible.

As an example of this effort to extend the decision model beyond the rationality framework, Wolfson and Carroll (1976) have introduced the concepts of ignorance (not knowing about certain pertinent alternatives) and error (believing certain alternatives exist when they do not) into the decision paradigm. Their approach promises to go beyond categorizing behavior as irrational and to begin to build a better understanding of these phenomena.

Given the atmosphere of uncertainty in decision theory research, and the apparent inadequacy of the two models discussed above, the Wolfson and Carroll program seems especially promising. It now appears prudent to encourage descriptive studies designed to test this new model, rather than expending further precious energy on tests of the predominant statistical and rational paradigms, which already appear in ruins. Another approach attempts to create a laboratory experiment in which persons' preferences for broad and specific data and index information can be studied (Sodt, 1979).

One other particularly appropriate direction would be to utilize a multidimensional scaling technique that would allow a person's information preferences to be mapped over time as he proceeds through an information-seeking problem. The potential for producing the predictive power needed by librarians and others who are involved in the improved delivery of information services may well be forthcoming from such a new approach.

SELECTED BIBLIOGRAPHY

Allen, T. J. (1967). "The Utilization of Information Sources During R & D Proposal Preparation." Working Paper No. 284-67. MIT Sloan School, Cambridge, Massachusetts.

Andrus, R. R. (1971). Approaches to information evaluation. *MSU Business Topics* **19**, 40-46.

Artandi, S. (1973). Opinion paper: information concepts and their utility. *Journal of the American Society for Information Science* **24**, 242–245.

Barefield, R. M. (1972). The effect of aggregation on decision making success: a laboratory study. *Journal of Accounting Research* **10**, 229–242.

Bar-Hillel, M. (1973). On the subjective probability of compound events. *Organizational Behavior and Human Performance* **9**, 396–406.

Beach, L. R. (1967). Multiple regression as a model for human information utilization. *Organizational Behavior and Human Performance* **2**, 276–289.

Beach, L. R., Wise, J. A., and Barclay, S. (1970). Sample proportions and subjective probability revisions. *Organizational Behavior and Human Performance* **5**, 183–190.

Becker, G. M. (1958). Sequential decision making: Wald's model and estimates of parameters. *Journal of Experimental Psychology* **55**, 628–636.

Becker, G. M., and McClintock, C. G. (1967). Value: behavioral decision theory. *Annual Review of Psychology* **18**, 239–286.

Brichacek, V. (1970). Use of subjective probability in decision making. *Acta Psychologica* **34**, 241–253.

Bruner, J. S., Goodnow, J. J., and Austin, G. A. (1956). "A Study of Thinking." Wiley, New York.

Bryden, M. P. (1967). A model for the sequential organization of behavior. *Canadian Journal of Psychology* **21**, 37–56.

Chaffee, S. H., and McLeod, J. M. (1973). Individual vs. social predictors of information seeking. *Journalism Quarterly* **50**, 237–245.

Chapman, C. R. (1973). Prior probability bias in information seeking and opinion revision. *American Journal of Psychology* **86**, 269–282.

Clarke, P., and James, J. (1967). The effects of situation, attitude intensity and personality on information-seeking. *Sociometry* **30**, 235–245.

Cohen, J. (1964). "Behavior in Uncertainty." Basic Books, New York.

Crawford, J. L., and Haaland, G. A. (1972). Predecisional information seeking and subsequent conformity in the social influence process. *Journal of Personality and Social Psychology* **23**, 112–119.

Davenport, W. G., and Middleton, M. A. (1973). Expectation theories of decision making for duplex gambles. *Acta Psychologica* **37**, 155–172.

Davis, D. J. (1966). An examination of human strategies for acquiring information. *Dissertation Abstracts* **26**, 7454–7455.

Davis, D. J. (1967). Structure of the environment and strategies for acquiring information. *Journal of Experimental Psychology* **73**, 227–231.

Davis, W., and Phares, E. (1967). Internal–external control as a determinant of information-seeking in a social influence situation. *Journal of Personality* **35**, 547–561.

Day, H. I., Langevin, R., Maynes, F., and Spring, M. (1972). Prior knowledge and the desire for information. *Canadian Journal of Behavioral Science* **4**, 330–337.

Donderi, D. C. (1967). Information measurement of single multidimensional stimuli. *Canadian Journal of Psychology* **21**, 93–110.

Donohew, L., and Tipton, L. (1973). A conceptual model of information seeking, avoiding, and processing. *In* "New Models for Mass Communication Research" (P. Clarke, ed.), pp. 243–268. Sage, Beverly Hills, California.

Donohue, J. C. (1972). Research on information-seeking—its place in the teaching of librarians. *International Library Review* **4**, 97–101.

Driscoll, J. M., and Lanzetta, J. T. (1964). Effects of problem uncertainty and prior arousal on pre-decisional information search. *Psychological Reports* **141**, 975–988.

Driscoll, J. M., and Lanzetta, J. T. (1965). Effects of two sources of uncertainty in decision making. *Psychological Reports* **17**, 635–648.

Driscoll, J. M., Tognoli, J. J., and Lanzetta, J. T. (1966). Choice conflict and subjective uncertainty in decision making. *Psychological Reports* **18**, 427–432.

Du Charme, W. M., and Donnell, M. L. (1973). Intrasubject comparison of four response modes for "subjective probability" assessment. *Organizational Behavior and Human Performance* **10**, 108–117.

Eden, C., and Harris, J. (1975). "Management Decision and Decision Analysis." Halstead Press, New York.

Edwards, W. (1954). The theory of decision making. *Psychological Bulletin* **5**, 380–417.

Edwards, W. (1961). Behavioral decision theory. *Annual Review of Psychology* **12**, 473–498.

Edwards, W., and Slovic, P. (1965). Seeking information to reduce the risk of decisions. *American Journal of Psychology* **78**, 188–197.

Edwards, W., and Tversky, A., eds. (1967). "Decision Making." Penguin, Baltimore, Maryland.

Edwards, W., Lindman, H., and Phillips, L. D. (1965). Emerging technologies for making decision. *In* "New Directions in Psychology II" (T. M. Newcomb, ed.), pp. 261–325. Holt, New York.

Feather, N. T. (1959). Subjective probability & decision under uncertainty. *Psychological Review* **66**, 150–164.

Feltham, G. A. (1964). The value of information. *Accounting Review* **43**, 684.

Ford, G. (1973). Progress in documentation: research in user behavior in university libraries. *Journal of Documentation* **29**, 85–106.

Fraser, D. A. S. (1973). Inference and decision. *Selecta Statistica Canadiana* **1**, 1–16.

Godden, D. (1976). Transition structure versus commitment in sequential subjective probability revision. *Acta Psychologica* **40**, 21–28.

Goodman, J. J. (1955). Determinants of choice-distribution in two-choice situations. *American Journal of Psychology* **68**, 106–116.

Green, B. F., Jr. (1968). Descriptions and explanations: a comment on papers by Hoffman and Edwards. *In* "Formal Representation of Human Judgement" (B. Kleinmuntz, ed.), pp. 91–96. Wiley, New York.

Green, P. E., Halbert, M. H., and Minas, J. S. (1964). An experiment in information buying. *Journal of Advertising Research* **4**,(3), 17–23.

Gustafson, D. H., Shukla, R. K., Delbecq, A., and Walster, G. W. (1973). A comparative study of differences in subjective likelihood estimates made by individuals, interacting groups, delphi groups, and nominal groups. *Organizational Behavior and Human Performance* **9**, 280–291.

Harwood, B. T. (1973). Expressed preferences for information seeking behaviors and their relationship to birth order. *Journal of Genetic Psychology* **123**, 123–131.

Hawkins, C. K., and Lanzetta, J. T. (1965). Uncertainty, importance, and arousal as determinants of predecisional information search. *Psychological Reports* **17**, 791–800.

Hays, W. L., and Winkler, R. L. (1970). "Statistics Probability, Inference, and Decision." Holt, New York.
Hilton, H. J. (1975). An ideal information access system: some economic implications. *In* "Information for Action: From Knowledge to Wisdom" (M. Kochen, ed.), pp. 205-219. Academic Press, New York.
Hoge, R. D., and Lanzetta, J. T. (1968). Effects of response uncertainty and degree of knowledge on subjective uncertainty. *Psychological Reports* **22**, 1081-1090.
Howell, W. C. (1966). Task characteristics in sequential decision behavior. *Journal of Experimental Psychology* **71**, 124-131.
Irwin, F. W., and Smith, W. A. S. (1957). Value, cost, and information as determiners of decision. *Journal of Experimental Psychology* **54**, 229-232.
Janis, J. R., and Mann, L. (1977). "Decision Making/A Psychological Analysis of Conflict, Choice, and Commitment." Free Press, New York.
Kahan, J. P., and Rapoport, A. (1974). Decisions of timing in bipolarized conflict situations with complete information. *Acta Psychologica* **38**, 183-203.
Kanarick, A. F., Huntington, J. M., and Peterson, R. C. (1969). Multi-source information acquisition with optional stopping. *Human Factors* **11**, 379-385.
Karlins, M., and Lamm, H. (1967). Information search as a function of conceptual structure in a complex problem-solving task. *Journal of Personality and Social Psychology* **5**, 456-459.
Kleiven, J., Fraser, C., and Gouge, C. (1974). Are individual and group decisions dependent on the available information? *Scandinavian Journal of Psychology* **15**, 178-184.
Klelter, G. D., and Wimmer, H. (1974). Information seeking in a multistage betting game. *Archiv für Psychologie* **126**, 213-230.
Kraft, D. H. (1973). A decision theory view of the information retrieval situation: an operations research approach. *Journal of the American Society for Information Science* **24**, 368-376.
Krantz, D. H., Atkinson, R. C., Luce, R. D., and Suppes, P., eds. (1974). "Contemporary Developments in Mathematical Psychology." Freeman, San Francisco, California.
Krivohlavy, J. (1970). Subjective probability in experimental games. *Acta Psychologica* **34**, 229-240.
Lanzetta, J. T. (1963). Information acquisition in decision making. *In* "Motivation and Social Interaction: Cognitive Determinants" (O. J. Harvey, ed.), pp. 239-265. Ronald Press, New York.
Lanzetta, J. T., and Driscoll, J. M. (1966). Preference for information about uncertain but unavoidable outcome. *Journal of Personality and Social Psychology* **3**, 96-102.
Lanzetta, J. T., and Driscoll, J. M. (1968). The effects of uncertainty and importance on information search in decision making. *Journal of Personality and Social Psychology* **10**, 479-486.
Lanzetta, J. T., and Kanareff, V. T. (1962). Information costs, amount of payoff, and level of aspiration as determinants of information seeking in decision making. *Behavioral Science* **7**, 459-473.
Levine, J. M., and Samet, M. G. (1973). Information seeking with multiple sources of conflicting and unreliable information. *Human Factors* **15**, 407-419.

Long, B. H., and Ziller, R. C. (1965). Dogmatism and predecisional information search. *Journal of Applied Psychology* **49**, 376–378.

McCall, J. J. (1965). The economics of information and optimal stopping rules. *Journal of Business* **38**, 300–317.

MacCrimmon, K. R. (1968). Descriptive and normative implications of the decision theory postulates. *In* "Risk and Uncertainty" (K. Borch and J. Mossin, eds.), pp. 3–32. St. Martin's, New York.

McGuire, C. B., and Radner, R. (1972). "Decision and Organization: A Volume in Honor of Jacob Marschak." American Elsevier, New York.

Marks, D. F., and Clarkson, J. K. (1973). Conservatism as nonBayesian performance: a reply to De Swart. *Acta Psychologica* **37**, 55–63.

Marschak, J. (1970). Economics of inquiring, communication, deciding. *In* "Introduction to Information Science" (T. Saracevic, ed.), pp. 697–706. Bowker, New York.

Messick, D. M., and Rapoport, A. (1966). A supplementary study of response uncertainty and relative expected value in multiple-choice decision behavior. *Psychonomic Science* **4**, 143–144.

Miller, G. A. (1956). The magical number seven, plus or minus two: some limits on our capacity for processing information. *Psychological Review* **63**, 81–96.

Miller, G. A., Galanter, E., and Pribram, K. (1960). "Plans and the Structure of Behavior." Holt, New York.

Mischel, W. (1973). Toward a cognitive social learning reconceptualization of personality. *Psychological Review* **80**, 252–283.

Mitroff, I. I. (1974). A Brunswik lens model of dialectical inquiring systems. *Theory and Decisions* **5**, 45–67.

Morris, J. R. (1975). The logarithmic investor's decision to acquire costly information. *Management Science/Application* **21**, 383–391.

Nauta, D., Jr. (1972). "The Meaning of Information." Mouton, The Hague.

Navon, D. (1975). A correlational approach to studying Bayesian inference in experimental settings. *Organizational Behavior and Human Performance* **13**, 318–329.

Newell, A., and Simon, H. A. (1972). "Human Problem-Solving." Prentice-Hall, Englewood Cliffs, New Jersey.

O'Connor, M. F., Peterson, C. R., and Palmer, T. J. (1972). Stakes and probabilities in information purchase. *Organizational Behavior and Human Performance* **7**, 43–52.

Orr, R. H. (1970). The scientist as an information processor: a conceptual model illustrated with data on variables related to library utilization. *In* "Communication Among Scientists and Engineers" (C. H. Nelson and D. K. Pollock, eds.), pp. 143–189. Lexington Books, Heath, Lexington, Massachusetts.

Paisley, W. J. (1966). Extent of information-seeking as a function of subjective certainty and the utility of the information. *Dissertation Abstracts* **26**, 4105–4106.

Parker, E. B., and Paisley, W. (1966). "Patterns of Adult Information Seeking." Stanford University, Stanford, California.

Payne, J. W. (1973). Alternative approaches to decision making under risk: moments versus risk dimensions. *Psychological Bulletin* **80**, 439–453.

Peterson, C. R., and Beach, L. R. (1967). Man as an intuitive statistican. *Psychological Bulletin* **68**, 29–46.

Pitz, G. F. (1966). The sequential judgment of proportion. *Psychonomic Science* **4**, 397-398.
Pitz, G. F. (1967). Sample size, likelihood, and confidence in a decision. *Psychonomic Science* **8**, 257-258.
Pitz, G. F. (1968). Information seeking when available information is limited. *Journal of Experimental Psychology* **76**, 25-34.
Pitz, G. F. (1969). The influence of prior probabilities on information seeking and decision-making. *Organizational Behavior and Human Performance* **4**, 213-226.
Pitz, G. F. (1970). On the processing of information: probabilistic and otherwise. *Acta Psychologica* **34**, 201-213.
Pitz, G. F. (1972). Simultaneous information integration in decisions concerning normal populations. *Organizational Behavior and Human Performance* **8**, 325-339.
Pitz, G. F., and Downing, L. (1967). Optimal behavior in a decision-making task as a function of instructions and payoffs. *Journal of Experimental Psychology* **73**, 549-555.
Pitz, G. F., and Geller, E. S. (1970). Revision of opinion and decision times in an information-seeking task. *Journal of Experimental Psychology* **83**, 400-405.
Pitz, G. F., and Reinhold, H. (1968). Payoff effects in sequential decision-making. *Journal of Experimental Psychology* **77**, 249-257.
Pitz, G. F., Downing, L., and Reinhold, H. (1967). Sequential effects in the revision of subjective probabilities. *Canadian Journal of Psychology* **21**, 381-393.
Pitz, G. F., Reinhold, H., and Geller, E. S. (1969). Strategies of information seeking in deferred decision making. *Organizational Behavior and Human Performance* **4**, 1-19.
Raiffa, H. (1968). "Decision Analysis: Introductory Lectures on Choices Under Uncertainty." Addison-Wesley, Reading, Massachusetts.
Rapoport, A. (1966). A study of human control in a stochastic multistage decision task. *Behavioral Science* **11**, 18-32.
Rapoport, A. (1967a). Dynamic programming models for multi-stage decision making tasks. *Journal of Mathematical Psychology* **4**, 48-71.
Rapoport, A. (1967b). Variables affecting decisions in a multistage inventory task. *Behavioral Science* **12**, 194-204.
Rapoport, A. (1968). Choice behavior in a markovian decision task. *Journal of Mathematical Psychology* **5**, 163-181.
Rapoport, A. (1970). What is information? *In* "Introduction to Information Science" (T. Saracevic, ed.), pp. 5-12. Bowker, New York.
Rapoport, A., and Tversky, A. (1966). Cost and accessibility of offers as determinants of optional stopping. *Psychonomic Science* **4**, 145-146.
Rapoport, A., and Tversky, A. (1970). Choice behavior in an optional stopping task. *Organizational Behavior and Human Performance* **5**, 105-120.
Rapoport, A., and Wallsten, T. S. (1972). Individual decision behavior. *Annual Review of Psychology* **23**, 131-75.
Rapoport, A., Lissitz, R. W., and McAllister, H. A. (1972). Search behavior with and without optional stopping. *Organizational Behavior and Human Performance* **7**, 1-17.
Rawls, J. (1971). "A Theory of Justice." Harvard University Press, Cambridge, Massachusetts.

Rhine, R. J. (1967). Some problems in dissonance theory research on information selectivity. *Psychological Bulletin* **68**, 21-28.
Savage, L. J. (1954). "The Foundations of Statistics." Wiley, New York.
Sayeki, Y. (1969). Information seeking for object identification. *Organizational Behavior and Human Performance* **4**, 267-283.
Schultz, C. B. (1974). Information seeking following the confirmation or contradiction of beliefs. *Journal of Educational Psychology* **66**, 903-910.
Shanteau, J. (1972). Descriptive versus normative models of sequential inference judgment. *Journal of Experimental Psychology* **93**, 63-68.
Shanteau, J. (1975). Averaging versus multiplying combination rules of inference judgment. *Acta Psychologica* **39**, 83-89.
Shaw, J. I. (1972). Reward size and game playing behavior. *Scandinavian Journal of Psychology* **13**, 131-132.
Sieber, J. E., and Lanzetta, J. T. (1964). Conflict and conceptual structure as determinants of decision-making behavior. *Journal of Personality* **32**, 622-641.
Sieber, J. E., and Lanzetta, J. T. (1966). Some determinants of individual differences in predecision information processing behavior. *Journal of Personality and Social Psychology* **4**, 561-571.
Simon, H. A. (1957). "Models of Man: Social and Rational." Wiley, New York.
Slovic, P., and Lichtenstein, S. (1968). Relative importance of probabilities and payoffs in risk taking. *Journal of Experimental Psychology Monographs* **78**, 1-18.
Slovic, P., Fischhoff, B., and Lichtenstein, S. (1977). Behavioral decision theory. *Annual Review of Psychology* **28**, 1-39.
Sodt, J. D. (1979). "The Effects of Metainformation Cost Change on Information and Metainformation Preference in a Decision Task." Unpublished dissertation, Syracuse University.
Steinmann, D. O., and Doherty, M. E. (1972). A lens model analysis of a bookbag and poker chip experiment: a methodological note. *Organizational Behavior and Human Performance* **8**, 450-455.
Stevens, S. S. (1959). Measurement, psychophysics, and utility. *In* "Measurement: Definitions and Theories" (C. W. Churchman and P. Ratoosh, eds.), pp. 18-63. Wiley, New York.
Suedfeld, P., and Streufert, S. (1966). Information search as a function of conceptual and environmental complexity. *Psychonomic Science* **4**, 351-352.
Suppes, P. (1960). Some open problems in the foundations of subjective probability. *In* "Information and Decision Processes" (R. E. Machol, ed.), pp. 162-169. McGraw-Hill, New York.
Suppes, P. (1966). Probabilistic inference and the concept of total evidence. *In* "Aspects of Inductive Logic" (J. Hintikka and P. Suppes, eds.), pp. 49-65. North-Holland Publishing Co., Amsterdam.
Teigen, K. H. (1974). Overestimation of subjective probabilities *Scandinavian Journal of Psychology* **15**, 56-62.
Toda, M. (1956). Information-receiving behavior of man. *Psychological Review* **63**, 204-212.
Tomasini, L. M. (1974). The economics of information: a survey. *Économie Appliquée* **27**, 319-337.

Tversky, A. (1967). Additivity, utility, and subjective probability. *Journal of Mathematical Psychology* **4**, 175–201.
Tversky, A. (1969). Intransitivity of preferences. *Psychological Review* **76**, 31–48.
Von Holstein, C. S. S. (1970). Measurement of subjective probability. *Acta Psychologica* **34**, 146–159.
Wald, A. (1950). "Statistical Decision Functions." Wiley, New York.
Wallsten, T. S. (1968). Failure of predictions from subjectively expected utility theory in a Bayesian decision task. *Organizational Behavior and Human Performance* **3**, 239–252.
Watanabe, S. A. (1969). "Knowing and Guessing: A Quantitative Study of Inference and Information." Wiley, New York.
Wendt, D. (1970). Utility and risk. *Acta Psychologica* **34**, 214–228.
Whittemore, B. J., and Yovits, M. C. (1973). A generalized conceptual development for the analysis and flow of information. *Journal of the American Society for Information Science* **24**, 221–231.
Winkler, R. L. (1972). "Introduction to Bayesian Inference and Decision." Holt, New York.
Winkler, R. L., and Murphy, A. H. (1973). Experiments in the laboratory and the real world. *Organizational Behavior and Human Performance* **10**, 252–270.
Wise, J. A., and Mockovak, W. P. (1973). Descriptive modeling of subjective probabilities. *Organizational Behavior and Human Performance* **9**, 292–306.
Wolfson, R. J., and Carroll, T. M. (1976). Ignorance, error, and information in the classic theory of decision. *Behavioral Science* **21**, 107–115.

Library Education in India, Pakistan, and Bangladesh

P. B. MANGLA

University of Delhi

I.	Scope	191
II.	Brief Historical Background	192
	A. General Information after 1947	193
III.	Library Education	195
	A. India	195
	B. Pakistan	219
	C. Bangladesh	229
IV.	Similarities and Variations	234
V.	Conclusion	236
	Appendix	237
	Selected Bibliography	238

I. SCOPE

The scope of this article is limited to the formal library education programs at the postgraduate level conducted by university departments, documentation centers, and research institutes in India, Pakistan, and Bangladesh.* Details about courses at the undergraduate

---

*Information given in this article about Pakistan and Bangladesh has been based on the printed literature available to the author. Certain material about Bangladesh was obtained through the courtesy of Messrs. Ivor Kemp and S. C. Biswas of the British Council, New Delhi, for which the author is thankful. Mr. J. L. Sardana, Lecturer, Department of Library Science, University of Delhi, made several positive suggestions in the finalization of this paper for which the author also is grateful.

level—usually conducted by library associations, teachers' training institutes, and libraries—are excluded. Also excluded are the short-term specialized courses conducted by university departments, research institutions, or organizations. The term "postgraduate" has been used in the British sense, implying the courses after the bachelor's degree. "Library education" includes library science training courses in the traditional sense as well as courses covering library and/or information science in the modern sense.

II. BRIEF HISTORICAL BACKGROUND

Historically speaking, India, Pakistan, and Bangladesh were one unified country, called India, until independence in 1947, when parts of Punjab and Bengal provinces as well as all of Sind and the North-West Frontier were constituted as a separate country, called Pakistan. Pakistan had two wings, West Pakistan and East Pakistan, each separated from the other by a distance of about 1000 miles of Indian territory. East Pakistan became an independent country in December 1971 and is now called Bangladesh. The history of these countries is therefore the history of India until 1947. Because of this history, these three countries not only have close cultural affinities, but also have inherited similar systems as well as traditions in administration, education, and research—including those in library services and library education.

The history of the Indian subcontinent dates back to over 5000 years when a well-developed civilization, called the Indus Valley Civilization, was in existence. "The Indus Civilization," writes Professor Childe (1943), "represents a very perfect adjustment of human life to a specific environment that can only have resulted from years of patient effort. And it has endured; it is already specifically Indian and forms the basis of modern Indian culture."

Although there is a definite sense of continuity between the Indus Valley Civilization and the present time, there is also a break or a gap in the historical information from the Indus Valley Civilization until the coming of the Aryans, around 1500 B.C. The history of the country after that presents a panoramic view of achievements and decline; unity as well as diversity; peace and conflicts—political, religious and economic—despotic rule as well as democracy; the coming of invaders resulting in massacres, turmoil and dislocation as well as of integration of different cultures, under Hindu, Buddhist, and Muslim rulers. The British, who came as traders in 1601 A.D. gradually brought the whole country under their colonial rule and from 1858 till independence, in August 1947, the British monarch was the ruler of India as well.

The progress and achievements made by the Indians during these centuries have received worldwide recognition. In his lectures delivered at the University of Cambridge in 1882, Max Muller, the famous scholar and orientalist, said, "If I were asked under what sky the human mind has most fully developed some of its choicest gifts, has most deeply pondered over the greatest problems of life, and has found solutions of them which well deserve the attention even of those who have studied Plato and Kant—I would point to India."

During the most recent two to three centuries, however, India had lagged behind in certain vital areas, such as education, scientific research, industrialization, and overall socioeconomic development because of obvious political reasons. After attaining independence, therefore, both India and Pakistan had to embark upon extensive programs of national development and reconstruction. The progress these countries have made during the past three decades really speaks well of these efforts.

General Information after 1947

1. INDIA

India is the most populous and seventh largest country in the world. It has an area of 38,87,782 km², with an estimated population in mid-1976 of 609 million. The per capita gross national product (GNP) in 1976 was U.S. $150. The country is a sovereign democratic republic and consists of 22 states and 9 union territories. The country has already progressed through five 5-year development plans and has made substantial progress in several areas, such as education, scientific and technological research, industrialization, agriculture, rural development, and other areas of socioeconomic development. Primary education is free in all states and compulsory in most of them. Overall literacy is about 30% and on October 2, 1978 the Government of India launched the massive National Adult Education Programme (NAEP) to eradicate illiteracy at a faster rate. The country has already developed a vast infrastructure of education and research facilities, consisting of schools, polytechnics, colleges, universities, institutions of higher learning, national laboratories, and research institutes/organizations. There are 105 universities, 9 institutions of national importance for higher learning, 10 institutions deemed to be universities, and more than 129 national laboratories, research institutions, or organizations. Several bodies, such as the Atomic Energy Commission, the Council of Scientific and Industrial Research, the Indian Council of Agricultural Research, and the Indian Council of Social Science Research, are engaged in developing and coordinating research activities in different sectors of science and technology, and social sciences. Several industrial organizations encourage and provide financial support for research and development activities in their respective areas of interest.

2. PAKISTAN

Pakistan has a total area of 796,095 km² and in 1977 had a population of 74.9 million people. It is a federal Islamic republic and the per capita GNP in 1976 was estimated to be U.S. $170. This country also has progressed through several development plans and has made substantial progress in several vital areas, such as education, scientific and technological research, industrialization, agriculture, rural development, and several other areas of socioeconomic development. The overall literacy is estimated to be about 25% and the government has extensive programs for the eradication of illiteracy in the country, particularly after the implementation of the New Education Policy (1972–1980). The infrastructure for education and research consists of schools, polytechnics, colleges, universities, laboratories, and research institutes. There are at present 13 universities and a large number of professional colleges, research institutes, and laboratories in the country. The laboratories and research institutes function under the umbrella of several bodies, such as the Pakistan Atomic Energy Council, the Pakistan Council of Scientific and Industrial research, the Pakistan Agricultural Research Council, and the Pakistan Medical Research Council. Research and development activities have been initiated in some of the industrial organizations as well. The New Education Policy (1972–1980) has opened up new vistas for educational development and research in the country.

3. BANGLADESH

Because until December 1971, the geographic area of Bangladesh was the eastern wing of Pakistan, its development occurred under the development plans of Pakistan. During this period, progress was made in several areas, such as education, research, and industrial and socioeconomic development, on almost the same lines as in the western wing of Pakistan. The country now has an area of about 88,956 Km² and the population is estimated to be around 79 million. It is a republic with a parliamentary system of government. The infrastructure for education and research in this country also consists of schools, polytechnics, colleges, universities, research institutes, etc. The country at present has six universities, the University of Dacca (founded 1921) being the oldest, and a number of research institutes in areas such as agriculture, sugercane, jute, technology, and medicine. The country took a few years to recover from the aftermath of the war of independence in December 1971 and is striving hard to make all-round progress at a faster rate. The per capita GNP in 1975 was U.S. $110. The Bangladesh Education Commission Report of 1974 has provided new directions for the development of education and research in the country.

III. LIBRARY EDUCATION

A. India

A study of library education in a country must necessarily be preceded by an overall view of its library and information services. This information is helpful in understanding the needs of the personnel at different levels so that the library education programs can be developed in a more realistic and objective manner, not only to meet immediate needs but also to plan for 8–10 years ahead.

1. LIBRARY SCENE

The past history of librarianship in India (as in several other countries in the east) is that of "having libraries," with little emphasis on library service in the modern sense. The recognition of the role libraries could play in the educational, scientific, industrial, and socioeconomic development of the country began to receive acceptance only as late as the 1940s.

a. Preindependence Period. Before independence, a public library system had been started in Baroda State in 1911 and a few good public libraries had been established at several other places, such as Lahore, Calcutta, Bombay, and Delhi. There were 18 universities in 1947 and some of these, such as Punjab University (Lahore), and the Dacca, Bombay, Madras, and Calcutta University libraries, had expanded in size and organized their collections and services on proper lines. Special libraries were small in number and size, however, and were attached to government departments, research institutions, organizations, etc.

b. Postindependence Period. After independence, the stimulus for the growth and development of libraries came from progress in and extension of education, scientific research, industrialization, and programs of socioeconomic development in the country. To highlight some of the achievements in this field, it may be mentioned that the country now has (1) four national libraries, viz., the National Library at Calcutta, the National Science Library and National Medical Library at Delhi, and the Indian Agricultural Research Institute Library at Delhi, which can also be considered as the national agricultural library; (2) an infrastructure of public library services in several states and union territories, with public library legislation in four states, viz., Tamil Nadu, Karnataka, Maharashtra, and Andhra Pradesh; (3) good libraries in colleges, universities, institutions of higher learning and laboratories, research institutions, and government ministries/departments; (4) bibliographic control of Indian publications with the publication of the Indian National Bibliography since 1958; (5) documentation services at the national level provided by the Indian National Scientific Documentation Centre (INSDOC) and the Defense Sciences Information and Documentation Centre (DESIDOC); and (6) library associations at the national and state levels.

In addition, the Government of India, Department of Science and Technology has already started the implementation of its plan for the National Information System in Science and technology (NISSAT) and four sectoral centers—Leather, Drugs and Pharmaceuticals, Food Technology, and Machine Tools—have been in operation since 1977. A proposal for establishing a national information system in the social sciences (NISS) is already under consideration by the Indian Council of

Social Science Research (ICSSR). Several institutions, such as Bhabha Atomic Research Centre (BARC) and the Indian Council of Agricultural Research (ICAR), are already functioning as national input centers for the international data bases, INIS and AGRIS, respectively. Collaboration with several other global information systems and programs, such as UNISIST and POPINS, is being developed in various ways so as to have all possible access to the information resources at the international level. Proposals to further develop and expand the library and information services in the country during the next plan period (1979-1984) are being finalized now.

It also is relevant that in order to meet the varied and complex needs of user groups, which consist of researchers, decision makers, managers, and planners, several libraries and documentation and information centers already provide such services as SDI, CAS, repackaging of information, and referral services. Computerized information services are already being planned or extended by several special libraries in the country.

2. CATEGORIES OF PERSONNEL

Manpower constitutes an important component of any library and information system. Professional staff at different levels and with requisite qualifications and aptitudes is needed in libraries and documentation and information centers in the country. Categories of personnel usually required are broadly classified as follows:

1. Professional personnel
2. Semiprofessional personnel
3. Other personnel, consisting of reprography technicians, translators, secretarial staff, typists, etc.

The University Grants Commission has categorized the professional staff in university and college libraries as follows:

1. Professional Senior: Level I
2. Professional Senior: Level II
3. Professional Junior
4. Professional Assistant

This categorization has been generally accepted for the personnel in other types of libraries and documentation centers, as well. Actual designations may differ, however, depending upon the staffing pattern in a library or documentation or information center.

The nature of responsibility and level of professional qualifications generally required for these categories of professional staff are as given in Table I. In the fourth column equivalence with teaching staff is indicated with regard to the status and salary scales in a university context. In other types of libraries and documentation centers equivalance in salary scales is generally decided in relation to other staff working in the parent body or organization.

3. COURSES IN LIBRARY SCIENCE

a. Preindependence Period. The need for professionally trained personnel to manage and run libraries effectively and efficiently was recognized during the first half of the present century and, consequently, library training programs were started at several places far before independence. The first formal library training course in the country was started at Baroda in 1911 by W. A. Borden, an American librarian and a student of Melvil Dewey, and C. A. Cutter, who in 1910, was invited by the ruler of the erstwhile Baroda State to organize a public library system there. This training course was continued until 1924. The second training course was started in 1915 at Punjab University, Lahore (now part of Pakistan), by Asa Dickinson, another American librarian and student of Melvil Dewey. Beginning in 1928, only graduates were admitted to this course and it continued until independence in 1947. In 1935, Khan Bahadur Asadullah Khan an alumnus of the Punjab University Library School, started a full-time undergraduate diploma course at the Imperial Library, Calcutta (now the National Library), which was continued until 1944. In 1931, the University of Madras took over the certificate course that had been started by the Madras Library Association in 1929. In 1937 this course was upgraded to a full-time postgraduate course of one academic year leading to the award of Diploma in Library Science. This course, under the dynamic stewardship of S. R. Ranganathan, attracted students from all over the country and has served in several ways as a model for the development of training programs during the pre and postindependence period in this country. In addition, short-term courses were

TABLE I
Responsibility, Professional Qualifications and Equivalent Status

Category	Responsibility in general terms	Generally required level of qualifications	Equivalence with the teaching staff
Professional Senior (level I)	To function in top positions in libraries/documentation/information centers of large size; teaching and research in library science	Doctorate in Library Science or equivalent; or Master's Degree in Library Science with a master's degree or doctorate in another subject	Professor
Professional Senior (level II)	To function as heads of divisions in libraries/documentation/information centers of large size; heads of medium size libraries/documentation/information centers; teaching and research in library science	Doctorate in Library Science or equivalent; or Master's Degree in Library Science with a master's degree or doctorate in another subject	Reader
Professional Junior	To function as heads of sections in medium-sized libraries/documentation/information centers; librarians or heads of small libraries/documentation/information centers; teaching in library science	Master's Degree in Library Science or its equivalent	Lecturer
Professional Assistant	To do professional work of routine nature in different types of libraries or in documentation or information centers	Bachelor's Degree in Library Science or its equivalent	Assistant Lecturer or Tutor, etc.

started by the Andhra Pradesh Library Association in 1920 and the Bengal Library Association in 1935.

Other courses generally patterned after the University of Madras diploma course at the postgraduate level were started in five more universities before independence: Andhra University in 1935, Banaras Hindu University in 1941, Bombay University in 1944, (which continued admitting undergraduates, as well, until the late 1950s), Calcutta University in 1945, and the University of Delhi in 1946.

b. Postindependence period. i. University courses. As the demand for professionally qualified personnel began to increase after independence, several universities started library courses, with the result that the number of library schools in the country today has risen to 43.

The Department of Library Science at the University of Delhi, although constituted in 1946, started admitting students for the postgraduate diploma course from 1947. S. R. Ranganathan functioned as a full-time Honorary Professor in the department during 1947–1955. In several respects this department has acted as a trend setter in library education, not only in India but perhaps in the whole of the British Commonwealth. This was the first department of library science to be constituted as a teaching department, like the other teaching departments in a university context. It was at this department that for the first time, in addition to the usual 1-year postgraduate diploma course, an advanced course leading to the degree of Master of Library Science (M. Lib. Sc.) was started in 1948. In addition, provision was made in the same year for research leading to the Ph. D. degree. This department again was the first to have started the 1-year M. Phil. course in the country in 1978.

While no new department of library science was established between 1948 and 1955, six departments came into existence between 1956 and 1959. In the 1960s 19 departments were established and during the past 8 years 12 more departments have been added to the list. Several more universities plan to start library science courses in the near future.

A list of the universities conducting library science courses, arranged chronologically on the basis of the establishment of the course, is given in Appendix I.

ii. Documentation/information science courses. With the advance and intensification of research activities the need for documentation/information services in research, technical, and several university libraries gradually became more pronounced from the early 1960s. This created a demand for qualified personnel with specialization in documentation/information science. To meet this demand, specialized courses in documentation/information science, such as "Information Storage and Retrieval," "Computer Application in Libraries," and "Documentation," were included in the curriculum, mostly at the master's level in some of the universities. Two institutions, namely, the Documentation

Research and Training Centre (DRTC), Bangalore, and the Indian National Scientific Documentation Centre (INSDOC), New Delhi, however, started conducting postgraduate courses in documentation/information science as such in 1961 and 1964, respectively. The course at Bangalore was started by S. R. Ranganathan, who remained closely associated with DRTC till his death in 1972.

4. LEVELS OF COURSES AND THEIR OBJECTIVES

The different courses being offered in the country at the postgraduate level, along with their overall objectives, are given in Table II.

5. ADMISSION REQUIREMENTS AND DURATION

Table III gives general details about the admission requirements and duration for the different courses. Because of recent improvements in the employment opportunities for qualified personnel, several library schools admit only those who possess at least a master's degree in an academic discipline. Such a trend is quite encouraging because candidates with higher academic qualifications are better equipped to provide specialized library and information services. The number of women candidates has been increasing during the past 10–15 years and they now constitute 60–70% of the total in almost all library schools. While admission to the bachelor's course is usually decided on the basis of academic merit, certain library schools have, in addition, a system of admissions tests and/or interviews for this purpose. Some library schools even ask for prior library experience as an essential condition. For admission to the master's course, an admission test is usually prescribed by most of the library schools. A few library schools also prescribe 1–2 year's professional experience as an essential requirement for admission to the master's course.

Admission to the M. Phil. and Ph. D. program is usually decided on academic merit.

For associateships in information science, admission is usually based on academic merit, and candidates with a bachelor's degree in engineering, technology, or medicine, with experience in information handling, are given preference.

TABLE II
Levels of Courses and Their Objectives

Degree/ Associateship	Sponsor	Overall Objectives	Remarks
University Level Courses: Bachelor of Library Science/Library and Information Science/ Library Science and Documentation (B. Lib. Sc./B. L. I. Sc./B. Lib. Sc.& Doc.)	University	(1) To give the student an understanding of the normative principles and theoretical foundations of library science; (2) to enable the student to understand and appreciate the functions and purpose of the library in the changing social and academic setup of the society; and (3) to train the student in the techniques of librarianship and management of libraries and documentation and information centers.	(1) It was called the diploma course until the late 1950s; (2) all the 43 library schools conduct this course
Master of Library Science/Library and Information Science/ Library Science & Documentation (M. Lib. Sc./M. L. I. Sc./ M. Lib. Sc. & Doc.)	University	(1) To acquaint the student with the organization, development, and structure of the universe of subjects; (2) to give the student specialized knowledge of the different kinds of documents, of the information needs of users, and of the theory and practice of dissemination of knowledge/information embodied in documents in different types of libraries, documentation and information centers; (3) to	(1) Started for the first time in 1948 at the University of Delhi and called B. Lib. Sc. degree course; Name changed to M. Lib. Sc. in 1949; (2) 16 library schools are conducting this course

Master of Philosophy (M. Phil.)		University	make the student proficient in the design, development, and use of advanced library techniques and tools and in the management of libraries and documentation and information centers; and (4) to acquaint the student with methods of research.	Only University of Delhi conducts this program at present
			(1) To make the student proficient in the methods and techniques of research and their application to problems in library science and service; (2) to give the student specialized knowledge in selected areas of library science; and (3) to train the student for doing further research work leading to a Ph.D. or other research degree	
Doctor of Philosophy (Ph.D.)		University	(1) To make the student proficient in selecting a topic in library science/ information science or other related disciplines for investigation; (2) to enable the student make a contribution in the advancement of knowledge on the basis of his research	Six library schools enroll students for research
Associateship: Associateship in Information Science		DRTC, Bangalore INSDOC, New Delhi	Similar to those for the master's degree (M. Lib. Sc.) given above with emphasis on advanced techniques for information handling and management of information centers and systems.	

203

TABLE III
Admission Requirements and Duration

Degree/Associateship	Minimum Admission Requirements	Duration	Remarks
University Degrees			
B. Lib. Sc./B. L. I. Sc./B. Lib. Sc. and Doc.	A Bachelor's degree (generally in second division)	One academic year	An academic year is usually 8–9 months long
M. Lib. Sc./M. L. I. Sc./M. Lib. Sc. and Doc.	B. Lib. Sc./B.L. I. Sc./B. Lib. Sc. and Doc. degree (generally in second division)	One academic year	(1) An academic year is usually 8–9 months long; (2) Calcutta University course is of 2 academic years; (3) students at Bombay University are required to attend classes only for a few weeks; thereafter they submit their Project Reports, without attending the classes in the University
M. Phil.	M. Lib. Sc/M. L. I. Sc./M. Lib. Sc. and Doc. degree (second division)	One calendar year	The calendar year consists of two parts, each of about 6 months duration. The course work is completed during the first part and the second part is utilized for dissertation work as a regular student
Ph.D.	As for an M. Phil. degree or an M. Phil degree	2–3 academic years	—
Associateship			
Associateship in Information Science	A bachelor's degree in (1) Library Science (2) A second-class master's degree in a subject, or (3) A Bachelor's Degree in Engineering or Medicine	About 2 calendar years	The DRTC has in addition prescribed 2 years of experience in information handling for (2) and (3).

6. MAIN FEATURES OF THE CURRICULA

a. Bachelor's Degree Course. The curriculum recommended by the Review Committee of the University Grants Commission (UGC) (of which S. R. Ranganathan was the chairman), in its report of 1965, is generally found to be followed in library schools in the country. The Review Committee recommended the following scheme of papers for the course:

1. Library Organization
2. Library Administration
3. Physical Bibliography and Book Selection
4. Document Bibliography and Reference Service
5. Library Classification (Theory)
6. Library Classification (Practice)
7. Library Catalog (Theory)
8. Library Catalog (Practice)
9. Record of Practical Work

Certain changes and modifications have been made in the above schema of papers by restructuring the contents, scope, and allocation of marks for purposes of evaluation by a few library schools during the past 8–10 years. For example, at the University of Delhi, besides the usual papers in Library Classification and Library Cataloguing, and one paper on Library Management and Administration, papers that expand the above scheme are: (1) Library and Society, (2) Reference and Information Sources, and (3) Reference and Information Service. A few library schools have included such topics as Documentation and History of Libraries, as well as options based on types of libraries, such as school libraries, public libraries, and academic libraries, either as separate papers or as part of the papers given in the above schema.

In certain library schools, particularly those in Maharashtra State, besides the library sciences, compulsory papers on such topics as General Knowledge, Sources of Books and Ideas, and Cultural History of India are also included in the curriculum. The inclusion of these non-library-science subjects might have had some justification during the past, when nongraduate students were generally admitted to library science courses. The situation has now changed, however, and continuing these topics in the curriculum only dilutes the teaching of the professional subjects within the limited time available for the course. The Review Committee strongly recommended the exclusion of these topics from the curriculum.

b. Master's Degree Course. The UGC Review Committee recommended the following scheme of papers for this course:

1. Universe of knowledge: Its Structure and Developments
2. Depth Classification (Theory)
3. Depth Classification (Practice)
4. Advanced Library Catalog (Theory)
5. Any one of:
    a. Public Library System
    b. Academic Library System
    c. Research and Technical Library System
    d. Documentation
6. Project during term time:
    a. Preparation of a project on an approved topic falling within the area of any one of the subjects offered as an optional paper under item 5 above
    b. Preparation of a documentation list on an approved topic on the basis of a set of approved periodicals for 1 year
7. Literature survey in one of the fields:
    a. Indology
    b. A subject in the humanities
    c. A subject in the social sciences
    d. one of the pure sciences
    e. one of the applied sciences
    f. government documents
    g. juvenile literature

The above scheme of papers remains that generally followed in library schools in the country. However, the library schools at Delhi and Madras have included certain areas of information science in their curriculum and have therefore changed the title of their degree to Master of Library and Information Science. Rajasthan University has designated its degree of Master of Library Science and Documentation. The University of Delhi has revised its scheme of papers as follows:

First Semester:

1. Universe of Knowledge: Its development and Structure
2. Depth Classification (Theory)
3. Library Systems Analsyis and Elements of Statistical Methods
4. Bibliography and Literature in any one of:

    a. The Humanities
    b. Natural Sciences
    c. Social Sciences
    d. Medical Sciences
    e. Agricultural Sciences
    f. Engineering and Technology

5. Current Problems in Library and Information Science

    a. Literature Surveys
    b. Field Surveys

Second Semester

6. Part

    a. Depth Classification (Practice) and
    b. Advanced Library Cataloguing (Practice)

7. Any one of:

    a. Information Storage and Retrieval Systems
    b. Reprography
    c. Computer Application in Library

8. Any one of:

    a. Public Library System
    b. Academic Library System
    c. Research and Technical Library System
    d. Medical Library System
    e. Agricultural Library System
    f. Engineering and Technological Library System

9. Current Problems in Library and Information Science: Project Report.

The University of Madras has the following scheme of papers:

First Semester:

1. Advances in Classification and Indexing
2. Advances in Cataloguing and Document Description
3. Library, Documentation, and Information Services
4. National, Regional, and Global Information Systems, Services, and Programs
5. Research Methodology

Second Semester

6. Library and Information Systems/Centers: Planning and Management
7. Computer Application in Library, and Information Storage and Retrieval
8. Project Work and Report
9. One of:

   a. University and College Library System
   b. Public Library System
   c. Industrial Information System
   d. Social Sciences Information System, etc.

As noted in Table III, Bombay University has a different pattern of conducting its M. Lib. Sc. course; unlike other library schools, regular attendance in class lectures is required only for a few weeks during the academic year. The scheme of papers is as follows:

Group A—Written papers:

1. Comparative Studies in Librarianship (two papers)
2. Research Methods and Documentation Techniques
3. Current Developments in Library Science

Group B—Dissertation
Group C—Oral and *viva voce*.

The project report or dissertation is an essential part of all the master's programs and provides the student a chance to study independently a topic under faculty guidance and so learn to apply his knowledge in a more fruitful and productive manner.

  c. M. Phil. Program. The course contents of the M. Phil. program at the University of Delhi are as follows:

Part I

1. Research Methods
2. Library Planning and Management
3. Any one of:
   a. University and College Library System
   b. Research and Technical Library System
   c. Public Library System
   d. Information Processing and Organization
   e. Information Transfer and Dissemination
   f. Comparative Librarianship
   g. Education for Library and Information Science

Part II: Dissertation

The above pattern is based on the overall pattern followed for M. Phil. courses in other subjects at the University of Delhi. This pattern had been recommended by the UGC.

  d. Ph.D. Program. The Ph.D. program in library science is generally governed by the overall rules and regulations of the concerned university as applicable to other subjects. Up to now only a few candidates have obtained their Ph.D. degrees from library schools at Delhi, Punjab, and Rajasthan Universities, and the research program is being gradually strengthened in all library schools. In addition, some candidates also have obtained Ph.D. degrees from other university departments by selecting library science topics such as Public Library Legislation from a department of political science, History of Libraries in India from a department of history, etc. The emphasis on research in library science is increasing and it is estimated that about two dozen candidates are presently working for their Ph.D degrees in the country.

  e. Associateship in Information Science. The syllabii of both DRTC and INSDOC are almost similar and consist of the following scheme of papers:

Area I: *Foundations*
  1. Foundation of Information Science
Area II: *Information Resources and Materials*
  2. Information Sources and communication Media
  3. Information Systems and Programs
Area III: *Methods of Information Handling*
  4. Information Processing and Organization
  5. Information Transfer and Dissemination
  6. Information Technology and Systems Design
Area IV: *Planning and Management*
  7. Information System/Center Planning and Management
Area V: *Electives (Illustrative)*
  8. a. Industrial Information Service
     b. Information System for Research and Development
     c. Information System for Planning, etc.
Area VI: *Guided Research Projects*
  9. and 10. Two such projects
Area VII: *Supporting Courses*
  Relevant selections from: (a) Research Methodology, (b) Statistical Methods, (c) Operations Research and Systems Analysis, (d) Linguistics, (e) Communication, and (f) Technical Writing

7. EVALUATION OF STUDENTS' PERFORMANCE

Until recently the practice in almost all library schools was to evaluate a student's knowledge and understanding of the subject by holding an examination at the end of the academic year. Each paper or course was generally credited at 100 points and the duration of the final examination for each paper or course was 3 hours. Although periodic class tests and/or terminal examinations were held, the points awarded in these tests or examinations were not counted in determining the final results.

This practice has now been changed in several library schools. A certain number of points, say 20-30, in each paper or course are set aside for the periodic assessment done by the respective teacher(s) and these are added to the points or grades obtained by a student in the final examination. In some library schools, a semester pattern has been introduced and the academic year is divided into two semesters, the first and second semester examinations being held in November/December and April/May, respectively. The system of periodic assessment has certainly brought a healthy change in the earlier system and enables students to utilize their study time in a more planned and consistent manner.

The system of preparing questions and the evaluation of answer books for these courses varies from one university to another. This work is done either by external examiners, or by external and internal examiners jointly, or by board(s) of examiners consisting of only internal or external teachers or a combination of both. Names of the examiners are generally kept secret. Besides the written examination, in a few library schools an oral examination is required, particulalry at the master's and M. Phil. levels.

Some library schools also award points to the various kinds of records that the students are required to maintain for the practical or observational work done during the academic year. These marks may also be added to the final score for the examination.

Almost all library schools award first division to grades of 60% or above, second division to 50–59% marks, and third division for less than 50% but with at least 35–40% marks in the aggregate. Some library schools have abolished the practice of awarding third division at the master's level. A few library schools have introduced the system of awarding grades in place of divisions.

For Ph.D. work the candidate has to submit a thesis that is evaluated by two or three examiners. After the thesis has been generally approved by the examiners there may be a condition for the candidate's qualifying in a comprehensive *viva voce* before he is finally awarded the Ph.D. degree.

8. TEACHING FACULTY

Up to the late 1950s the teaching faculty in library schools consisted of part-time teachers usually drawn from their respective university libraries. The university librarian invariably functioned as head of the department. The need for full-time teachers was duly recognized by the University Grants Commission (UGC) Review Committee (1965) which said:

> While we would welcome a close association between the departments of library science and the library in a manner to be determined by the universities, we are not in favour of the present practice of employing part-time teachers in the departments of library science drawn from the university libraries. This, in our view is not conduc-

tive to efficiency. Part-time use of the members of the university library staff for teaching library science was possible in the past when the annual library fund was low level and there was not much research work in many of the departments of study. These conditions have changed . . . . Therefore, it is not proper to continue any longer the practice of arranging the university library staff to be part-time teachers in the departments of library science.

The trend over the past several decades has been gradually to employ full-time teachers as well as department heads, in these library schools. Most of the library schools have a system of inviting senior staff members working in different types of libraries or in documentation and information centers either to offer certain courses or to deliver specialized lectures to the students.

The total number of full-time teachers working in Indian library schools is estimated at around 125, with 5 professors, about 25 readers, and about 95 lecturers. These teachers are at par with their counterparts in other teaching departments with regard to their status, salaries, study leaves, vacations, and other facilities. Qualifications and experience prescribed for the teaching positions in library schools are also generally at par with other teaching positions in the respective universities. A master's degree with a Ph.D. and teaching experience of 5–8 years is usually prescribed for teaching position of readers and professors in Indian Universities. Librarianship being a newly emerging discipline for study and research, and there being substantial demand for teachers, it has generally been difficult to recruit teachers with these qualifications and experience. The situation has improved somewhat during the past 3–5 years but a good deal remains to be done. Those Indian teachers who have had higher education in American or British universities have helped in strengthening the teaching programs in quite a few Indian library schools.

The UGC Review Committee had recommended that a department conducting only the B. Lib. Sc. course have a minimum of one reader (or associate professor) and two lecturers (or assistant professors), and a department with a master's course should have at least one professor, two readers, and four lecturers. At the workshop on the methods of teaching and evaluation in library science (1973) it was felt that in order to provide proper leadership and status to a library school a professor should be appointed even in those departments which offer the bachelor's degree course alone (Mangla, 1973).

9. MAJOR AREAS OF DISCUSSION

The vast expansion in library education programs and facilities has naturally raised numerous problems, which have been discussed in committee reports, conferences, seminars, and workshops over the past two decades or so. Some of the vital areas of concern are (1) levels of education, (2) selection of students, (3) course contents, (4) use of suitable teaching methods and aids, (5) dearth of properly qualified teachers, (6) accreditation, (7) continuing education for teachers, (8) need for developing research components, (9) the status and administrative organization of library schools, (10) employment opportunities, and (11) library science literature.

Although the Advisory Committee for Libraries, appointed by the Government of India, in its report (India, 1958, 1960) made several important recommendations for developing the training programs in the country, the Report of the UGC Review Committee (1965), called *Library Science in Indian Universities,* can rightly be considered as the first comprehensive document on the subject.

Important seminars and workshops that have discussed this subject in greater detail are: (1) Seminar on Education for Librarianship in India, held at Chandigarh in 1962, under the auspices of Indian Association for Special Libraries and Information Centre (IASLIC); (2) three seminars/workshops held at the University of Delhi, Department of Library Science; (*a*) Seminar on the Teaching of Library Science (1966), (*b*) Workshop on the Methods of Teaching and Evaluation in Library Science (1973), and (*c*) Library and Information Science Education in India held in (1977) (Mangla, ed.); (3) two National Conventions on Library Science Education held in 1976 under the auspices of the Indian Library Association (ILA); and (4) the Seminar on Library and Information Manpower Development held at Bangalore in 1976 under the joint sponsorship of DRTC and INSDOC. I acted as the Director of the 1973 and 1977 Workshop and Seminar at the University of Delhi, and of the two ILA Conventions of 1976. Several aspects of this subject also have been discussed at two international seminars held at Bangalore: the Meeting of the Supervisors of Library and Documentation Schools in the Asian Region (1976), under the sponsorship of UNESCO, and the Indo-U.S. Seminar on Scientific and Technical Information (1977), under the sponsorship of the Government of India, Department of Science and Technology.

In addition to these discussions of training, the UGC has appointed a Panel in Library and Information Science to review periodically different aspects of the existing library education programs in the country and make recommendations for future development.

a. Levels of Education. As in the United States, Canada, and even to some extent the United Kingdom, librarianship in India is largely a postgraduate profession. One of the issues often discussed is whether the present pattern of awarding bachelor's and master's degrees should be continued or should this be changed to a 2-year integrated master's degree course, parallel to the master's degree courses in several other academic as well as professional subjects? An analysis of the existing pattern indicates that it has certain advantages, particularly for those who, because of various economic and other reasons, do not want to continue for the master's degree and are more interested in securing a job after completing the bachelor degree course. At the same time, a 2-year master's degree course gives the library schools more teaching time so as to develop a more balanced structure of "core" and "optional" courses. Because the abolition of the bachelor's degree program at present is not desired, it would certainly be valuable if some of the better library schools were to experiment with conducting the 2-year master's course. Such an experiment, which may be spread over a period of, say 5-8 years, would give an ample opportunity to the teachers, librarians, and other employers to make a comparative evaluation of the products of the two systems. Such an evaluative study would certainly be useful for reorganizing the present pattern of education. It would be essential, however, to ensure that students completing their training programs under these two systems would not be at any employment disadvantage with respect to each other.

As another alternative it may also be suggested that, like other subjects, library science be offered as one of the subjects at the undergraduate level in colleges and universities, for the 3-year bachelor's degree, which may be called B.A. or B. L. S. degree. Those who would secure such a degree may later on be given preference for admission to the 2-year master's course in library science. Otherwise, with only the undergraduate degree, they should be considered as quite suitable for junior professional positions. The argument usually given against this pattern is that since a library or information scientist at a senior level deals with information or knowledge contained in documents as such, it would be more appropriate for the entrants to the profession to have a sound background and understanding of a subject. It is therefore advocated that a subject bachelor's degree with honours, or even preferably a master's degree in a discipline, should be considered essential for admission to the library schools at the university level.

The overall pattern of education and research for M. Phil. and Ph.D. programs follows the pattern of other subjects in universities or institutes of higher learning.

b. Selection of Students. The majority of the students joining the bachelor's degree course are fresh from the universities. It is usually felt that although students with better qualifications are joining the courses, many of them do not possess such traits as a proper aptitude for library work, a strong general background, an interest in books and users, and a good personality all of which are viewed as essential for being a competent professional librarian. Although many of these students, like their counterparts in other professional subjects, do gradually develop these essential traits after joining the profession and working under proper guidance and leadership, library schools certainly carry a heavy responsibility in selecting proper students for these courses. Besides an emphasis on good academic qualifications, screening of the applicants through a system of admission or aptitude tests followed by an interview could gainfully be used for this purpose. Such methods are already in issue for admission to other professional courses, such as medicine and business management, in the country.

An important point to be mentioned here is that, because of various historical and sociological reasons, top students with backgrounds in subjects in the natural and applied sciences—until recently even in the social sciences—do not generally choose librarianship as a career. Although this situation is gradually changing, there is a great need to attract such students by offering them various incentives, such as scholarships and fellowships. Such steps would certainly help in developing suitable personnel for scientific and research libraries and documentation centers in the country.

c. Course Contents. As mentioned in Section III, A, 6, significant changes or modifications have been introduced during the past few years in the curricula, particularly at the master's level, in some library schools. On the basis of their course contents the library schools in the country can be broadly classified into three categories: first, those which continue to follow the traditional type of courses, and these schools are in majority; second, those which are more progressive looking in their approach, so as to equip their students with knowledge of library science as well as information science (e.g., Delhi, Benaras, Madras, and Mysore); and third, the library schools offering courses in information science, such as DRTC and INSDOC.

Whereas students with education in information science would certainly be needed in certain special libraries or documentation and information centers, it is strongly felt that to meet the larger manpower needs in a developing country such as India the majority of the students should have a proper blending of education in library science as well as information science. It is because of this need that a few library schools not only have revised their curricula but also have redesignated their degrees as Bachelor's/Master's degree in Library and Information Science or Library Science and Documentation.

d. Teaching Methods and Aids. Until recently education in universities and colleges was largely imparted through class lectures and even dictation of class notes. The futility of these methods has largely been recognized in higher education in general, and in professional courses in particular, with the result that such methods as the seminar and tutorial colloquium are now being gainfully used for teaching purposes.Library science, as a professional subject, requires greater attention to methods innovations such as the case study, observation, role playing, clinical, seminars, and tutorials. The teaching in library schools should aim at stimulating the interest of each student in the subject, and creating in him a curiosity about exploring new ideas and information in an independent manner. Such teaching aids as audiovisual equipment are generally not used in the majority of the library schools at present but certainly could be used in a fruitful manner.

e. Research Component. As indicated in Section III, A, 6, *d,* a research component is still weak in the overall system of library education in the country and needs to be strengthened at a faster rate. The need for developing research activities in library schools has been emphasized by the UGC Review Committee as well as in the recommendations of the seminars and conferences mentioned earlier.

f. Administrative Organization of Library Schools. Almost all the library schools are already constituted as full-fledged teaching departments, like other teacher departments in their respective universities. About 50% of the library schools have full-time teachers as heads; the others still function under the respective university librarian, who has the additional responsibility of the school. As mentioned earlier, the trend now is to separate the schools from the administrative control of the university librarian and appoint full-time teachers. As in such countries as the United States, Canada, and the United Kingdom, this practice is gradually proving to be more conducive to the overall development of library science education and research in the country.

Certain standards with regard to the number of full-time teachers at different levels, their qualifications, teacher–student ratios, library science collections, number of nonteaching staff, and physical facilities have been discussed and useful recommendations are contained in the UGC Review Committee Report and in the proceedings of the Delhi University Workshop (Workshop on the Methods of Teaching, 1973). It has also been emphasized that library schools should conduct courses only at the postgraduate level, and that the undergraduate level courses should fall under the purview of library associations, women's polytechnics, and central libraries.

g. Accreditation. At present there is no system of accreditation of library schools at the national level. The UGC is charged with the responsibility of ensuring and maintaining proper academic standards of higher education in the country, but until now its role has generally been of a recommendatory nature rather than of an accrediting body. The need for creating a proper system of accreditation has therefore been felt but a suitable mechanism for this purpose has yet to be devised.

At present each university has its own system for giving equivalence to the degrees awarded by other universities. The Association of Indian Universities, the UGC, and the Government of India, Ministry of Education, also plays a role in granting recognition to the degrees awarded within the country as well as to the degrees awarded in other countries.

h. Employment Opportunities vis-à-vis Starting New Library Schools. The number of bachelor's degrees awarded annually from Indian library schools can be estimated at around 1250, master's degrees at about 100, and associateships not more than 25. Because there still is no system of manpower planning for the profession, the vast annual increase in the number of library science graduates has gradually led to a situation of unemployment or under employment for the qualified personnel in the country. It is therefore essential that before a new library school or course is started, or the enrollment in an existing one is increased, the overall need for more librarians be considered in an objective manner. The two important factors that must be given due consideration before a new school is started or the existing ones are expanded are: (1) a survey of the already existing library school(s) and their facilities in the state or region; and (2) manpower needs at different levels, in the state, region, or the country as a whole.

Also, it is strongly felt that no new library school should be started without first ensuring the availability of adequate resources, such as teaching staff, books, and buildings. A library school certainly should not be started merely because it adds (if at all it does) to the personal prestige of the individual(s) involved. The urgent need certainly is for consolidation and improvement rather than expansion of the existing training programs in the country.

i. Continuing Education for Teachers of Library Science. The need of continuing education for teachers of library science and library staff has already been well recognized. During the 1960s Ranganathan directed such a program, on an annual basis at the DRTC which was attended by four or five teachers. The emphasis in the program was on various aspects of teaching methodology. Continuing education programs for teachers and professional staff are generally organized by library schools these days, usually with financial assistance from the UGC.

j. Library Science Literature. As in other professional subjects, most of the texts or recommended books used in teaching are those published in the United States or the United Kingdom. Among the Indian publications, Ranganathan's are the most important works and are used widely by students and teachers. In addition, during the past 10–15 years a good number of books, including textbooks, written by Indians also have been published. Although quite a few of these books have proved quite valuable; others are based on class notes, or are of general nature and usually have been of poor quality.

Because English is gradually being replaced by Hindi or regional languages as a teaching medium, library science books either are being translated from English or written in these languages. Much remains to be done in this field, however.

The total number of library science journals dealing with Indian library problems in English and other languages is estimated at not more than 15. The number of journals in English which contain articles of good quality and research value is quite small and includes: *Library*

Science with a Slant to Documentation (DRTC), *Journal of Library and Information Science* (Delhi University, Department of Library Science), *Annals of Library Science and Documentation* (INSDOC), and *Herald of Library Science* (Varanasi).

B. Pakistan

1. LIBRARY SCENE

At the time of her emergence as an independent sovereign state in August 1947, Pakistan inherited four libraries of significance. Three of these, viz., Punjab University Library (founded 1908), Punjab Public Library (founded 1884), and Punjab Civil Secretariat Library (founded 1885), were located at Lahore, a city which was once called the "city of libraries" and the "cradle of library movement in India"; and the fourth was Dacca University Library (1921, now in Bangladesh). Of these the Punjab University Library was the largest with a collection of 105,300 printed books and 15,000 manuscripts.

Although the country embarked upon extensive programs of national development and reconstruction soon after 1947, in the field of libraries and library education the pace of development at the initial stages was rather slow. As in other developing countries, the planners, decision makers, and bureaucrats showed the usual apathy in recognizing the role libraries could play in the overall socioeconomic development programs of the country. The leading English daily, *Dawn,* commenting on the overall position of libraries in the country in one of its editorials in 1953, said:

> Libraries and reading room facilities in our Federal Capital are utterly inadequate to meet the needs of even a fraction of its population. Since the advent of Pakistan, nothing substantial has been added to the existing meagre facilities in this respect.

It further added:

> The attitude of the Government in the matter is reflected in the treatment of the Khaliqdina Hall Library (founded 1856), an institution of a record of service for over nearly a century . . . . In Karachi the dearth of library facilities has the effect of inducing people to make ever increasing use of libraries and reading rooms sponsored and maintained by foreign agencies, which incidently also serve as centres of subtle foreign propoganda. This is the direct result of the Government's attitude of apathy towards libraries and reading rooms.

This position gradually improved from the early 1960s, and significant progress has been made in different types of libraries and information services, particularly in university and special libraries, during the past two decades or so. Until the projected national library comes into operation at Islamabad, the Liaquat National Library at Karachi will continue functioning as the national library for the country. The copyright law, which came into force on February 27, 1967, requires copies of books published in the country to be deposited in libraries designated for this purpose. It was estimated that in 1977 that there were 132 special libraries in the social sciences and 110 in sciences and Technology, with a total book stock of 1,900,478. The total number of college libraries in 1970 was 325 which is expected to be more than 400 by 1980. According to 1973–1974 budget estimates, out of a sum of Rs. 97,933,980* allocated for the eight Universities, a total of Rs. 3,222,710 (3.3%) was utilized for their libraries. While Islamabad University spent 9.9% of the budget on its library, Peshawar University's expenditure was only 1.1%. Under the New Educational Policy much development was expected in public, educational, and research libraries during the years 1972–1980. In 1972, the New Educational Policy announced plans for the establishment of a system of 50,000 people-oriented public libraries during 1972–1980 to combat illiteracy in the country and for the placement of public librarians along with librarians of colleges and universities at the status and salary level of teachers. The Karachi Metropolitan Public Library System is one offshoot of the New Educational Policy. Much, however, remains to be done to improve the school libraries and the working conditions, salary, and status of the school librarians.

The Pakistan National Scientific and Technical Documentation Centre (PANSDOC) was established in 1957. The Pakistan Scientific and Technological Information Centre (PASTIC) was established in 1974 with its base at Islamabad. The new system has been planned to include PANSDOC together with a National Science Reference Library and Scientific Statistical Division and is directly under the control of the Pakistan National Science Foundation (founded in 1973). The system will use a computer for sorting and retrieving scientific information and services such as SDI. Each province will have a provincial center under

---

*One United States dollar = 10 rupees.

its control with two separate branches: (*a*) a library, and (*b*) a scientific and technical information center. The entire system is expected to be completed by 1982 at a cost of Rs. 10,170,000.

Library Associations, such as the Pakistan Library Association and several others; the Society for the Promotion and Improvement of Libraries (SPIL), foreign assistance and experts, library schools, and several international organizations, such as Asia Foundation, and the United Nations and its agencies have played an important role in the development of libraries and information services in Pakistan during this period.

2. COURSES IN LIBRARY SCIENCE

As mentioned in Section III, A, 3, *a,* the Library School at Punjab University Library, Lahore, was started by an American, Asa Dickinson, in 1915. It was closed in 1947 and therefore Pakistan had no library training course at the time of her emergence. Until 1956, courses at the undergraduate level leading to Certificate in Library Science were conducted by library associations as well as at Punjab, Dacca, and Peshawar Universities.

The first postgraduate diploma course in library science was started in the country in 1956 at Karachi University. The Universities of Punjab and Dacca (now in Bangladesh) started the course at diploma level in 1959 followed by the University of Peshawar in 1962 and Sind University in 1970. In 1962 master's degree programs were added at the universities of Karachi and Dacca, followed by Punjab University in 1974. A Ph.D. program was started at the University of Karachi in 1967 and remains the only research degree program in the country. There are now therefore four universities conducting the 1-year postgraduate diploma course and two of them have advanced courses for the master's degree as well.

3. LEVELS OF COURSES, OBJECTIVES, DURATION, AND ADMISSION REQUIREMENTS

The different courses and their overall objectives, duration, and admission requirements, which are largely similar to those conducted in Indian universities, are as given in Table IV.

TABLE IV

Levels, Objectives, Duration, and Admission Requirements[a]

Levels of training and duration	Diploma/degree awarded	Library cadres for which training designated	Admission Requiremets
Research course of 2 or more years duration	Ph.D.	Library educators; library theoreticians, senior specialist librarians	Master's degree in Library Science or equivalent.
Master's degree course of 1 academic year duration	M. A. in Library Science	Librarians and specialists	Postgraduate Diploma in Library Science or equivalent, which is also regarded as the first year of the M. A. in Library Science course
One-year beginning course	Postgraduate diploma in library science	Library associates; assistant librarians; junior assistant librarians, and technologists	A Bachelor's Degree

[a] Based on Khurshid (1977a, p. 297).

4. ENROLLMENT

Candidates holding a good bachelor's degree with superior qualifications are generally able to secure admission in the diploma course. For admission to the master's degree course, in addition to possessing the diploma, a candidate is usually required to have at least 1 year's postdiploma experience in a library of good standing. The number of women students has been gradually increasing in almost all the four library schools during the past 8–10 years.

The annual enrollment for the diploma and master's courses is about 144 and 75, respectively. By 1974, 1144 students had obtained the diploma and 239, the master's degree. On the basis of the annual enrollment the number of graduates through 1979 would be about 1860 and 620, respectively. An idea of the annual enrollment in the different universities and other details can be obtained from Table V.

5. MAIN FEATURES OF THE CURRICULA

a. Diploma Course. The majority of the courses being taught at the diploma level can be grouped broadly into four areas: (1) bibliography and book selection, (2) classification and cataloguing, (3) organization and administration/management, and (4) reference service. In addition, the University of Karachi has compulsory courses, such as "History of Books and Libraries," "Foundations of Librarianship," and "History of Libraries and Librarianship" (Sind University calls it "Development of Libraries and Librarianship"). These subjects are included by other universities as topics under different courses such as "Library Administration and Organization." The Karachi Library School even uses such titles as "Applied Cataloguing" and "Applied Classification," for its courses dealing with theory of classification and cataloguing. It has also prescribed knowledge of a modern language other than English and mother tongue, as an essential reqirement for the completion of the training program. Until 1977, the total number of compulsory courses prescribed by the different universities for this training program were Karachi, 2; and Peshawar, Punjab, and Sind, 5 each.

Commenting on the changing trend in the curricula at this level, Anis Khurshid (1977a) says:

> The area of similarities of these core courses is now beginning to narrow down. The Lahore School proposes to offer 16 elective courses, including Library Architecture,

TABLE V
Annual Enrollment Until 1974 and the Total Number of Diploma/Degree Holders[a]

University	Annual Enrollment		Ph.D. Enrollment	Number of students already graduated		Expected no. of graduates upto 1979	
	Diploma	Master's degree		Diploma	Master's degree	Diploma	Master's degree
Karachi	75	55	5	561	239	931	514
Punjab	27	20	—	293	Started in 1974	428	100
Peshawar	17	—	—	201	—	286	—
Sind	26	—	—	89	—	219	—
Total	144	75	5	1144	239	1864	614

[a]Figures are based on Khurshid (1977a) and other references

Documentation and Information Retrieval, and even a thesis, in its beginning programme, that is, at the level of diploma. These courses will again be repeated in its second year programme, i.e., at the level of M. A.

b. Master's Degree Course. The master's degree program consists of a combination of "core" courses and "electives" at Karachi and Punjab Universities. Each of these two library schools has a set of five compulsory courses. Whereas the Karachi school requires 5 electives out of a total of 14, at Punjab a student is required to choose only 1 elective out of 4 offered for the course. The combined main areas of the "core" courses at both these library schools are (1) Advanced Bibliography; (2) Advanced Cataloguing and Advanced Classification; (3) Library Resources; (4) Management of Libraries; (5) Methods of Research; and (6) Library and Society. Electives include such areas as (1) those based on types of libraries: (*a*) academic librarianship, including school, college, and university library services and/or systems, (*b*) public library systems, and (*c*) special libraries; (2) those based on literature in different subject fields, such as the humanities, pure sciences, applied sciences, and social sciences; (3) Archives Management; (4) Information Science and Communication; (5) Planning or History of Library Services; and (6) Public Documents. A thesis and *viva voce* examination is also included as an elective at Karachi. As part of its compulsory course, "Research and Investigation," the Karachi school requires each student to prepare and submit a thesis on a subject approved by the school and some of these dissertations have even been published.

c. Ph.D. Degree. Like other countries of the subcontinent, there are no course requirements for the Ph.D. degree in Pakistan. Some of the topics assigned for research at Karachi are:

1. Growth of Periodical literature in West Pakistan from 1857 to 1957
2. Evolution of Calligraphy in the Muslim World
3. Library Investment and Intellectual Return
4. Islamic Libraries (749 A.D.–1257 A.D.)
5. Public Libraries: A National Strategy to Combat Illiteracy in Pakistan
6. Book Production and Distribution in Pahalvi Period from 1925 to 1972

6. EVALUATION OF STUDENTS' PERFORMANCE

Until recently, a student's knowledge and understanding of the subject was judged mainly by his performance at the final examination held at the end of the course. This practice has now been changed and a semester system has been introduced in most of the universities in the country. Other aspects, such as test preparation and evaluation, are almost the same as described in Section III, A, 7.

7. TEACHING FACULTY

The Karachi Library School, which was started as the first university library school in 1956, conducted the diploma classes with part-time teaching staff headed by the university librarian. The same pattern was followed by the other library schools at the initial stages of their development. The position gradually changed, however, and a decade later Moid (1966) reported that there were 33 teachers in the four library schools, as given in Table VI.

The university librarian, however, remained the head of the library school in all these universities as late as 1966. The majority of teachers had obtained their Master's degree from other countries, mostly from the United States, and one had obtained a Ph.D. in Library Science as well.

Describing the situation a decade later, Anis Khurshid (1977a) said that the Karachi school had a full-time faculty of five and the Lahore

TABLE VI
Teaching Strength (1966)

University	Full time	Part time[a]	Cooperative[b]	Total
Karachi	4	2	5	11
Dacca (now in Bangladesh)	3	11	—	14
Punjab	2	3	—	5
Peshawar	2	1	—	3
Total	11	17	5	33

[a]Those teachers who were drawn from the university library and were paid extra renumeration for their teaching work on a monthly basis.

[b]Those teachers who were drawn from outside the university and were paid on a lecture basis.

school had three. The Peshawar and Sind schools were still completely part-time schools.

As is true of other developing countries, Pakistan faces difficulties in recruiting suitable library science faculty with proper qualifications and experience. The trend is now toward fullfledged departments with full-time heads as well as teachers, so that these departments can conduct their courses in a more comprehensive and efficient manner. Practicing librarians are still found to be helpful in teaching certain papers and/or supplementing the work of the full-time faculty, by giving extension lectures and seminars.

The library school at Karachi has an enrollment of 129 students for the diploma and master's courses, which gives a teacher–student ratio of 1:26—certainly on the high side for a professional course. Moreover, some teachers have the additional responsibility of acting as supervisors for the research students.

8. CERTAIN OBSERVATIONS

As in other developing countries, library science education has certainly been an important area of discussion at professional conferences and seminars in Pakistan during the past two decades or so. On the basis of the available literature, it is somewhat difficult to say whether there have been much of a concerted effort at the national level to develop and organize the training programs in a more cohesive and well-planned manner. Also, authoritative guidelines or norms have not yet evolved for use by existing library schools as well as new library schools in developing their programs, course contents, and for resources such as teaching staff, nonteaching staff, physical facilities, and financial requirements. The University Grants Commission of Pakistan could possibly play a vital role in this respect.

a. Course Contents. While a few new areas have already been included in the course contents, particularly at the Master's level, as in several Indian library schools, emphasis continues to be mostly on the traditional subjects. Because the country plans to have a network of information services as well as to develop its university and special libraries on modern lines, it certainly seems urgent that such areas as "Computer Application in Libraries" and "Information Storage and Retrieval" be given due emphasis in the training programs. Also, there is an urgent need to review and revise the existing syllabii of most of the library schools at the diploma level, as well. Perhaps specialized agencies, such as PANSDOC or PASTIC, should conduct courses in information science as is done by INSDOC in India.

  b. Teaching Methods and Aids. According to Moid (1966) the methods of instruction used in these library schools consist of lectures, discussions, reports, and practical work. In addition, visits to important libraries are also arranged. The university library is generally used as a laboratory. The Karachi Library School organizes colloquia periodically where participation by the students is compulsory. Other methods that can be used profitably are tutorials, role playing, and case studies.

  c. Research Component. Although the Karachi Library School has provision for the Ph.D. degree, the research component in library schools, like that in India, is quite weak. Special efforts need to be made in this respect by utilizing local talent and other resources and/or through assistance from various other agencies outside the country.

  d. Accreditation. At present in Pakistan there is no system of accreditation as such. It would perhaps be much easier to evolve such a system at the present stage, when only four library schools are functioning in the country.

  e. Manpower Survey and Employment. In order to estimate manpower requirements, say, for the next 5–8 years, it would certainly be relevant for a library school or a professional association to conduct a comprehensive manpower survey. The findings of such a survey would be helpful in planning the training programs in a more objective manner. It appears that because of such expansion in library services during the past two decades or so, finding jobs for the diploma and master's degree holders has not been much of a problem during this period. However, expansion in training programs should, as far as possible, be correlated with the employment opportunities in the country.

  f. Library Science Literature. A glance through the catalogs of these library schools indicates that most of the text books and other books, as well as journals, used in the teaching of the courses are American and British publications. Quite a few Pakistani authors have also produced books that are useful for the students. The Karachi Library School and its alumni have played a vital role in this respect. They have already produced several books and occasional papers, some of which are *Cataloguing of Pakistani Names,* 1964; *Library Services to Children in Pakistan,* 1964; *Reader in Cataloguing,* 1972, by A. H. Akhtar; *Librarianship in Pakistan: fifteen years work,* 1947–62, by Anis Khurshid and S. I. Ali; and *Studies in Pakistan Librarianship,* 1971, by J. Haider and A. Hanif.

In addition, the Pakistan Library Association has produced several publications, such as conference proceedings, indexes, and directories. Its *PLA Journal* serves as an important medium for dissemination of articles written by Pakistani authors and others and maintains high academic standards. The *Pakistan Library Bulletin,* is published by a private organization called the Library Promotion Bureau.

C. Bangladesh

1. LIBRARY SCENE

From August, 1947 until December, 1971, Bangladesh was the Eastern Wing of Pakistan; therefore, the development of libraries and library education in this country for those 24 years was dependent upon the libraries and library education development policies in Pakistan, as a whole. At the time of her emergence as an independent sovereign republic in 1971, Bangladesh had no national library as such. The overall library infrastructure in 1973 included: (1) about 114 public libraries of varying sizes and at different stages of development, with three government-sponsored and well-organized public libraries at Dacca, Chittagong, and Khulna; (2) six university libraries, Dacca University Library being the oldest with over 300,000 printed books and 20,000 rare manuscripts in Bengali, Sanskrit, Arabic, and Persian; (3) about 285 college libraries, most of them in disorder; (4) a few libraries in schools; and (5) about 100 special libraries attached to government departments, research institutes, and organizations. Most of these special libraries are located at Dacca and are well organized and mostly staffed by trained personnel. The Pakistan National Scientific Documentation Centre (PANSDOC) had in 1963 opened a branch office at Dacca, which was designated the Bangladesh National Scientific and Technical Documentation Centre (BANSDOC) in 1971.

During the past 5-6 years good progress has been made in developing libraries and documentation services in the country. The report of the Bangladesh Education Commission of May 1974 (see Husain, 1976) contains one full chapter called "Granthagar" (Library) and its recommendations for: (1) developing libraries in schools, colleges, research institutes, and universities; (2) the salary, status and qualifications of library personnel; and (3) public libraries, national library, library training program, etc., are of far-reaching significance for the development of library and information services in the country. These recommendations have been accepted by the government, and it is expected that in due course Bangladesh will have a network of library and information services on modern lines. An important recommendation of the commission report is that the Central Public Library at Dacca be converted into a Bangladesh national library. Another national library, called National Medical Library and Documentation Centre, was established at Dacca in 1974.

BANSDOC was granted a sum of 3 million Takas* under the first 5-year plan and has been developed and equipped on modern lines. It is already playing a significant role by providing such services as bibliographic searches and reprography to the researchers in the country.

Among the well-organized special libraries that have developed good documentation services mention may be made of those attached to the Bangladesh Institute of Development Studies (BIDS), the Bangladesh Bank, the Bangla Academy of Rural Development, the Bangladesh Agricultural Research Council, the Bangladesh Atomic Energy Commission, and the Bangladesh Bureau of Educational Information and Statistics. The recently established Social Sciences Research Council is expected to collect and disseminate information in social sciences in the country. In addition, libraries of foreign countries or such organizations as the British Council and United States Information Service are playing an important role in providing library services as well as assistance to the libraries in the country.

2. COURSES IN LIBRARY SCIENCE

Although certificate and other specialized courses are conducted by the Library Association of Bangladesh and several other institutions, the University of Dacca is still the only university conducting postgraduate library science courses in the country. As mentioned in Section III, B, 2, it started the diploma course in 1959 and the master's degree course was added in 1962. The M. Phil. course is planned for the near future.

*One United States dollar = 16 Takās.

3. LEVELS OF COURSES, OBJECTIVES, DURATION, AND ADMISSION REQUIREMENTS

The different courses and their objectives, duration, and admission requirements are on similar lines to those in Pakistan or India and are given in Table VII.

4. ENROLLMENT

The average annual enrollment now is 70 in the diploma course and 50 in the master's course. The total number of diploma holders through 1979 can be estimated around 650 and master's degree holders, around 400.

5. MAIN FEATURES OF THE CURRICULA

a. Diploma Course. The majority of the courses included at this level can be broadly grouped into four main areas: (1) Classification and Cataloguing; (2) Evaluation and Selection of Library Materials; (3) Library Administration and Organization; and (4) Use of Books and Libraries. In addition, other compulsory courses are Archives and Preservation of Books, History of Books and Libraries, and, Paleography. The number of compulsory courses included in the diploma course is 10.

b. Master's Course. The master's program consists of a combination of "core" and "elective" courses. The "core" courses consist of such areas as (1) Advanced Cataloguing and Classification; (2) Advanced Reference Service, including Research Methods; (3) Documentation and

TABLE VII
Courses, Duration, and Admission Requirements

Diploma/Degree	Duration	Admission Requirements	Remarks
M. A. in Library Science	One academic year	Postgraduate Diploma in Library Science	The Diploma course is considered as the first year of the M. A. in Library Science
Diploma in Library Science	One academic year	A Bachelor's Degree	—

Information Retrieval; and (4) Development in the Field of Librarianship from 1940 to date. In addition, there are "Guided Dissertation," "*viva voce*" and "In-service Training" as compulsory requirements. Electives include library administration, of either academic or public or special libraries. The total program consists of seven compulsory courses and one elective.

6. EVALUATION OF STUDENTS' PERFORMANCE

Bangladesh has in general inherited the Indian system of education, including that of evaluation of student's performance. Therefore the information about the system given earlier under India and Pakistan is largely applicable to Bangladesh as well.

7. TEACHING FACULTY

The Dacca Library School opened in 1959 with part-time teachers, and the university librarian was designated as head of the school. The school at present has a full-time teaching staff of six, consisting of one associate professor and five assistant professors. A full-time professor is yet to be appointed. It is no longer under the control of the university librarian but the classes continue to be held in the evenings. Since the annual enrollment is about 120, the average teacher–student ratio is 1:20. Recruiting teachers with suitable qualifications and proper experience is quite difficult in Bangladesh as well.

8. CERTAIN OBSERVATIONS

A glance through the issues of the *Eastern Librarian,* an official organ of the Library Association of Bangladesh, indicates that library education in the country has been an important subject for discussion during the past 5–6 years. The Education Commission also reviewed library education in detail and made recommendations for the expansion and development of library education facilities in the country. In its Recommendation 30:54, the Education Commission emphasized the need for trained manpower by saying:

> For running libraries of higher standard, according to our Recommendations, a few thousand of trained librarians and library personnel will be needed. To meet the demand for trained library staff, both at the semiprofessional and professional levels,

the Education Commission recommended expansion of the existing training facilities: (i) of those undergraduate courses run by Library Association of Bangladesh, and (ii) by starting library science courses at the postgraduate levels in Rajshahi, Jahangir Nagar and Chittagong universities. With regard to the status, salary, etc., the Education Commission in its Recommendation 30:58 said: "We therefore recommend that in matters of status and emoluments, librarians and library personnel of comparable qualifications and training should be equated with teachers. To class the librarians with administrative officers will be unreasonable and contrary to the national interests. The entire responsibility and control of libraries should be left to librarians with requisite qualifications."

Because only one university at present conducts the training programs and vast expansions are expected in the future, a few observations may be made as follows:

a. Course Contents. The course contents at both the diploma and the master's levels are mostly based on a traditional outlook in library science. Certain courses, such as Archives and Preservation of Books, and Paleography, included at the diploma level may be important areas of study in their own right but it is doubtful whether they are really of much use to the general student who seeks employment in college, public, university or other types of libraries. Such areas require specialized knowledge on the part of the library staff which may be made available by the library school via refresher courses, or short-term intensive programs for those who are working or plan to work in manuscript libraries or archival collections. Similarly, at the master's level the existing course contents need to be reviewed and certain areas, such as "Bibliography and Literature" in different disciplines such as social sciences, science and technology, and humanities, as well as areas of information science, need to be included. The existing work load at both these levels also needs to be reexamined in the light of the objectives as well as the duration of these courses. "In-service training" is certainly an important element in a professional course, but it could possibly be more helpful in the form of a posttraining apprenticeship rather than during the formal training program.

It would certainly be more helpful if a sort of model syllabus was developed through joint effort of teachers, librarians, and information scientists for the training courses at different levels: undergraduate as well as postgraduate, to meet not only the present needs but also the needs of the future.

b. Teaching Methods and Aids. The various points discussed earlier under India and Pakistan are applicable for the Dacca Library School, as well. It would certainly be desirable for the courses to be conducted as full-time daytime courses rather than as evening programs, particularly when the school has full-time teachers on its staff.

c. Research Component. In view of the fact that the government has vast plans to expand the library and information service infrastructure in the future, there is need not only to expand the training facilities but also to develop research activities in the country. The development of research activities would not only help individual(s) to gain more experience and knowledge of different problems but would also help them in developing the infrastructure along proper lines.

d. Accreditation. No system of accreditation is in existence at present in Bangladesh. It may be added, however, that because a few more library schools are planned for the future, it is essential that the authorities concerned and/or the Library Association of Bangladesh evolve guidelines or standards for organizing these library schools.

e. Library Science Literature. As in India and Pakistan, American and British texts and journals are generally used. The number of good publications in this field published in Bangladesh in English and Bengali languages is still quite limited. *The Eastern Librarian,* an official organ of the Library Association of Bangladesh, serves as the most important medium for dissemination of professional literature and information in the country.

IV. SIMILARITIES AND VARIATIONS

On the basis of the preceding discussion it can be seen that there are more similarities than differences in the various aspects of the systems of library education in India, Pakistan, and Bangladesh. An important factor in these similarities is that the three countries share a common and long historical, cultural, and educational background. Although library education had been started in India as early as the 1920s, it must be noted that in India and Pakistan (including the east wing, now Bangladesh), major expansion took place, only after independence, and particularly after the mid-1950s. The number of library schools in India multiplied at a rather rapid rate, however, because of such factors as the size of the country, its large population, expansion in educational and research facilities, early recognition of the role of libraries and professionally trained staff in the industrial education and socioeconomic development of the country, and professional leadership.

The overall pattern of the courses and their levels, objectives, durations, and admission requirements share many features in all the three countries. Also, these countries all have (1) limited research activity in the library schools; (2) no system of accreditation at the national level; (3) no comprehensive manpower, surveys and manpower planning for librarianships; and (4) a shortage of suitable faculty for the different levels in the library schools. Training courses were started with part-time teachers, usually drawn from the university libraries and with university librarians as heads of the library schools, but now the trend in these countries is to have full-time faculty of the same caliber and enjoying the same status, facilities, and priviliges as in other departments of the universities.

India certainly had a great advantage in the person of S. R. Ranganathan, who played a vital role in the development not only of library education, but also of libraries and the library profession as a whole, in the country. His writings, consisting of more than 50 books and about 2000 articles, constitute an important contribution in the field from this country. His Colon Classification scheme is widely recognized all over the world. Besides his writings, there are quite a few other publications that have appeared during the past 10–15 years and are of good quality. An important trend in publishing library science documents is that of issuing text books for students at different levels. Some of the library associations are also bringing out publications of good quality, not only in English but also in several other languages. A few journals have high academic standards. In Pakistan, the Karachi Library School and its alumni, the Pakistan Library Association, and a few other organizations have brought out useful publications but the number is quite limited. In Bangladesh publication activity remains inadequate.

Whereas in India, information science is taught at DRTC and INSDOC and in some of the library schools at the master's level, in Pakistan and Bangladesh emphasis on this new area in the curriculum has somewhat limited coverage. This new area requires further attention from the teachers and other professionals, for all these countries have taken steps to develop an information service network at the national level.

In India, the University Grants Commission (UGC) has played an important role in designing the curricula and in providing guidelines or norms for developing library education programs in the country. At present, its Panel on Library and Information Science is reviewing the existing course curricula so as to provide for the changing and varied needs of the professional personnel working in libraries and documentation and information centers. Pakistan and Bangladesh would also benefit from a system, at the national level, which could help in designing uniform, standardized, and accepted guidelines for the overall system of library education in their respective countries.

V. CONCLUSION

Librarianship as a profession has largely emerged from the adolescent stage in India, Pakistan, and Bangladesh, and library schools have certainly made a vital contribution in this process. In order for the momentum of development in library and information services to be properly maintained, library schools must carry a still heavier responsibility in providing high quality and relevant education. In this context, much help and guidance should be obtained by the library schools from a system of regular contacts with the employers and the users of the library and information services. Such a system would help the library schools a great deal in the process of designing their course contents and pattern of education in a more logical and pragmatic manner. Although several library schools do have informal contacts with employers and users, it would be useful if these contacts were more formal and regular in nature.

Because of their close geographic proximity and similarities in their systems as well as in their problems, the library schools in these countries can certainly gain a great deal, if various ways and means can be explored and used to develop a system of mutual cooperation among them. Some ideas in this respect might be regional seminars on topics of common interest, exchanges of teachers, and exchanges of course materials. With such a system of cooperation the library schools can play more effective roles not only in their respective countries, but also possibly in the South Asia region, and even in the developing countries of the world.

APPENDIX I

List of University Library Schools Arranged According to the Year They Started diploma/B. Lib. Sc. course

Name of the University	Year of starting:			
	Diploma/ B. Lib. Sc.	Master's degree	M. Phil.	Ph.D.
1. Andhra University, Waltair	1935	—	—	—
2. University of Madras	1937	1977	—	—
3. Banaras Hindu University, Varanāsi	1941	1965	—	—
4. University of Bombay	1944	1968	—	—
5. Calcutta University	1945	1975	—	1972
6. University of Delhi	1947	1948	1978	1948
7. M. S. University Baroda	1956	—	—	—
8. University of Nagpur	1956	—	—	—
9. Vikram University, Ujjain	1957	1971	—	1976
10. Aligarh Muslim University	1958	1972	—	—
11. Poona University	1958	1979	—	—
12. Osmania University, Hyderabad	1959	1979	—	—
13. Panjab University, Chandigarh	1960	1972	—	1972
14. University of Rajasthan, Jaipur	1960	1974	—	1975
15. University of Kerala, Trivandrum	1961	1979	—	—
16. Karnataka University, Dharwar	1962	1971	—	1974
17. I. T. College, Lucknow (Lucknow University)	1962	—	—	—
18. S.N.D.T. Women's University, Bombay.	1962	1978	—	—
19. A.E.C. Training College, Panchmarhi (under University of Saugar).	1962	—	—	—
20. Burdwan University	1964	—	—	—
21. Gujarat University, Ahmedabad	1964	—	—	—
22. Jadavpur University, Calcutta	1965	—	—	—
23. Jiwaji University, Gwalior	1965	—	—	—
24. University of Mysore	1965	1971	—	—
25. Shivaji University, Kohlapur	1965	—	—	—
26. Gauhati University	1966	—	—	—
27. Varanaseya Sanskrit Vishwavidyalaya, Varanasi	1967	—	—	—
28. Marthwada University, Aurangabad	1967	—	—	—

(*cont.*)

APPENDIX I (CONT.)

Name of the University	Year of starting:			
	Diploma/ B. Lib. Sc.	Master's degree	M. Phil.	Ph.D.
29. Kurukshetra University	1968	—	—	—
30. A.P.S. University, Rewa	1968	—	—	—
31. Panjabi University, Patiala	1969	—	—	—
32. Bhopal University	1970	—	—	—
33. University of Saugar	1971	—	—	—
34. Ravishankar University	1971	—	—	—
35. Kashmir University	1971	—	—	—
36. Jabalpur University	1971	—	—	—
37. Bhagalpur University	1973	—	—	—
38. Bangalore University	1973	1975	—	—
39. Guru Nanak Dev University, Amritsar.	1973	—	—	—
40. University of Madurai	1974	—	—	—
41. S. V. University, Tirupati	1974	—	—	—
42. University of Udaipur	1975	—	—	—
43. Sambalpur University	1975	—	—	—

SELECTED BIBLIOGRAPHY

Alam, A. K. M. S. (1973). Libraries and library problems in Bangladesh. *Unesco Bulletin for Libraries* **27**, 262–264.

Axford, H. W. (1966). Library education at the University of Punjab: American influence. *Journal of Education for Librarianship* **6**, 280–289.

"Bangladesh Directory and Yearbook, 1976" (1977). Associated Book Promoters, Calcutta.

Childe, G. (1943). "What Happened in History." Pelican Books, Middlesex, England.

Documentation Research & Training Centre (DRTC) (1979). "Courses in Documentation & Information Science: Prospectus and Syllabus." Bangalore.

Gelfand, M. A. (1967). Survey of University of Delhi Department of Library Science. *Indian Library Association Bulletin* **3**, 114–134.

Husain, A. (1976). English rendering of the "Chapter 30—Granthagar" (Library) of the Report of the Bangladesh Education Commission dated May, 1974. *Eastern Librarian* **10**, 171–193.

"India—A Reference Annual, 1977 & 78" (1979). India, Ministry of Information & Broadcasting, New Delhi.

India. Advisory Committee for Libraries (1958). "Report." Manager of Publications, Delhi. (Second ed., 1960.)

Indian National Scientific Documentation Centre (INSDOC) (1978). "Training Course in Information Science: Prospectus and Syllabus." New Delhi.
Indo-U.S. Seminar on Scientific and Technical Information (1977). "Papers and Recommendations." Bangalore (Unpublished report).
Isaac, K. A. (1969). "Developments in Library Education in India." (Paper presented at Education for Librarianship and Librarianship for Education, a British Council Seminar, Madras, November 11–13.) (Mimeograph copy.)
Kabir, A. F. M. (1966). Library education and training in East Pakistan. *Eastern Librarian* **1**, 39–44.
Kaula P. N. (1967). An evaluation of education for librarianship in India. *Unesco Bulletin for Libraries* **21**, 182–189.
Khurshid, A. (1969). "Standards for Library Education in Burma, Ceylon, India and Pakistan." University of Pittsburgh, Pittsburgh, Pennsylvania.
Khurshid, A. (1970). Library education in South Asia. *Libri* **20**, 59–76.
Khurshid, A. (1977a). Library education in Pakistan. *In* "Encyclopedia of Library and Information Science," Vol. 21, pp. 282–299. Dekker, New York.
Khurshid, A. (1977b). Libraries in Pakistan. *In* "Encyclopedia of Library and Information Science," Vol. 21, pp. 255–281. Dekker, New York.
Krishan Kumar and Sardana, J. L. (1977). "Research in Library and Information Science in Indian Library Schools." (Paper presented at the Seminar on Library and Information Science Education in India, University of Delhi, October 3–8, 1977) (Mimeograph copy.)
Library Education in Pakistan (1971). *International Library Review* **3**, 83–88.
Mangla, P. B. (1967). Survey of University of Delhi, Department of Library Science (1966) by M. A. Gelfand—An evaluation. *Indian Library Association Bulletin* **3**, 137–147.
Mangla, P. B. (1973). Workshop on the methods of teaching and evaluation in Library Science: A report. *Indian Association of Special Libraries and Information Centres (IASLIC) Bulletin* **18**, 115–138.
Mangla, P. B. (1974). University libraries in India: Their development and proposals for the fifth Five-Year Plan. *International Library Review* **6**, 453–470.
Mangla, P. B. (1976). Library science faculty. *Indian Librarian* **31**, 80–84.
Mangla, P. B. (1977). "Master's Course in Library and Information Science." (Paper presented at the Seminar on Library and Information Science Education in India, University of Delhi, Delhi, October 3–8, 1977) (Mimeograph copy.)
Mangla, P. B. (1978). Levels of training in library and information science: Admission requirements and duration. *Library Science with a Slant to Documentation* **15**, 125–131.
Mangla, P. B., ed. (in press). "Library and Information Science Education in India: Papers and Recommendations of an all-India Seminar held at the University of Delhi, Department of Library Science, October 3–8, 1977." Macmillan, New Delhi.
Mangla, P. B., and Sardana, J. L. (1970). Development of university and college libraries in India during the 4th Five-Year Plan: Suggestions. *Indian Library Association Bulletin* **6**, 109–134.
Mangla, P. B., and Vashishtha, C. P. (1976). Library and information science education in India. *Journal of Library & Information Science* **1**, 127–160.

Meeting of the Supervisors of Library and Documentation Schools in the Asian Region (Bangalore) (1976). "Library and Information Manpower Development in the Asian Region: Report." DRTC, Bangalore.

Mirza, Q. (1972). Some reflections on the new education policy and libraries. *Pakistan Library Bulletin* **5**, 7–10.

Moid, A. (1966). Library education and training in Pakistan. *In* "Library Education and Training in Developing Countries" (G. S. Bonn, ed.), pp. 81–95. East–West Centre Press, Honolulu.

Neelameghan, A. (1974). Education for librarians and documentalists in India. *In* "Encyclopedia of Library and Information Science," Vol. 11, pp. 312–349. Dekker, New York.

Neelameghan, A. (1977). "Integrated Course for Master's Degree in Library and Information Science: Design Considerations." (Paper presented at the Seminar on Library and Information Science Education in India, University of Delhi, Delhi, October 3–8, 1977). (Mimeograph copy.)

"Pakistan Yearbook, 1974" (1975). East & West Publishing Corporation, Karachi.

Ranganathan, S. R. (1973). Productivity in library education. *Herald of Library Science* **12**, 1–8.

Ranganathan, S. R. (1966). Vitalizing the university education for librarians. *Library Science with a Slant to Documentation* **3**, 293–315.

Seminar on Library and Information Science Education in India (Delhi) (1977). "Papers and Recommendations." University of Delhi, Department of Library Science, Delhi. (Unpublished report.)

Seminar on Library and Manpower Development: National, Regional and International Aspects (Bangalore) (1976). "Papers and Recommendations." DRTC, Bangalore.

Seminar on the Teaching of Library Science (Delhi) (1966). "Papers and Recommendations." University of Delhi, Department of Library Science, Delhi. (Unpublished report.)

Statesman's Yearbook: "Statistical and Historical Annual of the States of the World for the Year 1978–79" (1979). Macmillan, London.

University Grants Commission (UGC) (India), Review Committee (1965). "Library Science in Indian Universities." UGC, New Delhi.

University of Delhi, Department of Library Science (1978). "Prospectus: 1978–79." Delhi.

University of Madras (1979) "Regulations for Master of Library and Information Science." Madras.

Workshop on the Methods of Teaching and Evaluation in Library Science (Delhi) (1973). "Papers and Recommendations." University of Delhi, Department of Library Science, Delhi. (Unpublished report)

Subject Index

A

Academic library management studies, status quo and, 39–43
Access points, *AACR 2* and, 16
Allocations, collection development and, 120–123
Anglo-American Cataloguing Rules 2
  assumptions—tenets—attitudes
    direct and collocative functions, 24–26
    explicit statement of principles, 18–19
    provision of options, 21–23
    recognition of user needs, 19–21
  content of catalog codes, 4
    access points, 16
    authorship principle, 5–10
    choice of main entry, 14–16
    description, 17–18
    form of heading for corporate bodies, 11–14
    form of heading for persons bodies, 10–11
  external influences
    international agreement, 28
    technology, 26–27
  future of
    bibliographic milieu, 28–31
    implementation and influence of the code, 31–36
Authorship principle, *AACR 2* and, 5–10
Automated data in budget formulation, 107

B

Bangladesh, library education in, 229–234
Beyesian model, individual decision theory and, 174–183
Bibliographic instruction
  assumptions and rationales, 66–68
  educational environment and,
    measures of library proficiency, 71–72
    perceptions and commitment, 68–69
    precondition, proficiencies and predictions, 69–71
  evaluation and research,
    design and assessment, 72–73
    research: gospel or gossamer, 74–75
  instructional patterns
    externally stimulated and self-regulated instruction, 78–79
    levels of instruction, 76–78
    mediated and computer-assisted learning, 79–80
    organizational setting, 76
  literature reviews and bibliographies, 64–66
Bibliographic milieu, future of *AACR 2* and, 28–31
Blanket order arrangement, collection development and, 127–128
Budgets, limited, effects on collection development, 116–117
Budget format, 102–103
Budget formulation and presentation
  arguments for increasing materials funding, 113–114

241

Budget formulation and presentation (cont.)
  budget format, 102–103
  budgeting cycle, 101–102
  budget presentation, 110–111
  communication process, 103–104
  documentation, 104–105
  faculty participation, 112
  library as funding priority, 112
  Materials budget for 1978–1979, 113
  meeting university guidelines, 111–112
  participants, 102
  rationale for modifying a request, 114–116
  sources of funding, 105–106
  staff participation, 110
  uses of automated data, 107
  use of national indexes and local data, 108–109
Budgeting cycle, 101–102
Budgeting literature, library materials and, 91–96
Budget presentation, 110–111

C

Collection development and materials budget
  allocations, 120–123
  blanket order arrangement, 127–128
  conclusions, 129–131
  duplication and, 123–124
  economic conditions and, 118
  effects of limited budgets on, 116–117
  foreign materials, 126–127
  increases in twelve libraries, 119–120
  mechanics of spending materials fund, 128–129
  methods of reducing expenditures, 123
  microforms, 126
  priority of materials budget, 117–118
  responses to economic conditions, 118–119
  selectivity and patterns of purchasing, 124–125
  serials, 125–126
  serials review, 124
Collection use studies, management challenges to status quo and, 57–59
Collocative functions, of AACR 2, 24–26
Communication process in budget formulation, 103–104

Cooperation, interlibrary, 138–139
Corporate bodies, form of heading for, 11–14

D

Description, *AACR 2* and, 17–18
Direct functions, of *AACR 2*, 24–26
Documentation in budget formulation, 104–105
Duplication, collection development and, 123–124

E

Economic conditions, increased materials budgets and, 118
Educational environment, bibliographic instruction and, 68–72
Environment, budgeting process and, 96–97
  effects of environment, 100–101
  library materials budgeting constraints, 98–99
  university budgeting constraints, 97–98
Expenditures, reduction of, 123

F

Faculty participation in budget formulation, 112
Financial implications, of interlibrary cooperation, 137
Foreign materials, collection development and, 126–127
Funding sources, 105–106

I

India, library education in, 195–219
Individual decision theory
  background literature, 156
  Baysian model, 174–183
  optimism and, 156–163
  subjective expected utility model, 163–174
Interlibrary cooperation and materials fund, 131–132
  cost reductions, 133

Subject Index   243

financial considerations, 137
interlibrary loans and, 138–139
mechanics of, 133–135
other cooperative measures, 138
political implications, 135–136
rationale for cooperation, 132
Interlibrary loans, materials budget and, 138–139
International agreement, influence on *AACR 2*, 28

L

Library as funding priority, 112
Library education in India, Pakistan and Bangladesh, 195–234
 brief historical background, 192–195
 scope of article, 191–192
 similarities and variations, 234–236
Library materials budgeting constraints, 98–99
Library materials budgeting literature, 91–96
Library proficiency, measures of, 71–72
Literature reviews, bibliographic instruction and, 64–66
Local data in budget formulation, 108–109

M

Management Review and Analysis Program and beyond
 management studies and change, 51–53
 methodology, 44–45
 origins, 43–44
  Pittsburgh study and the National Enquiry into Scholarly communication, 53–54
 results, 45–51
 use and value, 54–56
Materials budget
 economic conditions and, 118
 priority of, 117–118
Materials budget and collections development
 allocations and, 120–123
 blanket order arrangement, 127–128
 conclusions, 129–131
 duplication and, 123–124

economic conditions and, 118
effects of limited budgets on, 116–117
foreign materials, 126–127
increases in twelve libraries, 119–120
mechanics of spending materials fund, 128–129
methods of reducing expenditures, 123
microforms, 126
priority of materials budget, 117–118
responses to economic conditions, 118–119
selectivity and patterns of purchasing, 124–125
serials, 125–126
serials review, 124
Materials budgets for 1978–1979, 113
Materials fund, mechanics of spending, 128–129
Materials fund and interlibrary cooperation, 131–132
 cost reductions, 133
 financial considerations, 137
 interlibrary loans and, 138–139
 mechanics of, 133–135
 other cooperative measures, 138
 political implications, 135–136
 rationale for cooperation, 132
Materials funding, arguments for increasing, 113–114
Microforms, collection development and, 126

N

National Enquiry into Scholarly Communication, MRAP and, 53–54
National indexes in budget formulation, 108–109

O

Optimism, individual decision theory and, 156–163
Options, provision of, by *AACR2*, 21–23

P

Pakistan, library education in, 219–229
Persons, form of heading for, 10–11

Pittsburgh study, MRAP and, 53–54
Political implications, of interlibrary cooperation, 135–136
Principles, of *AACR2*, explicit statement of, 18–19
Purchasing, selectivity and patterns of, 124–125

S

Serials, 125–126
 review of, 124
Staff participation in budget formulation, 110

Sujective expected utility model, individual decision theory and, 163–174

T

Technology, influence on *AACR 2*, 26–27

U

University, budgeting constraints of, 97–98
University guidelines in budget formulation, 111–112
User needs, recognition of by *AACR 2*, 19–21

Cumulative Subject Index Volumes 1-10

A

Abilene Christian College Library, **3**, 120, 123, 126, 127
Abridged Index Medicus, **2**, 50, 69, 81
Abstracting services, **2**, 13; **5**, 4-5, 10-11
Abstracts of Mycology, **2**, 73
Academic environment, **8**, 10
Academic institution, **8**, 293-303
Academic libraries, **8**, 9, 93, 184-187
Academic library management studies, **10**, 39-43
Access points, *AACR 2* and, **10**, 16
Access to information, **2**, 1-38; **5**, 1-52
Acquisition(s), **1**, 37-55; **2**, 18-22, 26; **5**, 125-127, 134-135
Acquisition environment, **8**, 12-20
Added entries, **1**, 12-13, 19
Administration, **6**, 253-274
Adult education, **2**, 271; **3**, 67-68; **5**, 245
Adult Education Association, **8**, 255
Adult Functional Competency, **8**, 260
Adult learning, **8**, 256-258
Advisory Council of Library Education in New Jersey, **8**, 310
Aerospace Research Applications Center, **4**, 28
Affirmative action, **8**, 81-128
Affirmative Action and Equal Employment: A Guidebook for Employees, **8**, 105
Affirmative Action Plan Development, **8**, 103-112
Africa, **1**, 249-251, 254-255; **2**, 330
Age Discrimination in Employment Act, **8**, 85

Aggression, **6**, 167-172
Agricultural-Biomedical Literature Exploitation, **2**, 58
Agricultural Information and Documentation Service Netherlands, **5**, 26
Agriculture Library Network, **5**, 33-35
Agricultural Sciences Information Network, **2**, 58
Agriculture, **5**, 32-35
Air-conditioning, **3**, 111
Akron University, **3**, 251
Akwesasne Library-Culture Center, **8**, 157-159
Alaska, **5**, 222
Alaska University, **3**, 91
Alberta University, **8**, 204, 214
Albuquerque Model Cities Library, **3**, 24
Alcoholism and Drug Rehabilitation Program, **8**, 161
Allocations, collection development and, **10**, 120-123
Amarillo College Library, **3**, 66
American, **see also** National *and* U.S.
American Academy of Arts and Sciences, **7**, 193
American Archivist, **3**, 246, 250, 264
American Association for the Advancement of Science, **4**, 122
American Association of Community and Junior Colleges, **5**, 242
American Association of Junior Colleges, **3**, 33-34, 37, 44, 48, 51-58, 61, 64
American Association of Law Libraries, **4**, 108; **8**, 276, 278, 288-289

American Association of Library Schools, **5**, 175; **8**, 284
American Association of School Librarians, **1**, 141–144, 146–147, 162, 163; **5**, 241
American Association of School Libraries, **6**, 13–15, 20–23
American Association of State and Local History, **3**, 258–259, 262–263
American Bar Association, **4**, 122
American Bibliography of Agricultural Economics, **2**, 59
American Copyright League, **2**, 319
American Council on Education, **3**, 48; **5**, 142
American Documentation Institute, **2**, 184
American Federation of Teachers, **4**, 122, 131
American Historical Association, **3**, 258, 269
American Hospital Formulary Service, **2**, 78
American Indian, **8**, 145–146, 167
American Indian Center, **8**, 143
American Indian Historical Society, **8**, 147
American Indian Law Newsletter, **8**, 146
American Indian Libraries Newsletter, **8**, 167
American Indian Library Service, **8**, 135–174
American Indian library technical assistants, **8**, 102
American Indian Policy Review Commission, **8**, 169
American Institute of Physics, **3**, 251
American librarianship, **8**, 90–94
American Libraries, **7**, 161
American Library Association, **1**, 85, 98, 103, 108, 109, 209, 219–220; **2**, 113–114, 168–169, 175, 176, 200, 242, 247–249, 256–257; **3**, 7, 17, 25, 48, 50–59, 64, 70, 77, 84, 131, 169, 184–185, 197–203, 259, 269, 274; **4**, 4, 8, 78–79, 83–87, 90–98, 104, 107–108, 111, 117, 122–123, 125, 127, 131, 136, 137, 140–141, 149–150, 163, 164; **5**, 116, 119, 125–131, 141–142, 169, 172–173, 176, 177, 234–236, 239, 241, 244–246, 297; **6**, 14; **7**, 145–176; **8**, 63–65, 67, 88–90, 94, 97–100, 102, 126, 127, 147, 167–168, 191, 204, 257, 276, 279–282, 296, 306; **9**, 11–12
American library education, **8**, 243–255, 258–264
American library history, **8**, 181–195
American Library in Paris, **1**, 245
American Library Institute, **2**, 229
American Library Trustee Association, **2**, 239
American Medical Association, **2**, 78

American National Standards Institute, **2**, 158–159, 177; **3**, 189; **4**, 7; **5**, 116
American Political Science Association, **4**, 122
American Psychological Association, **2**, 83–84; **3**, 251–252
American Services Technical Information Agency, **7**, 6–7, 47
American Society for Information Science, **4**, 29; **5**, 19, 297; **7**, 268; **8**, 288
American Society for Metals, **5**, 5
American Society for Testing Materials, **2**, 159
American Society of Hospital Pharmacists, **2**, 78
American Sociological Association, **4**, 122
American Standards Association, **1**, 99
American Telephone and Telegraph Company, **5**, 27–28
American University, **3**, 270, 274
Amherst College Library, **3**, 120, 128, 130, 131
Andrés Bello Convenio, **5**, 6, 66, 81–82
Anglo-American Cataloging Rules, **2**, 123; **3**, 167–190, 239, 259, 262–263; **4**, 8; **5**, 309
Anglo-American Cataloguing Rules 2, **10**, 4–36
Anglo-American Conference on the Mechanization of Library Services, **3**, 187
Ann Arbor Public Library, **3**, 204–207
Approval book acquisition programs, **1**, 51
Archives, **3**, 245–275
Archivists, **3**, 268–275
Area programs, **5**, 136–137
Area Program for Enrichment Exchange, **1**, 155
Arizona, **8**, 161–162, 166
Arizona Department of Libraries and Archives, **8**, 143
Arizona State University, **3**, 120; **8**, 102, 166
Art, **7**, 182, 215–216
Art Research Libraries of Ohio, **2**, 20
ASEAN program, **5**, 6
Asian American Librarians Caucus, **8**, 88
Associación Nacional de Bibliotecarios, **5**, 83
Associated Colleges of the Midwest, **5**, 325
Association des Bibliothecaires Suisses, **5**, 95
Association for Educational Communications and Technology, **3**, 54–56; **5**, 218–219, 242, 298
Association for Recorded Sound Collections, **2**, 285; **5**, 286, 298, 300, 302–304, 313
Association of American Library Schools, **7**, 166; **8**, 191, 269, 276, 296, 299

Association of Assistant Librarians, **6**, 221
Association of College and Reference Libraries, **3**, 49–50
Association of College and Research Libraries, **3**, 47–56, 64, 76, 85, 262; **4**, 122; **5**, 242; **8**, 90, 95
Association of Educational Communications and Technology, **6**, 15; **8**, 262
Association of Hospital and Institution Libraries, **1**, 178
Association of International Libraries, **5**, 27
Association of Jewish Libraries, **8**, 276
Association of New York Libraries for Technical Processes, **2**, 11
Association of Research Libraries, **2**, 12, 18–19, 168, 172, 175, 180; **4**, 116; **5**, 128, 130, 142–143; **6**, 27; **8**, 2, 4, 105, 108
Association of Scientific Information Dissemination Centers, **4**, 29
Association of Southeastern Research Libraries, **4**, 14
Association of State, County and Municipal Employees, **4**, 131
Association of Universities and Colleges of Canada, **5**, 73
Association Suisse de Documentation, **5**, 95
Atlanta University, **5**, 327–328, 338, 342–343, 346, 350
Atlanta University Affiliation, **5**, 327–328, 342
Atlanta University Center, **5**, 323, 328, 342–343, 346, 348, 350, 380
Atlantic Provinces Library Association, **8**, 232
Atomindex, **5**, 24
Attitude, **6**, 176–193
Auckland, New Zealand Public Library, **5**, 86
Audio-Visual materials, **1**, 133–156; **2**, 86–88; **3**, 8, 22, 72, 90–91, 124–125; **5**, 206–207, 214–215, 231–246, 249–277
Audiovisual services, **5**, 231–246
Austin Peay State College Library, **3**, 121, 131
Australian Advisory Council on Bibliographic Services, **5**, 67–68
Australian Libraries, **5**, 67–69, 86
Australian library services, **9**, 258–284
Australian National Bibliography, **3**, 170
Author abstracting and indexing, **2**, 25
Authority files, **1**, 82; **3**, 241
Authors, **2**, 305–349
Authorship principle, *AACR 2* and, **10**, 5–10

Automated data in budget formulation, **10**, 107
Automatic Subject Citation Alert, **2**, 76; **4**, 28

B

Baker report, **2**, 31
Baldwin Wallace College Library, **3**, 121
Balliol College, **5**, 336
BALLOTS system, **8**, 35, 37
Baltimore County Public Library, **1**, 8
Baltimore Enoch Pratt Free Library, **2**, 257–258; **3**, 173; **4**, 81; **8**, 182, 188
Bancroft, Hubert Howe, **2**, 277
Bangladesh, library education in, **10**, 229–234
BASIC, **2**, 13
Beaver College Library, **3**, 121, 130
Behavioral criteria, **9**, 120–123
Beloit College Library, **3**, 120–121, 126
Bertalan, F. J., **3**, 61–62
Beverly Hills Unified School District, **1**, 153
Beysian model, individual decision theory and, **10**, 174–183
Bible, **2**, 218
Bibliographic Classification of Bliss, **7**, 60–62
Bibliographic control of archives and manuscripts, **3**, 253–268
Bibliographic control of microforms, **2**, 169–172
Bibliographic data base, **4**, 32–33
Bibliographic instruction, **10**, 64–80
Bibliographic milieu, **10**, 28–31
Bibliographic organization, **2**, 7, 10
Bibliographic records, **3**, 221–242; **4**, 1–18
Bibliographic searching, **5**, 134–135
Bibliography courses, **3**, 88–90
Bibliography of Agriculture, **2**, 37, 55–59
Bibliography of the History of Medicine, **2**, 84
Bibliometrics, **6**, 102–106
Biblioteca Benjamin Franklin, **1**, 245
Bibliotekstjänst, **5**, 94
Bibliothèque Nationale, **7**, 109
Bibliotherapy, **1**, 171–186; **6**, 193–199
Binary searches, **1**, 67–69
Binding records control, **2**, 141–145
Biological Abstracts, **2**, 13, 31, 72–73, 78
Biological Abstracts-Previews, **2**, 73; **4**, 33
Biological Sciences Information Services, **2**, 31, 72–73; **4**, 35; **5**, 39

Biomedical Communications Network, **2**, 54–57
Biomedical conference proceedings, **2**, 85
BioResearch Index, **2**, 73
Birmingham Libraries Cooperative Mechanisation Project, **4**, 9, 16
Birmingham University Library, **3**, 109
Black Caucus, **8**, 88, 94
Black librarians, **8**, 94
Black studies, **3**, 252
Blanket order arrangement, **10**, 127–128
Board of Education for Librarianship, **7**, 167
Boeing Scientific Research Laboratories Library, **1**, 9
Bolivia, **5**, 81–82
Book acquisitions, **1**, 37–55
Book catalogs, **1**, 2, 8–34
Book order files, **1**, 46, 48
Book order forms, **1**, 44
Book purchase funds, **1**, 45
Book Review Digest, **3**, 97, 101
Book Review Index, **3**, 97
Book Reviews in the Humanities, **3**, 97
Book selection in California, **2**, 243
Bookmobile services, **8**, 143
Bossier City Educational Resource Center, **1**, 142
Boston Atheneum, **4**, 124
Boston Public Library, **4**, 124
Boston University Library, **3**, 124
Bowling Green State University Library, **3**, 121–122, 131
Bradford Law, **6**, 103–104
Brain Information Service, **2**, 60
Brazil, **5**, 69–71
Brigham City Indian collection, **8**, 145
Brigham Young University, **3**, 124; **8**, 203, 209, 242
British, *see also* Great Britain, United Kingdom
British Columbia University, **2**, 135–136; **8**, 203, 209, 242
British Columbia University School of Librarianship, **3**, 169
British Council, **1**, 260–264
British Library Association, **4**, 122
British Museum, **3**, 170; **5**, 14, 98–100
British National Bibliography, **3**, 170, 180–181, 187, 189, 227; **4**, 5–9; **7**, 53
British Society of Metals, **5**, 4

British Standards Institution, **3**, 189
Bronx Community College Library, **3**, 66
Brookings Institution, **8**, 66
Brooklyn Community Coordinator Project, **2**, 255
Brooklyn Public Library, **4**, 86
Brown University Library, **3**, 120, 126, 129, 131
Browsing, **2**, 27
Bryn Mawr College Library, **3**, 127
Budgets, **1**, 221–222; **10**, 116–117
Budget allocation formulas, **8**, 15–16
Budget format, **10**, 102–103
Budget formulation and presentation, **10**, 101–116
Budgeting cycle, **10**, 101–102
Budgeting literature, **10**, 91–96
Budget presentation, **10**, 110–111
Bureau of Indian Affairs, **8**, 140, 144, 146, 161, 171, 173
Bureau of Libraries and Educational Technology, **8**, 267

C

California Association of School Librarians, **1**, 143–144
California Bureau of Audio-Visual and School Library Education, **6**, 16
California Commission for Accrediting Junior Colleges, **3**, 50
California Community College, **8**, 102
California Fair Employment Practices Commission, **8**, 115
California Institute of Technology Library, **3**, 122
California Library Association, **8**, 100–101
California State College Library, **2**, 115; **3**, 89–91, 120, 121; **4**, 151
California State Library, **8**, 101
California University School of Librarianship, **5**, 171, 243
California, University of, Irvine, **1**, 53
California University Libraries, **2**, 66–68, 77, 109–115, 124–134, 136–152, 155–156, 282–286; **3**, 56, 57, 77, 84, 92–104, 120–126, 129, 131, 173, 242, 274; **4**, 11–12, 15, 17, 36, 111, 117–119; **5**, 331–332, 338; **8**, 146, 293

Callison College, **5**, 332
Cambridge Language Research Unit, **7**, 30
Cambridge University, **5**, 323, 333–337, 348, 350, 352
Cameras, **1**, 2–3; **2**, 178–179
Canada, **2**, 17, 89, 238, 313; **3**, 170, 263–267; **8**, 202–204
Canada National Libraries, **4**, 16–17, 29, 48; **5**, 37, 71–74
Canadiana, **3**, 170
Canadian Association of College and University Libraries, **5**, 73; **8**, 232
Canadian Association of Library Schools, **8**, 231
Canadian Association of University Libraries, **8**, 205
Canadian culture, **8**, 201–204
Canadian Library Association, **3**, 184; **8**, 88, 208, 217, 222–224
Canadian library associations, **8**, 231–233
Canadian library education, **8**, 201–238
Canadian Selective Dissemination of Information Project, **4**, 36
Card catalogs, **1**, 4–8
Carlsbad Unified School District, **1**, 141
Carnegie Commission on Higher Education, **5**, 242
Carnegie Corporation, **1**, 248–251; **2**, 280, 281, 284; **3**, 34, 46, 61; **5**, 164, 175, 234; **7**, 158–159, 162, 166
Carnegie United Kingdom Trust, **6**, 221–222; **7**, 158–159, 168
Carrolton Press, **2**, 173
Cartridge teaching materials, **1**, 140–141
Case Institute of Technology, **5**, 330
Case studies, **6**, 147–148
Case Western Reserve University Libraries, **5**, 166, 171, 330–331
Catalog(s), **3**, 111, 179–184, 195–215, 221–242
Cataloging, **2**, 10–12, 16, 64–67, 123, 169–172; **3**, 167–190, 253–268; **4**, 1–18; **5**, 125–127, 134–135, 309–310; **6**, 66–74
Cataloging, Centralized, **1**, 105–106
Cataloging, Descriptive, **1**, 5
Cataloging-in-Publication program, **8**, 61–62
Catalogue & Index, **3**, 170, 185
Cathode-ray tubes, **1**, 33
Catholic University of America, **8**, 313, 315
Censorship, **2**, 215–249
Center for Research Libraries, **2**, 19–20; **3**, 123; **5**, 325; **8**, 34–35

Central Florida Junior College Library, **3**, 66
Centralized processing centers, **2**, 11; **5**, 138–139
Central Michigan University Library, **3**, 121, 128
Cerritos College Library, **3**, 66
Certification, **9**, 235–236
Ceylon libraries, **5**, 74–75
Chabot College Library, **3**, 124
Chain printers, **1**, 23
Chalmers Institute of Technology, **5**, 94
Chamberlayne College Library, **3**, 77
Chemical Abstracts, **2**, 13, 74–75; **4**, 29
Chemical Abstracts Condensates, **2**, 74; **4**, 33, 43; **5**, 121
Chemical Abstract Service, **2**, 13, 30–31, 74; **4**, 29, 35; **5**, 4, 6, 20–21, 36, 38–39
Chemical-Biological Activities, **2**, 13, 74, 78
Chemical literature, **4**, 157
Chemical Titles, **2**, 13, 27, 74
Chemistry information systems, **5**, 38–39
Chicago City Junior College Library, **3**, 66
Chicago Public Library, **2**, 19, 257–259, 271
Chicago Public Library, The, **8**, 188
Chicago University, **3**, 120, 125–128, 130, 131, 183–184, 197, 203, 213; **4**, 4; **5**, 125, 137–138, 171; **6**, 222; **7**, 167–168
Chief Officers of State Library Agencies, **8**, 311
Children's library services, **1**, 159–169; **3**, 1–10
Chile, **1**, 256; **5**, 81–82
Choice, **2**, 168; **3**, 62
Christian College Library, **3**, 66
Chronicle of Higher Education, **8**, 8, 11
Churchill College, **5**, 337
CIPP model, **8**, 266–267
Circulation, **4**, 63–71; **6**, 29–30, 43
Citation analysis, **7**, 299–335; **9**, 241–242
Citation indexing, **2**, 13, 75–76; **4**, 47–48
Civil rights, **4**, 83–85, 88–89
Civil Rights Act, **8**, 84, 118
Civil Service Commission, **8**, 84
Civil service systems, **8**, 116–117
Claremont College libraries, **5**, 323, 326–327, 339–340, 343–347, 349–352
Claremont Men's College, **5**, 326, 349–350
Claremont University Center, **5**, 326–327, 339–340, 343
Clark College, **5**, 328, 343, 350
Clark University Library, **3**, 121, 124
Classification, **2**, 64–65; **5**, 311–312; **7**, 41–103

Clearinghouses, **2**, 14–18
Clemson University Library, **3**, 121–122, 126, 128
CLENE Directory of Continuing Education Opportunities, **8**, 292, 297
CLENE Institute for State Library Agency Personnel Responsible for Continuing Education, **8**, 267
Clerk, **9**, 76–81
Cleveland Indian Center, **8**, 143
Cleveland Public Library, **8**, 182
COBOL, **1**, 47, 52; **3**, 227; **4**, 5
Code International de Catalogage de la Musique, **3**, 188
CODEN, **2**, 159
Code of Professional Ethics, **9**, 11–12
Cognition, **4**, 177
Collaborative Library System Development, **4**, 16
Collation, **1**, 112
Collection control, **9**, 239–243
Collection development, **7**, 299–335; **8**, 1–40
Collection development and materials budget, **10**, 116–129
Collection use studies, **10**, 57–59
Collective bargaining, **8**, 117–119
College & Research Libraries, **4**, 123
College and Research Libraries News, **8**, 37, 187, 194
College and Seminary Library, **5**, 324–325, 340, 344, 347, 349
College and university libraries, **1**, 113–131, 263–264; **3**, 107–117, 119–131; **4**, 149–169; **5**, 338–348, 351–352; **6**, 25–27, 54–75, 227
College of Librarianship, **6**, 233
College of Library Studies, **6**, 233
College of Physicians of Philadelphia Library, **2**, 68–69
Collocative functions of *AACR 2,* **10**, 24–26
Colombia, **5**, 81–82
Colon Classification, **7**, 62–65
Colorado Academic Libraries Book Processing Center, **2**, 11
Colorado Division of State Archives, **3**, 270
Colorado River Tribes Public Library, **8**, 143
Colorado State University Library, **3**, 128
Colorado University libraries, **3**, 124, 126
COLT Directory, **8**, 289
Columbia University, **2**, 62, 276–283, 286–288, 291, 294–298; **3**, 120, 270; **4**, 126; **5**, 138, 142, 169, 171; **7**, 166; **8**, 101, 107

Comic books, **7**, 179
Commission on Civil Rights, **8**, 118
Commission on Intructional Technology, **5**, 245; **8**, 258
Commission on Junior College Terminal Education, **3**, 34
Committee for International Cooperation in Information Retrieval among Examining Patent Offices, **5**, 26
Committee on Accreditation, **8**, 99
Committee on Institutional Cooperation, **5**, 163
Committee on National Library Information Systems, **2**, 5, 32–33
Committee on Scientific and Technical Information, **2**, 25–26, 32–33, 36; **7**, 7
Committee on the Status of Women in Librarianship, **8**, 88
Communication, **1**, 180–181; **5**, 207–210; **6**, 82, 87–89, 91–94, 139–202; **7**, 181–182; **9**, 227–228
Communication process in budget formulation, **10**, 103–104
Community antenna television, **5**, 215–224, 239
Community colleges, **3**, 29–77
Community projects, **3**, 9
Comprehensive Employment and Training Act, **8**, 112–113
Computer(s), **2**, 103–161, 210; **3**, 124–125, 221–242; **4**, 8, 63–71; **5**, 137, 140, 141
Computerized Agricultural Research Information System, **5**, 34
Computerized Engineering Index, **4**, 33, 43; **5**, 20
Computer-produced catalogs, **1**, 3–4, 8–27 30, 32–34, 59–94
Computers collating sequences, **1**, 60–62, 68
Computers in acquisition, **1**, 37–55
Computers in cataloging, **1**, 1–34
Computers in school libraries, **1**, 151, 154, 165–166
Computers off line, **1**, 42, 44–49
Computers on line, **1**, 42, 49–53, 92–94
Conference of Librarians, **4**, 127
Conference on Student use of Libraries, **1**, 162
Conference on the Use of Computers in Medical Education, **2**, 65–66
Congress for Change, **4**, 93
Connecticut, **2**, 191
Conservation, **8**, 30–32

Conservative Library Association, **2**, 239
Content analysis, **6**, 148, 189–190
Context evaluation, **8**, 266
Contingency approach, **9**, 131–132
Continuing competence, **8**, 247–250
Continuing education, **8**, 241–323
Cooper, Alice, **7**, 178
Cooperation, **1**, 189–205, 230–232
Cooperation, interlibrary, **10**, 138–139
Cooperation cataloging, **2**, 10–12
Cooperative programs, **8**, 32–37
Copyright, **2**, 305–349
Cornell University, **1**, 49; **4**, 151
Corporate bodies, **10**, 11–14
Cost-benefit analysis, **9**, 125–126
Cost studies, **1**, 95–110
Council for Mutual Economic Assistance, **5**, 5–6, 28–30
Council for National Academic Awards, **6**, 224
Council on Biological Sciences Information, **2**, 31
Council on Library Resources, **1**, 253–254; **3**, 54, 56, 258, 266, 271; **4**, 2, 14, 163–164; **5**, 66; **8**, 20
Council on Library Technical Assistants, **5**, 169; **8**, 120, 289
Council on Library Technology, **5**, 168–169; **8**, 289
County libraries, **1**, 191–193
County library systems, **1**, 193
Courses, **9**, 236–237
Coxe, H. O., **7**, 151
Cranfield Project, **6**, 98
Crawford report, **2**, 31
Cumulative Book Index, **3**, 170
Current Bibliography on Science & Technology, **2**, 184
Current Contents, **2**, 76; **4**, 36
Current List of Medical Literature, **2**, 49
Current literature alerting search services, **2**, 73
Cuyahoga Community College Library, **3**, 66
Cybernetics, **6**, 113–114

D

Dalhousie University, **8**, 203, 224–225
Dana, John Cotton, **7**, 154
Danish Library Association, **5**, 76; **6**, 249
Data banks, **1**, 54
Data base, **9**, 229–232

Data base for serials, **2**, 12–13
Data conversion to machine form, **3**, 221–242
Dayton and Montgomery County Public Library, **8**, 107
Decision making in libraries, **1**, 214; **6**, 273–278; **9**, 154–174
Deganawidah-Quetzalcoatl University, **8**, 146
Degrees conferred, **8**, 11
Delaware University Library, **3**, 121
Delta College Library, **3**, 66
Demand, **9**, 50–53
Denmark, **2**, 310; **5**, 75–76
Denmark National Technological Library, **4**, 48
Denver University, **5**, 221, 224
Denver University courses for archivists, **3**, 270, 274
Denver University Library, **2**, 130; **4**, 153
Departmental libraries, **9**, 242–243
Deprivation, **3**, 2–3
Derwent, **4**, 49
Description, *AACR2* and, **10**, 17–18
Detroit Institute of Arts, **3**, 253
Detroit Public Library, **3**, 248; **8**, 182, 188
Developing countries, **2**, 306–307, 328–329, 333–345
Developing country libraries, **1**, 241–281
Dewey Decimal Classification, **7**, 51–53, 60; **8**, 62, 190
Dewey, Melvil, **7**, 149, 151, 152, 165–166, 170
Diabetes Literature, **2**, 76
Dial access information systems, **1**, 151–154; **3**, 124
Dial-Access Library, **2**, 86–87
DIALOG, **5**, 20
Dictionary of American Biography, **3**, 257
Dime novels, **2**, 226–227
Direct Access to Reference Information, **4**, 33
Direct functions of *AACR2,* **10**, 24–26
Disadvantaged, **2**, 253–273; **3**, 1–10
District of Columbia Library, **8**, 107
Divided catalogs, **1**, 15–16
Document delivery, **9**, 214–218
Documentation Center, **5**, 37
Documentation in budget formulation, **10**, 104–105
Documentation Research and Training Center, **7**, 65
Domain of Instructional Technology, **8**, 262
Domestic publications, **8**, 21–22
Dougherty Report, **5**, 129–131, 136, 141, 144
Dow Chemical Company, **4**, 29

Drug information, **2**, 77–79
Drug Information Association, **2**, 77
Duke University, **3**, 123, 128; **8**, 107
Du Page College Library, **3**, 66
Duplication, **8**, 28
Duplication in collection development, **10**, 123–124
DuVal Report, **2**, 48

E

Earlham College Library, **3**, 89
East African Academy, **5**, 6
East Anglia University Library, **3**, 116
Eastern Washington State College Library, **3**, 124
Eastman Kodak Company, **2**, 175; **4**, 29
Economic Commission for Latin America, **5**, 6
Economic conditions, **10**, 118
Ecuador, **5**, 81–82
Edinburgh University Library, **3**, 116
Education, **5**, 32–33; **6**, 11, 243–245
Educational environment, **10**, 68–72
Education Amendments, **8**, 244
Education of State Library Personnel, **8**, 307
Education for librarianship, **1**, 220, 250, 252–254
Educational communications, **5**, 203–228
Educational programs, **8**, 88–90
Educational technology, **5**, 203–228
EDUNET, **2**, 30
Edwards, Edward, **7**, 149
Efficiency, **9**, 108
Elbert Covel College, **5**, 332
El Camino College Library, **3**, 66
El Centro College Library, **3**, 65
El Centro College of the Dallas Junior College District, **1**, 9, 27
Electronic Components Data bank, **5**, 20
Emory University Library, **3**, 122, 126, 127, 130, 131
Employment, **8**, 90–97
Employment procedures, **8**, 124–126
Encyclopedia Britannica, **2**, 171–172, 179
Engineering Index, **2**, 13, 27; **4**, 35; **7**, 16
Engineers Joint Council, **2**, 31
England, **2**, 309
Environment, **1**, 218–223; **10**, 96–101
Environmental criteria, **9**, 117–120

Epilepsy Abstracts, **2**, 61
Equal employment opportunity, **8**, 82, 113–114
Equal Employment Opportunity Coordinating Council, **8**, 119
Equal Employment Opportunity Guidelines, **8**, 98–99, 103, 105–106, 108, 263
Equal Pay Act, **8**, 84
Erotic stimuli, **6**, 159–165
Essex University Library, **3**, 116
Ethnic cultures and library materials, **3**, 5, 8
Ethnicity, **3**, 4–5
European Atomic Energy Community, **5**, 18, 19, 22–23, 32
European Bureau of Adult Education, **5**, 33
European Coal and Steel Community, **5**, 22
European Documentation and Information System for Education, **5**, 32–33, 46
European Economic Community, **5**, 22; **6**, 245–247
European Nuclear Documentation Service, **5**, 18–23
European Scientific and Technical Information and Documentation Networks, **5**, 46
European Scientific Information Dissemination Centers, **4**, 29; **5**, 21
European Space Research Organization, **5**, 18–22, 36, 46
European Translations Center, **2**, 17
European Vehicle Launcher Development Organization, **5**, 20
Evaluation of Adult Basic Education: How and Why?, **8**, 268
Evangelical Theological Seminary, **5**, 324–325, 340, 349
Everett Junior College Library, **3**, 66
Exchanges, **8**, 27–28
Exerpta Medica, **4**, 33; **5**, 36, 39
Excerpta Medica Foundation, **2**, 61, 70–72
Exchange system, **9**, 33–37
Exeter University Library, **3**, 109, 116
Expanded Journals Project, **8**, 34
Expenditures, reduction of, **10**, 123

F

Facsimile transmission, **2**, 22–23
Facts on File, **2**, 173

Faculty participation in budget formulation, **10**, 112
Faculty status, **9**, 244–245
Fairmount Heights High John Library, **5**, 166
Farmington Plan, **2**, 18–19; **5**, 138–139; **8**, 6
Farmington Plan Newsletter, **8**, 33
Fashion Institute of Technology Library, **3**, 66
Fast Access Information Retrieval, **2**, 90
Federal aid to libraries, **1**, 231–232; **3**, 137–165
Federal library funding, **3**, 141, 142, 144; **8**, 9
Federal government, **8**, 311–314
Federal Library Committee, **8**, 313
Federal Register, **8**, 114
Fédération Internationale de Phonothèques, **5**, 299
File conversion, **2**, 118
Filing, **1**, 59–94
Filing rules, **1**, 65–66, 85, 87–89, 92–94
Films, **5**, 234–236, 254–255, 266–272
Filmstrips, **5**, 255–257
Financial implications of interlibrary cooperation, **10**, 137
Findlay College Library, **3**, 121
Finland, **5**, 77–78
Finnish Association for Documentation, **5**, 78
Finnish Library Association, **5**, 78; **6**, 249
First Amendment, **9**, 4–10
Five Associated University Libraries of New York State, **4**, 14
Florida Atlantic University Library, **1**, 10, 87–88; **2**, 66, 110, 131
Florida Southern College Library, **3**, 121
Florida State Library, **8**, 312
Food and Agriculture Organization, **5**, 7, 34–35, 46
Food Science and Technology Abstracts, **4**, 33
Forbes Library, **5**, 325
Ford Foundation, **1**, 253–256; **2**, 256, 280; **5**, 219
Ford Motor Company, **2**, 282
Foreign acquisitions, **8**, 4–5
Foreign Acquisitions Newsletter, **8**, 33
Foreign materials in collection development **10**, 126–127
Foreign Newspaper Microfilm Project, **2**, 175
Forest Press, **7**, 51–53
Format recognition, **3**, 237–242
FORTRAN, **1**, 52; **3**, 227; **4**, 5
Foundations, **1**, 247–256

France, **2**, 310, 317; **5**, 102
Freedom to Read Foundation, **2**, 241–242
Fullerton Junior College Library, **3**, 65
Fund for Adult Education, **5**, 239
Funding sources, **10**, 105–106
Funding variations, **8**, 9, 28–29

G

Ganado College, **8**, 161–162
Gatekeepers, **7**, 275–279
Gathings Committee, **2**, 234–235
General Electric Company, **2**, 282
General Electric vs. Gilbert, **8**, 114
General Telephone and Electronics, **4**, 49
Geological Archives, **4**, 33
Geological Reference File, **4**, 33
Geophysical Abstracts, **4**, 35
George Peabody College, **5**, 324, 340, 344, 349, 351
Georgetown University Library, **3**, 131
Georgia Institute of Technology Library, **3**, 128
Georgia University, **3**, 120, 121, 131; **4**, 29
German Foundation for Developing Countries, **5**, 7
Germany, **2**, 310
Gifts, **8**, 26–27
Gilman, Daniel Coit, **7**, 149
Glasgow University Library, **3**, 116
Goal achievement, **9**, 107–108
Goal model, **9**, 111–117
Government document depositories, **2**, 36
Government Reports Announcements, **4**, 33
Graduate Theological Union, **5**, 327, 339, 344–349
Grant, Seth Hastings, **7**, 149
Graphic arts composing equipment, **1**, 23
Graphic Arts Composing Equipment, **2**, 50
Great Britain, *see also* British, United Kingdom
Great Britain, **2**, 17, 313, 318
Great Depression, **8**, 190
Great Lakes International Council, **8**, 165
Great Society Program, **2**, 254–255; **8**, 143
Greece, **2**, 218–220
Grossmont College Library, **3**, 66
Group therapy, **1**, 174–175
Growth, **9**, 249–250
Guelph University Library, **3**, 120, 127, 130

Guidelines for the Training of Library Technicians, **8,** 217–218
Guide to Microfilms in Print, **2,** 172
Guild, Reuben, **7,** 149
Gulf Coast Junior College Library, **3,** 66

H

H. W. Wilson Foundation, Inc., **5,** 148, 153–154, 176
Haifa University, **5,** 81
Hamilton College, **4,** 157
Hampshire Inter-Library Center, **2,** 21; **5,** 325
Handbook of Medical Library Practice, **2,** 48
Hardin-Simmons University Library, **3,** 120
Harvard University, **1,** 8, 85–86, 114, 115, 122; **2,** 67, 175; **3,** 121, 125, 242; **8,** 65–66
Harvey Mudd College, **5,** 326, 349–351
Hawaii University, **1,** 40
Health and Rehabilitation Services Division, **8,** 99
Hebrew University, **5,** 80–81
Helsinki University Library, **5,** 78
Henry Ford Community College Library, **3,** 66
Herman Miller Company, **3,** 126–127
Higher education, **8,** 8
Higher Education Guidelines: Executive Order 11246, **8,** 105
Hines, Theodore, **1,** 89
Historical Abstracts, **4,** 33
Historical societies, **3,** 248–250
History of Science Society, **3,** 251
Hofstra University Library, **3,** 122
Holley, Edward G., **7,** 150
Honduras, **5,** 79
Hoover commissions, **2,** 192
Hospital librarians, **1,** 178
Hospital libraries, **1,** 171–186; **2,** 79–81
Hou Kola, **8,** 155
House Labor-HEW Appropriations Committee, **8,** 101
Hull University Library, **3,** 116
Human Relations Area Files, **5,** 312
Huntsville Public Library, **5,** 221

I

Integrated Scientific Information System, **5,** 26–27

Idaho University Library, **3,** 121
Illinois Annual Conference on Junior College Libraries, **3,** 57–58
Illinois Association of School Librarians, **1,** 144–146
Illinois Central College Library, **3,** 65
Illinois Minorities Manpower Project, **8,** 100
Illinois State Library, **8,** 100
Illinois Technical Research Institute, **4,** 29; **5,** 329, 342, 346, 348
Illinois University, **2,** 66, 110, 131; **3,** 120, 121, 123, 254, 270, 274; **4,** 156; **5,** 113, 164–165, 171, 176
Image Transmission Conference, **2,** 177
Images Enterprises, Inc., **2,** 179
Imprint, **1,** 12
Income distribution, **3,** 2
Index Medicus, **2,** 48–52, 64, 69–70, 75; **5,** 36
Index to Dental Literature, **2,** 50
Indexing, **2,** 13–14, 172–173; **4,** 47
India, **2,** 19, 306; **10,** 195–219
Indian Americans, **8,** 137–142
Indiana University, **3,** 120, 123–124, 126, 128–131; **5,** 312; **8,** 24, 40
Indian Historian Press, **8,** 147
Indian Technical Assistance Center, **8,** 165
Individual decision theory, **10,** 156–183
Inferential statistics, **6,** 38–39
Information, **2,** 1–38, 45–92, 265, 270; **3,** 25–26; **4,** 25–52, 175–228, 198–225; **5,** 1–52, 280–281; **6,** 80–135, 183–185
Information broker, **7,** 283–286
Information Center for Hearing, Speech and Diseases of Communication, **2,** 60
Information Center for Vision and Diseases of the Eye, **2,** 60
Information industry, **9,** 44–45
Information Industry Association, **2,** 37; **5,** 4
Information libraries, **1,** 261, 266
Information Médicale Automatisée, **5,** 37
Information policy, **9,** 45–46
Information retrieval, **7,** 1–103, 299–335
Information Service for Physics, Electro-Technology Computers and Control, **4,** 33, 46, 48; **5,** 6, 20, 36, 39
Information transfer, **7,** 257–291
Information Transfer Experiments, **2,** 28
Inner cities, **2,** 258–273
Innovators, **7,** 271
Input evaluation, **8,** 266

Institute for Scientific Information, **2**, 27, 76, 78; **4**, 28, 37, 40, 49
Institute of Electrical and Electronics Engineers, **5**, 5
Institute of Electrical and Electronic Engineers Retrieval from the Literature on Electronics and Computer Sciences, **4**, 35
Institute of Food Technology, **5**, 26
Institute of Medical Research, **5**, 37
Institute of Professional Librarians of Ontario, **8**, 227–229
Institut für Documentationswesen, **5**, 26
Institution librarians, **1**, 178
Institution libraries, **1**, 171–186
Institution of Electrical Engineers, **5**, 5
Institut National de Recherche et de Documentation Pédagogiques, **5**, 33
Instituto Nacional do Livro, **5**, 70
Instruction, **5**, 259–260
Instructional materials centers, **1**, 135–156, 162; **3**, 68–69, 72–73; **5**, 204–205
Instructional methods, **3**, 45; **4**, 160–162
Instruction in library use, **3**, 83–104; **4**, 149–169
Intellectual Freedom, **2**, 215–249; **4**, 82–83; **9**, 27–28
Interdenominational Theological Center, **5**, 328
Interlibrary cooperation and materials fund, **10**, 131–139
Interlibrary loan, **2**, 21–22, 61–64; **10**, 138–139
Intermountain Union List of Serials, **2**, 122
International agreements, **10**, 28
International Association of Music Libraries, **5**, 299
International Association of Sound Archives, **5**, 299, 303–304
International Association of Technological University Libraries, **5**, 7
International Atomic Energy Agency, **5**, 18, 23–24
International Book Year, **5**, 3
International Business Machines Corporation, **1**, 23; **2**, 160; **4**, 27–28, 49
International Center of Scientific and Technical Information, **5**, 28
International Classification: Journal on Theory and Practice of Universal and Special Classification Systems and Thesauri, **7**, 89–92

International Conference on Cataloging Principles, **3**, 187–189
International Conference on the Development of Documentation and Information Network in East Africa, **5**, 6–7
International Congresses and Conferences, **2**, 105
International Council of Scientific Unions, **5**, 7, 9–11, 41, 44
International Development Research Center, **5**, 7
International Documentation Network on Economic and Social Development, **5**, 33
International Encyclopedia of the Social Sciences, **4**, 138
International Federation for Documentation, **7**, 49, 81, 87–89
International Federation for Information Processing, **5**, 7
International Federation of Library Associations, **3**, 188; **4**, 7; **5**, 7, 27, 41, 103
International Federation of Professional Librarians of Ontario, **8**, 216
International Filmbook Corporation, **2**, 180
International Food Information Service, **5**, 26
International Information System for the Agricultural Sciences and Technology, **5**, 33–35, 46, 49
International information systems, **5**, 1–52
International Institute for Educational Planning, **5**, 65
International Labor Office, **5**, 26–27, 33
International library programs, **1**, 241–281
International Meeting of Cataloging Experts, **3**, 188
International Nuclear Information System, **4**, 33; **5**, 12, 14, 18–20, 23–24, 34, 46, 49
International Nursing Index, **2**, 180
International Organization for Standardization, **5**, 7, 11, 24, 41
International Patent Institute, **5**, 26
International Pharmaceutical Abstracts, **2**, 78
International Research Associates, **4**, 84
International School of Librarianship, **6**, 245
International Serials Data System, **5**, 30–32
International Standard Bibliographic Description, **4**, 9–11; **5**, 139
International Standard Book Number, **4**, 9–10
International Standard Serial Number, **4**, 9–10; **5**, 30–31

International Standards Organization, **1**, 99; **4**, 7
International System of Scientific and Technical Information, **5**, 28–30
Internships, **9**, 237–238
Interuniversity Communications Council, **2**, 30
Iowa Department of Public Instruction, **6**, 16
Iowa Drug Information Service, **2**, 79
Iowa University Library, **3**, 123, 126
Israel, **5**, 79–81
Italian Library Association, **6**, 228, 249

J

J. Morris Jones/World Book Encyclopedial ALA Goals Award, **3**, 58; **5**, 55
Jamaica, **1**, 261–263
Japan, **1**, 252–253, 279–280
Japan Information Center for Science and Technology, **2**, 184
Jast, Jouis S., **7**, 152
Jefferson library, **8**, 57
Jewett, Charles Coffin, **7**, 150
Jewish National and University Library, **5**, 80
Jobs in Instructional Media Study, **6**, 22–23; **8**, 262
Joeckel, Carlton B., **7**, 154
John Carroll University Library, **3**, 121, 130
John Crerar Library, **2**, 17, 19; **5**, 329, 342, 345–348; **7**, 316
Johns Hopkins University Library, **3**, 125, 126
Johnson-O'Malley Act, **8**, 155
Johnston College, **5**, 331–332
Joint Commission on Scientific and Technical Communication, **2**, 32
Jones, J. Winter, **7**, 151
Journal of Education for Librarianship, **8**, 286, 302
Journal of Librarianship, **7**, 161
Junior colleges, **3**, 29–77

K

Ka Ri Wen Ha Wi Newsletter, **8**, 158
Kansas City Junior College Library, **3**, 66
Karolinska Institutet, **4**, 29
Kent at Canterbury University Library, **3**, 109, 116

Kentucky University, **8**, 310
Keyword-in-context index, **2**, 13; **3**, 266
Knapp Foundation of North Carolina, Inc., **5**, 173
Kutztown State College Library, **3**, 121

L

Lafayette College Library, **3**, 121
Lakehead University, **8**, 218
Lakota Higher Education Center, **8**, 146
Lancaster University Library, **3**, 116; **6**, 26
Language, **4**, 170–180, 222–226
LARC Association, **2**, 115–116
Latin American Centre for Economic and Social Documentation, **5**, 6
Latin American Cooperative Acquisitions Project, **2**, 19; **8**, 33
Laval University Library, **2**, 131–132, 148; **3**, 173
Leadership, **6**, 266–272
Learning laboratories, **3**, 90–91
Learning resources, **3**, 68–69; **4**, 149–169
Lehigh University libraries, **3**, 121, 125
Leona Johnson Memorial Library, **8**, 159
Letter recognition, **4**, 184–197
Librarian(s), **2**, 203–207; **3**, 33; **4**, 77–99, 103–141; **5**, 147–179, 181–188, 244–245, 300–302; **6**, 217–249, 265–266; **7**, 145–176; **8**, 90–94, 96, 110, 241–323; **9**, 69–88, 238–239
Librarian(s) as planners, **1**, 219–221, 225–230
Librarian exchanges, **1**, 264
Librarian of Congress, **8**, 56
Librarianship, **2**, 48; **4**, 103–141; **6**, 236–238; **8**, 81–128, 219–222, 247–250; **9**, 64, 175–178, 186–207
Librarianship as a profession, **1**, 219–220
Librarianship philosophies of service, **1**, 160–162
Libraries, **1**, 207–238, 249, 254, 256, 261–263; **2**, 187–212; **3**, 4, 111–113; **4**, 77–99, 130–131; **5**, 107–120, 141–144, 321–352; **6**, 1–46, 54–55, 253–274; **7**, 41–103, 199–202, 216–224, 231–255, 299–335; **8**, 243; **9**, 40–41, 91–95, 107–127, 132–137, 144–154
Library Administration Division, **8**, 282
Library as funding priority, **10**, 112
Library Association, **2**, 223; **3**, 169, 170–171, 185–186; **6**, 219, 221, 223–225, 247–248; **7**, 145–176; **8**, 190–191

Library Association of Australia, **2**, 242-243; **3**, 173; **5**, 69
Library Association Record, **7**, 161
Library automation, **2**, 27-28; **4**, 1-18
Library Bibliographic Classification, **7**, 66-67
Library Bill of Rights, **2**, 231-232; **4**, 83; **9**, 10
Library budgets, **1**, 221-222
Library buildings, **3**, 107-108, 111-116, 120-130
Library Chronicle, **7**, 161
Library collections, **6**, 42-43; **7**, 299-335
"The library-college," **4**, 163
Library committees, **3**, 111
Library consultants, **2**, 198-209; **3**, 143
Library cooperation, **2**, 28-34; **4**, 12-17; **5**, 138
Library demonstration projects, **1**, 250
Library development assistance, **1**, 241-281
Library education, **8**, 191-192, 201-238; **9**, 88-89
Library education in India, Pakistan and Bangladesh, **10**, 191-236
Library Employees Union, **4**, 131
Library General Information Survey Project, **5**, 117-119; **6**, 17-18; **8**, 123
Library Information System for Swedish Libraries, **5**, 26-27, 94
Library Journal, **4**, 85; **7**, 161; **8**, 33, 127
Library Literature, **3**, 62, 88, 246; **8**, 233
Library materials, **3**, 9-10, 22-23; **9**, 23-27
Library materials budgeting constraints, **10**, 98-99
Library materials budgeting literature, **10**, 91-96
Library Network Analysis Theory, **2**, 57
Library networks, **2**, 28-34, 52-64, 210; **4**, 12-17
Library Networking in the West, **8**, 291
Library of American Civilization, **2**, 171, 172, 179
Library of Congress Classification, **7**, 56-60
Library personnel resources, **5**, 150-152, 172-173, 181-188
Library planning, **1**, 207-238; **5**, 61-103
Library profession, **8**, 99
Library proficiency, **10**, 71-72
Library Quarterly, **7**, 161
Library research, **2**, 202-203
Library schools, **5**, 152-256, 189-198; **6**, 238-242; **7**, 145-176
Library services, **2**, 211, 253-273; **3**, 1-10; **4**, 86-87; **5**, 61-103, 107-120; **9**, 41-44

Library Service for American Indian People, **8**, 147
Library statistics, **1**, 108
Library surveys, **1**, 103-104, 232-233, 249
Library systems, **1**, 189-205, 232; **2**, 29
Library technical assistants, **3**, 70; **4**, 139; **5**, 167-169, 184-185; **6**, 234-235, 246; **9**, 72-76
Library tours, **3**, 86-87
Library Trends, **7**, 161; **8**, 3, 194, 283
Library-user-funder, **9**, 33-37
Library users, **3**, 3; **9**, 27-28
LIBRAS group, **2**, 20
Lifelong learning, **8**, 244
Lister Hill National Center for Biomedical Communications, **2**, 54-57
Lists of Serial Publications of Foreign Governments, **2**, 105
Literature reviews, **10**, 64-66
Local data in budget formulation, **10**, 108-109
Lockheed Aircraft Company, **5**, 20
London University, **5**, 33, 333-335, 338, 348
Los Angeles City College Library, **3**, 65, 66
Los Angeles County Public Library, **8**, 107, 112, 115
Los Angeles Times Index, **3**, 103
Loughborough University of Technology Library, **2**, 116; **4**, 15-16
Louisiana State University, **4**, 153; **8**, 112
Louisville University School of Medicine Library, **2**, 67, 134
Loyola College, **5**, 324-341
Loyola-Notre Dame Library, **5**, 324, 340-341, 344, 347, 349
Loyola University, **5**, 329-330, 341, 347-348
Luhn's Business Intelligence System, **4**, 27-28, 30
Luther College Library, **3**, 120, 131

M

MacAllister, J. Y. W., **7**, 152, 159
McColvin Report, **7**, 155
McGill University, **8**, 203, 207, 209, 213
Machine Readable Cataloging, **2**, 11, 12, 65, 105, 123, 158; **3**, 186-187, 189, 226-228, 232-242; **4**, 1-18, 33, 37; **5**, 20, 140-141; **7**, 53; **8**, 62, 67
Main Street, **7**, 148-149
Madrid University, **4**, 152

Main entries, **1**, 11, 18
Malaya University, **5**, 83
Malaysia, **5**, 82-83
Malaysian Library Association, **5**, 83
Management in libraries, **1**, 207-238; **6**, 266-272
Management Review and Analysis Program, **8**, 281; **10**, 43-56
Manitoba Institute of Technology, **8**, 217
Manuscripts, **3**, 245-275
Marquette University Library, **3**, 120
Maryland, **2**, 191; **6**, 15-16
Maryland Hall of Record, **3**, 270
Maryland University Library, **3**, 274; **4**, 113, 132; **5**, 166, 174
Marymount College, **5**, 329, 341-342, 347-348
Mass media, **6**, 141-142
Massachusetts Central Library Processing Center, **4**, 16
Massachusetts Historical Society, **3**, 248
Massachusetts Institute of Technology, **2**, 28; **7**, 318; **3**, 125
Massachusetts University Library, **3**, 122; **5**, 325
Master List of Medical Index Terms, **2**, 71
Materials budget, **10**, 117-118
Materials budget and collection development, **10**, 116-129
Materials budgets for 1978-1979, **10**, 113
Materials fund, **10**, 128-129
Materials fund and interlibrary cooperation, **10**, 131-139
Materials funding, **10**, 113-114
Mead, Margaret, **1**, 243
Meaning, **4**, 181-184, 222-226
Media, **9**, 234-235
Media Evaluation and Development by American Indians, **8**, 167
Medical information, **2**, 45-92, 70-79
Medical libraries, **2**, 51-54, 63, 65-70, 80-81, 88-92; **5**, 114; **7**, 281-282; **9**, 213-250
Medical Library Assistance Act, **2**, 52; **8**, 312
Medical Library Assistance Extension Act, **2**, 52-53
Medical Library Association, **2**, 65; **8**, 100, 276, 277, 287; **9**, 246-247
Medical Library Association News, **8**, 287
Medical Library Center of New York, **2**, 12, 63
Medical Literature Analysis and Retrieval System, **2**, 28, 31, 49-52, 57, 60-61, 64, 65, 69, 76, 78, 81, 89-90, 92; **4**, 33, 46; **5**, 6, 26, 36-37, 48, 49, 86; **8**, 313

Medical society libraries, **2**, 82
Medicine history, **2**, 84; **3**, 251
Medicine information systems, **5**, 36-37
MEDICO, **2**, 77-78
Menominee County Library, **8**, 165
Mental patients, **1**, 182
Metallurgy, **5**, 32
Metals Abstracts Index, **4**, 33; **5**, 20
Mexico, **5**, 83-84
Miami-Dade Junior College Library, **2**, 108-109, 125, 132-133, 150-151; **3**, 66, 67
Michigan Library Association, **8**, 100
Michigan State University, **8**, 181
Michigan Technological University Library, **3**, 121, 128
Michigan University, **1**, 44, 117-120, 122; **3**, 120, 123, 203-207, 211; **5**, 171; **6**, 269; **8**, 102
Microcard Corporation, **2**, 172, 175
Microcards, **2**, 177-178
Microfiche, **2**, 177-179, 183
Microfilm, **2**, 149, 177-178
Microfilm book catalogs, **1**, 33
Microfilming Corporation of America, **2**, 166
Microform(s), **2**, 23-24, 165-185; **3**, 125; **10**, 126
Microform readers, **2**, 177-178
Microformats, **2**, 177-180
Microforum, **2**, 166
Micrographics News & Views, **2**, 166
Micrographics Weekly, **2**, 166
Micropublication, **2**, 23-24, 165-185
Micropublisher, **2**, 166
Middle management, **6**, 253-274
Midwest Inter-Library Center, **5**, 325
Milam, Carl, **7**, 153
Minicomputers, **2**, 234
Minnesota University, **5**, 172; **8**, 147, 150-151, 168
Minnesota University Biomedical Library, **2**, 67-68, 124, 137-140, 150-151, 155-156
Minnesota University Center for Immigration Studies, **3**, 252
Minnesota University Library, **3**, 108, 121, 126, 131; **4**, 159
Minorities, **8**, 94-96, 110-111, 114-116, 123-124
Mission, **9**, 12-14
Missouri State Department of Education, **6**, 16
Missouri University, **1**, 37, 43; **4**, 65
M.L.S. degree, **8**, 120, 126

Modern Practice of Adult Education, The, **8**, 257
Mohrhardt, F. E., **3**, 46, 61
Mountain-Plains Library Association, **8**, 100, 292
Montclair Public Library, **8**, 107
Monterey Public Library, **5**, 209
Montreal Université, **8**, 203, 207
Morehouse College, **5**, 327–328, 343, 350
Morris Brown College, **5**, 328, 343, 350
Mount Holyoke College Library, **5**, 325
Mt. St. Scholastica College Library, **3**, 120–121
Mt. San Antonio College Library, **3**, 39, 65–68, 77, 91
Mt. San Jacinto College Library, **3**, 67
Mt. Sinai Hospital Library, **2**, 67
Multi-media, **3**, 124–125
Museum of the American Indian, **8**, 146
Music Library Association, **5**, 297–298, 300–301, 315

N

National, *see also* American, Federal and U.S.
National Academy of Sciences, **2**, 25–26, 32–33, 36
National Advisory Commission on Libraries, **2**, 5, 32–34, 261–262; **7**, 174
National Aeronautics and Aerospace Administration, **2**, 27
National Archives, **8**, 147
National Association for the Advancement of Colored People, **3**, 252
National Association of Spanish-Speaking People, **8**, 88
National Association of State Libraries, **2**, 195
National Book Committee, **5**, 242
National Cancer Institute, **2**, 77
National Center for Atmospheric Research Library, **2**, 130
National Center for Biomedical Communications, **2**, 54–57
National Center for Educational Statistics, **2**, 201; **6**, 17
National Commission on Libraries and Information Science, **7**, 174; **8**, 263, 274, 302, 306–309, 316–317
National Conference on Library Statistics, **5**, 116
National Council of Teachers of English, **6**, 14

National Education Association, **1**, 149–150; **4**, 120; **5**, 246; **6**, 15; **8**, 262
National Endowment for the Arts, **7**, 194
National Endowment for the Humanities, **2**, 286; **8**, 24
National Enquiry into Scholarly Communication, **10**, 53–54
National Federation of Science Abstracting and Indexing Services, **5**, 10
National indexes in budget formulation, **10**, 108–109
National Indian Education Association, **8**, 147, 167, 169
National Indian Education Association Library Project, **8**, 149–152, 154, 164
National Indian Law Library, **8**, 147
National Information System for Psychology, **2**, 26
National Institute of Neurological Diseases and Stroke, **2**, 60–61
National Lending Library for Science and Technology, **2**, 21
National libraries, **7**, 105–143; **8**, 65, 192, 313
National Libraries Task Force, **2**, 12, 65
National Library Advisory Board, **8**, 66
National Library of Medicine, **7**, 281–282; **8**, 263
National Medical Audiovisual Center, **2**, 64, 87
National Microfilm Association, **2**, 177–178
National Press Club, **4**, 122
National Program for Acquisitions and Cataloging, **2**, 10–11; **5**, 139; **8**, 62
National Register of Master Microforms, **2**, 172; **8**, 32
National Standard Reference Data System, **2**, 16
National Technical Information Service, **5**, 20
National Translations Center, **2**, 17
National Union Catalog, **2**, 12; **3**, 180, 182; **4**, 7, 17; **5**, 139
National Union Catalog of Manuscript Collections, **3**, 256–263, 267
National University Extension Association, **8**, 255
Native American Evaluation of Media Materials, **8**, 167
Navajo Community College, **8**, 146, 161
Navajo Health Authority, **8**, 162
Navajo Tribal Museum, **8**, 162
Nebraska University College of Medicine, **2**, 87
Nebraska University Library, **3**, 121, 128

Neighborhood centers, 2, 255
Neighborhood Youth Corps, 2, 256
Netherlands, 5, 84–85
Network for Continuing Medical Education, 2, 87
Networks, 2, 29
Nevada University Library, 3, 121
Nevins, Allan, 2, 277–283, 293, 297
Newberry Library, 2, 19; 18, 166
Newcastle upon Tyne University Library, 3, 109
New England Library Association, 8, 101, 292
New England Library Board, 8, 292
New England Library Information Network, 2, 11; 4, 14
New England Regional Medical Library Service, 2, 53–54
New Haven Public Library, 2, 256; 4, 86
New Mexico, 8, 162–164
New Mexico State Library, 8, 164
New Mexico University Library of Medical Sciences, 2, 66, 67
Newport Beach High School, 1, 141
New Serial Titles, 2, 105
Newsletter on Intellectual Freedom, 2, 234–239
Newspapers in Microform, 8, 32
Newspapers on microfilm, 2, 175
New York libraries, 2, 12, 54, 66, 69, 135, 137, 144, 147, 152, 255, 259–260
New York Metropolitan Reference and Research Library Agency, 2, 21
New York Public Library, 3, 248; 8, 188
New York State Library, 4, 126–127
New York (State) library systems, 1, 194–197
New York State University Library, 3, 20–21, 122, 124
New York Times, 2, 167–168, 173, 175
New York Times Index, 3, 85, 102
New Zealand, 2, 243; 3, 170; 5, 85–87
New Zealand National Library, 3, 170, 178
Nicholson, E. B., 7, 150
Nigeria, 1, 254–255, 5, 87–88
Non-book materials in libraries, 1, 134–156
Nondiscrimination, 8, 82
NORDFORSK, 5, 94
NORDOK, 5, 94
North Carolina State University Library, 3, 144, 274
North Carolina University, 8, 107
North Central College, 5, 324–325, 349

North Dakota State University Library, 3, 120
Northern Illinois University, 4, 150
Northern Iowa University Library, 3, 120, 128, 131
Northern Ohio University Library, 3, 120, 127, 128
North Texas University Library, 3, 121
Northwestern University Library, 3, 120, 122, 130; 4, 37, 68
Norway, 5, 88–90
Notes in cataloging, 1, 12
Notre Dame College, 5, 324, 341
Notre Dame University Library, 3, 122
Nuclear research indexes, 5, 22–24
Nuclear Science Abstracts, 2, 76; 4, 33, 36; 5, 22–23
Numeric name interpolation systems, 1, 83–84
Nursing libraries, 2, 81–82

O

Oak Park High Schools, 1, 154
Oakland Community College Library, 3, 67
Obscenity, 6, 151–165
Occidental College Library, 3, 123
Office for Civil Rights, 8, 84, 86
Office for Federal Contract Compliance, 8, 85
Office for Library Personnel Resources, 8, 88, 123–124, 147, 168
Office of Libraries and Learning Resources, 8, 267
Office of Library and Information Services, 8, 173
Office of Library Service for the Disadvantaged, 8, 147
Oficina de Educacion Iberoamericana, 5, 6, 66, 81–82, 102–103
Ohio Association of School Libraries, 6, 16
Ohio College Library Center, 4, 5, 13–14, 17; 5, 140
Ohio Historical Society, 3, 252
Ohio Library Center, 2, 11
Ohio State University, 3, 125; 6, 268–269
Oklahoma Christian University Library, 3, 127
Oklahoma City University, 8, 102
Oklahoma Department of Libraries, 4, 14–15, 37
Oklahoma State University Library, 3, 124
Oklahoma University, 5, 171

Oklahoma University Medical Center, **2**, 88
Ontario Hydro Library, **1**, 10
Ontario New Universities Library Project, **1**, 8, 16–23
Operations research, **6**, 25–27; **9**, 144–179
Operators of Chemical Information Systems, **4**, 29
Opinion leaders, **7**, 274–275
Optical character recognition, **4**, 11
Optical character scanning, **3**, 240
Optimism, **10**, 156–163
Options, **10**, 21–23
Oral history, **2**, 275–301
Oral History Association, **2**, 276, 278, 281–283, 291, 293, 300–301; **5**, 298
Orange Coast College Library, **3**, 66
Orange County Community College, **5**, 168
Orange County Library, **8**, 107
Oregon State College Library, **3**, 124
Oregon State System of Higher Education, **6**, 23
Oregon State University Library, **3**, 121, 125; **4**, 156
Oregon University Library, **3**, 121, 123, 127, 274
Organization, **9**, 214
Organization for Economic Cooperation and Development, **5**, 5–7, 11, 18–25
Organization of American States, **1**, 259–260; **5**, 6, 66, 102–103
Organization of information, **2**, 6–8
Ortega y Gasset, **7**, 191
Oslo University, **5**, 90
Otlet, Paul, **7**, 54
Ottawa University, **8**, 207
Outreach, **3**, 3–4
Outreach programs, **9**, 219–223
Overhead transparencies, **5**, 257
Oxford University, **5**, 323, 333–338, 347–348

P

Pacific Lutheran University Library, **3**, 120, 124, 131
Pacific Northwest Association, **8**, 291
Pacific University, **5**, 331–332
Pacy, Frank, **7**, 160
Pädogogishes Zentrum, **5**, 33
Pakistan, **2**, 19; **10**, 219–229

Palomar College Library, **3**, 66
Pan American Union, **1**, 243
PANDEX, **2**, 13; **4**, 33
Paraprofessionals, **9**, 67–88
Paris Union for the Protection of Industrial Property, **2**, 329–330
Parkinson's Disease Information Center, **2**, 60
Parry Report, **3**, 110–112
Pasadena City College Library, **3**, 67
Patent indexes, **5**, 25–26
Peabody Library Information Test, **4**, 156
Pennsylvania Department of Education, **6**, 16
Pennsylvania library systems, **1**, 194–197
Pennsylvania University Library, **3**, 128
Performance measurement, **6**, 1–46
Performance standards, **1**, 100–102
Periodicals, **2**, 13
Personnel, **9**, 109
Personnel utilization policy, **9**, 88–91
Persons, form of heading for, **10**, 10–11
Persuasion, **6**, 180–181
Pertinence, **6**, 108
Peru, **5**, 81–82
Pesticides Documentation Bulletin, **2**, 59
Philadelphia Bibliographical Center, **2**, 172
Philadelphia College of Pharmacy and Science, **4**, 156
Philadelphia Free Library, **3**, 7, 173, 178; **6**, 28
Phillipine Libraries Association, **5**, 91
Phillipines, **5**, 90–91
Philosophy of access to information, **2**, 4–5
Phoenix College Library, **3**, 66
Photocopies, **2**, 22
Photocopying for interlibrary loans, **2**, 61–64
PHOTON ZIP 901, **2**, 50
Physics history, **3**, 251
Physics Information Exchange, **2**, 26
Picture collections, **5**, 257–259
Pirie, J. W., **3**, 62
Pittsburgh study, **10**, 53–54
Pittsburgh University, **3**, 122, 126; **4**, 29, 156; **7**, 18
Pitzer College, **5**, 326, 345, 349
PL 1 (computer language), **1**, 52
Planning, **1**, 208–218; **9**, 226–227
Political implications of interlibrary cooperation, **10**, 135–136
Politics and libraries, **2**, 203–207, 209–210
Polk Junior College Library, **3**, 66
Pomona College, **5**, 326, 348–349

Poole, William, F., 7, 150–151
Popular culture and libraries, 7, 188–216, 224
Popular Culture Association, 5, 298; 7, 198, 209
Popular Culture Association Journal, 7, 209
Pornography, 6, 151–165
Portugal, 5, 91–92
Poverty, 3, 2–3
Pratt Institute, 8, 102
Predicasts, 4, 33
Prejudice, 6, 176–193
Preprints, 2, 86
Presidential libraries, 3, 247–248
President's Committee on Employment of the Handicapped, 8, 108, 127
Pricing patterns, 9, 53–56
Prince George Memorial Library, 5, 166
Princeton Microfilm Corporation, 2, 173
Princeton University Library, 3, 123
Principles of *AACR2,* 10, 18–19
Process evaluation, 8, 266
Product evaluation, 8, 266
Productivity, 6, 54–75
Professional associations, 8, 274–292
Professional education, 6, 222–223
Professionalism, 8, 251–255
Professional Women's Caucus, 4, 140
Program planning and budgetary systems, 5, 211–212
Progressive Librarians' Council, 4, 98
Project Discovery, 1, 151–152
Project INTREX, 2, 28
Project MARC, 1, 27–32, 34, 52–53, 76, 80, 85
Project Springboard, 1, 152–153
Psychological Abstracts, 4, 33
Psychology, 7, 310–311
Psychology history, 3, 251–252
Public Affairs Information Service, 3, 99–100
Public Health Service Act, 2, 52
Public libraries, 1, 166–167, 189–205; 2, 196–198, 253–376; 3, 1–10, 15–26, 137–165; 5, 114–115; 6, 27–29; 7, 153–156, 198–202, 216–224, 231–255; 8, 91, 93, 187–190; 9, 12–14
Public Library Association, 8, 99, 284
Public Library Inquiry, 7, 180
Public Library Measurement Study, 6, 33–36
Public library systems, 1, 190–194; 2, 29
Publishers Weekly, 8, 9–10

Punched cards in acquisitions, 1, 2–3
Punched tapes in acquisitions, 1, 47–48
Purchasing, 10, 124–125
Purdue University, 2, 107; 6, 26

Q

Quantitative methods, 8, 37–39
Queens, New York, 2, 255
Queen's University School of Library Studies, 3, 122

R

Racial and Ethnic Data for Institutions of Higher Education, 8, 89
Racism, 8, 99–100; 9, 14–16, 23–27
Radcliffe College Library, 3, 122
Raking the Historic Coals, 8, 189
Ranganathan, Shiyali Ramamrita, 7, 43, 60, 62
Raymond College, 5, 332
Reader services, 2, 253–273
Reader's Guide to Periodical Literature, 3, 85, 89, 99–100
Reading, 1, 171–186; 4, 175–228; 6, 139–202
Reading University Library, 3, 109
Ready Store, 4, 186–197, 214–217
RECON, 5, 19–21
Recordak Corporation, 2, 175
Recordings, 5, 279–320
Recurring Bibliography of Hypertension, 2, 50
Redlands University, 5, 331–332
Reed College Library, 2, 114
Refereeing, 2, 24–25
Reference collections in school libraries, 1, 164
Reference services, 1, 159–169; 2, 68–70; 6, 31–32
REFORMA: National Association of Spanish-Speaking Librarians, 8, 88
Regional library systems, 1, 193–197, 235–236
Regional Medical Libraries, 2, 51–54, 63, 81, 92
Register catalogs, 1, 26–27, 31
Relevance, 6, 80–135
Remote access systems, 2, 28
Remote Information Systems Center, 2, 28
Reprints, 2, 24, 85–86
Research, 6, 145–148; 9, 227, 239–241

Research in Education, **3,** 7
Research in librarianship, **9,** 190–207
Resource sharing, **9,** 228–229
Retrieval systems, **2,** 70–79
Revenue sharing, **3,** 145–147, 150–163
Reverse discrimination, **8,** 114–116
Rice University, **1,** 52–53; **3,** 126
RINGDOC, **2,** 78
Riverside Junior College Library, **3,** 77
Roads, **5,** 25
Rochester Public Library, **2,** 259–260
Rochester University, **1,** 9; **3,** 122, 129; **4,** 153
Rockefeller Foundation, **1,** 251–253; **5,** 234
Rosary College School of Library Science, **8,** 100
Rough Rock Community School Library, **8,** 152–154
Royal Australian Chemical Institute, **5,** 68
Royal Danish Library School, **6,** 232–233, 249
Royal Institute of Technology, **5,** 94
Royal Society of Medicine Library, **2,** 116
Rutgers University, **4,** 156; **8,** 107
Rutgers University Graduate School of Library Service, **2,** 205

S

Sacramento City-County Library, **8,** 120
St. Louis, **5,** 221
St. Louis Junior College Library, **3,** 66
St. Petersburg Junior College Library, **3,** 66
St. Regis Akwesasne Mohawk Reservation, **8,** 157
Salaries, **8,** 90–95
Sampling, **5,** 118–119; **6,** 38
San Bernardino Valley College Library, **3,** 66
San Bruno, **5,** 219
San Diego City College Library, **3,** 66
San Diego College for Women, **5,** 330
San Diego University, **5,** 330–331
San Francisco Public Library, **2,** 134–135, 150–151, 155
San Gabriel Community College Library, **3,** 77
Santa Clara Community Library, **8,** 163
Santa Fe College Library, **3,** 121, 127
Saskatchewan University, **4,** 16–17
Savage, E. A., **7,** 158
Save the Children Foundation, **8,** 143

Scarritt College for Christian Workers, **5,** 324, 340, 344, 349, 351
School librarians, **1,** 169
School libraries, **1,** 133–156, 162–164, 166–167; **2,** 196; **6,** 1–47; **8,** 93
School Library Association of California, **3,** 50
School Library Journal, **1,** 156
School Library Manpower Project, **8,** 251
School Library Personnel Task Analysis Survey, **8,** 262
School of Library and Information Science, **8,** 203, 210, 214–216
School of Social Studies, **6,**249
Science Citation Index, **2,** 13, 75–76
Science Information Exchange, **2,** 17
Scientific Activity predictor form Patterns with Heuristic Origins Project, **7,** 272
Scotland National Library, **3,** 170
Scripps College, **5,** 326, 349–350
Search argument, **1,** 66
Seattle Indian Center, **8,** 143
Seattle Public Library, **5,** 235
Selection priorities, **8,** 20–24
Selective dissemination of information, **2,** 27, 73, 76–77, 108, 120; **4,** 15–17, 25–52
Selective Permutation Index, **3,** 266–268
Selectivity, **1,** 113–114
Self-determination, **8,** 140–142
Seminars on Acquisition of Latin American Library Material, **2,** 19
Serials, **2,** 12–13, 16, 61–64, 66–68, 103–161; **5,** 30–32, 130; **8,** 24–26, 35–36; **10,** 124–126
Sexism, **6,** 188–192; **8,** 99–100; **9,** 14–16, 23–27
Sexual behavior, **6,** 151–165
Shachtman Report, **5,** 127–129, 131, 144
Shared cataloging, **2,** 10–12, 64
Shared Systems Program, **5,** 19, 25–26
Share Research Corporation, **4,** 29
Sheffield University, **2,** 90; **3,** 109; **7,** 318
Short-Term Memory, **4,** 194–195, 217–221
Shoshone-Bannock Library and Media Center, **8,** 160–161
Simmons College, **5,** 172
Sinte Gleska College, **8,** 146
Sioux City Public Library Indian Library Project, **8,** 159–160
Slides, **5,** 272–273
Sloan Commission on Cable Television, **5,** 219

Smithsonian Institution, **3**, 267
Smithsonian library, **8**, 61
Social change, **8**, 128
Social classes, **7**, 213–214
Social mobility, **7**, 212–213
Social responsibility, **4**, 78–80
Social Sciences and Humanities Index, **3**, 93, 99–100; **4**, 33
Society for Ethnomusicology, **5**, 298
Society of American Archivists, **2**, 283; **3**, 258–259, 262–263, 269–274; **5**, 298
Socioeconomic trends, **8**, 86–97
Sociological Abstracts, **4**, 33
Sociology, **7**, 311–312
Sort tags, **1**, 77–80, 86, 87–89
Source and Citation, **4**, 33
South Dakota University, **3**, 121, 123, 130, 131; **8**, 147
Southampton University Library, **2**, 116; **4**, 16
Southern Colorado College Library, **3**, 121–122
Southern Education Reporting Service, **2**, 173
Southern Illinois University Library, **3**, 89, 120; **4**, 65
Southern Oregon College Library, **3**, 120
Southwestern Library Association, **4**, 14; **8**, 290, 292
Southwestern Library Interstate Cooperative Endeavor, **4**, 14–15; **8**, 290
Southwest Museum, **8**, 146
Space Documentation Service, **4**, 48; **5**, 18–22
Space research indexes, **5**, 19–22
Space technology, **2**, 193–194
Spain, **5**, 92–93
Spanish-speaking librarians, **8**, 88, 95
Speaker, The (film), **9**; 17–23
Special Interest Group on Education, **8**, 288
Special Libraries Association, **1**, 104; **2**, 17, 113–114, 200; **4**, 108, 111, 117; **5**, 297; **7**, 154; **8**, 95, 100, 226, 289
Speech Communication Association, **5**, 298
Spelman College, **5**, 327–328, 343, 350
Spengler, Oswald, **7**, 191
Staff, **9**, 64–67
Staff Committee on Mediation, Arbitration and Inquiry, **8**, 99
Staff development, **8**, 246–247
Staff participation in budget formulation, **10**, 110
Standardization, **1**, 98; **2**, 11
Standards of library service, **1**, 95–110, 209, 221–222, 231

Standing Conference of Librarians of the Libraries of the University of London, **5**, 335, 338
Standing Conference of National and University Librarians, **3**, 109–110, 116
Standing Rock Tribal Library, **8**, 154–157
Standing Rock Tribal Library Newsletter, **8**, 155
Stanford University Herbert Hoover Archives, **3**, 263, 268
Stanford University Library, **5**, 138
Stanford University Meyer Library, **1**, 9, 17–20, 88–89, 123–124; **3**, 121–122, 124, 126
State government, **2**, 189–193
State libraries, **2**, 187–212; **3**, 142–145, 149–150
State library systems, **1**, 194–197, 235
State University of New York, **2**, 28
Statistics, **6**, 38–39
Stephens College Library, **3**, 46–47, 62, 66; **4**, 151–152, 158
Steroid Conjugates, **2**, 74
Stevens, Henry, **7**, 167
Storage libraries, **2**, 20–22
Story telling, **3**, 7–8
Story Up to Now, The, **8**, 65
Structural criteria, **9**, 123–124
Students, **3**, 83–86
Subject bibliographers, **8**, 5–6
Subject entries, **1**, 13–14, 20–21; **3**, 242
Subject-field competition, **8**, 23–24
Subjective expected utility model, **10**, 163–174
Suffolk University, **4**, 156
SUPERMARC, **4**, 7–8
Supervision, **6**, 255–259
Surveys, **6**, 146–147; **7**, 231–252
Sussex University Library, **3**, 116
Swarthmore College Library, **3**, 129
Sweden, **5**, 93–95
Swedish Agency for Administrative Development, **5**, 27
Swedish Library Association, **5**, 94
Swedish School for Social Sciences, **5**, 78
Swiss Library Association, **6**, 249
Switzerland, **5**, 95–96
Symposium on Computer-Based Chemical Information, **4**, 29
Syracuse Public Library, **2**, 260
Syracuse University School of Library Science, **3**, 270; **5**, 166
System goals, **9**, 109–110

System of Documentation and Information for Metallurgy, **5**, 32
Systems, **1**, 199–201; **5**, 132–134
Systems analysis, **1**, 39–40
Systems concept, **9**, 130

T

Table argument, **1**, 66
Tabulating machines in acquisition, **1**, 40–49
Tacoma Public Library, **8**, 107
Tampa University Library, **3**, 121–131
Tampere University, **5**, 78; **6**, 233
Tape recorders, **2**, 279–288
Task Force, **8**, 68–78
Task Force ABLE, **2**, 58
Task Force on Women, **8**, 88, 99
Teaching needs, **8**, 22–23
Technical education, **3**, 42
Technical reports, **2**, 85
Technical services, **1**, 95–110; **5**, 123–144; **6**, 30–31
Technical services cost ratio, **1**, 106
Technician, **9**, 81–88
Technology, **10**, 26–27
Tekniska Hogskolans Bibliotek, **4**, 29
Telefacsimile transmission, **2**, 56
Teletypewriters, **2**, 22, 63
Television in school libraries, **1**, 153; **5**, 238–239
Temple University Library, **3**, 120, 124
Terminology, **1**, 107–108
Texas A&M University Library, **2**, 107, 110, 131
Texas Instruments Library, **2**, 125
Texas University, **1**, 123; **2**, 107, 282; **3**, 122, 270
Textile Information Treatment User's Service, **5**, 37–38
Textile technology, **5**, 37–38
Textual data, **3**, 223–225
Thesauri, **2**, 25; **7**, 1–40
Thesaurus of Engineering and Scientific Terms, **7**, 47
Thunderbird Graduate School of International Management Library, **3**, 121
Time horizon, **9**, 131
Title entries, **1**, 13, 19–20
Title transcription, **1**, 11

Toledo University, **5**, 167
Toronto Faculty of Library Science, **8**, 210, 231
Toronto Public Library, **8**, 222
Toronto University, **3**, 169, 173; **5**, 333–334; **8**, 229, 231
Toscanini Society, **5**, 299
Toxicity Bibliography, **2**, 77
Tracings (in cataloging), **1**, 12
Training, Appraisal and Promotion Program, **8**, 109
Translations, **2**, 17, 85, 335–336
Traveling libraries, **2**, 191
Trinity College, **4**, 67; **5**, 336–337
Tucson Public Library, **8**, 101
Tufts University Library, **3**, 121, 128
Tulane University Library, **3**, 120, 126
Turkey, **1**, 254

U

Uncataloged library materials, **1**, 46–47, 96
Undergraduate libraries, **1**, 113–131; **3**, 83–85
UNESCO, **1**, 242–243, 256–259; **2**, 200, 236, 323–324, 333, 340, 342, 348; **5**, 3, 5–7, 27–32, 41, 44, 46, 65–66, 70, 74, 79, 81–82, 102–103; **8**, 243
UNESCO Bulletin for Libraries, **1**, 242
UNIDO, **5**, 46
Union catalogs, **2**, 12, 16; **3**, 111
Union list, **9**, 223–226
Union List of Microfilms, **2**, 172
Union List of Serials, **2**, 105
Union lists of serials, **2**, 12, 16, 61–64, 105, 121–123
Union of Soviet Socialist Republics, **5**, 63–64
Unit cards, **1**, 5, 20
United Nations Educational and Cultural Organizaton, **8**, 243
United Arab Republic, **2**, 19
United Auto Workers, **2**, 284
United International Bureau for the Protection of Intellectual Property, **5**, 25
United Kingdom, *see also* British, Great Britain
United Kingdom, **5**, 25, 34, 96–100; **9**, 206–207
United Kingdom Chemical Information Service, **4**, 49
United Nations, **2**, 6, 12, 27–28, 321

United Nations in Scientific and Technical Information, **5**, 3–5, 9, 11, 21, 24, 30–31, 34, 42, 44–45, 49, 51, 82; **7**, 48, 70–80, 82, 84
United Nations Institute for Training and Research, **5**, 27
United States, **2**, 318–321; **8**, 241–323
U.S., *see also* American, Federal, National
U.S. Allied Health Act, **3**, 43
U.S. Appalachian Regional Development Act, **3**, 138
U.S. Argonne National Laboratory, **4**, 5
U.S. Army Electronics Command, **4**, 49
U.S. Atomic Energy Commission, **2**, 13–14
U.S. Bureau of Labor Statistics, **4**, 107
U.S. Bureau of Libraries and Educational Technology, **3**, 6, 160–161
U.S. Chace International Copyright Act, **2**, 318–319
U.S. Civil Rights Act, **4**, 85
U.S. Commission on Civil Rights, **8**, 118
U.S. Commission on Obscenity and Pornography, **6**, 155–156
U.S. Comstock Act, **6**, 152
U.S. Constitution Bill of Rights, **2**, 221
U.S. Copyright laws, **2**, 318–321, 325
U.S. Copyright Offices, **8**, 61
U.S. Department of Defense, **2**, 14, 176
U.S. Department of State, **5**, 66
U.S. Economic Opportunity Act, **5**, 158; **8**, 312
U.S. Education Professions Development Act, **5**, 158; **8**, 312
U.S. Education Revenue Sharing Act, **3**, 155–158
U.S. Elementary and Secondary Education Act, **5**, 158–160; **6**, 17; **8**, 312
U.S. Equal Employment Opportunity Act, **8**, 84
U.S. Equal Employment Opportunity Commission, **8**, 84, 119
U.S. Federal Communications Commission, **5**, 220, 285
U.S. Federal work-study program, **3**, 59–60
U.S. G.I. Bill of Rights, **3**, 43
U.S. Health, Education and Welfare Department, **8**, 85, 99
U.S. Higher Education Act, **2**, 19, 29; **3**, 42–43, 46, 53, 58–60, 137; **5**, 158, 166–167; **8**, 101–102, 124, 244, 312
U.S. Higher Education Facilities Act, **3**, 137–138
U.S. History, **2**, 221
U.S. House of Representatives, **2**, 234–235
U.S. Information Agency, **1**, 264–267
U.S. Interior Department, **8**, 173
U.S. Labor Department, **8**, 87
U.S. Library of Congress, **1**, 2, 5, 54, 85; **2**, 19; **3**, 170, 180–186, 190, 222, 225–226, 237, 242, 249, 252–255, 263–267; **4**, 5, 7–11, 12; **5**, 139, 140–141, 307–308; **8**, 55–78, 109–112
U.S. Library Services and Construction Act, **2**, 29, 256; **3**, 137–165; **4**, 12, 86; **5**, 158–160, 162, 166; **8**, 143, 164–165, 312
U.S. Lifelong Learning Act, **8**, 260
U.S. Medical Library Assistance Act, **2**, 31, 52; **3**, 138; **5**, 158; **8**, 312
U.S. Model Cities Program, **3**, 138
U.S. National Aeronautics and Aerospace Administration, **2**, 13–14; **4**, 33; **5**, 20, 36
U.S. National Agricultural Library, **2**, 58–59; **3**, 170; **5**, 34
U.S. National Archives, **2**, 286
U.S. National Archives and Record Service, **3**, 245, 247–249, 255, 263, 266–270, 273
U.S. National Center for Educational Statistics, **5**, 119
U.S. National Commission for UNESCO, **5**, 66
U.S. National Commission on the Causes and Prevention of Violence, **6**, 166–172
U.S. National Commission on Libraries and Information Services, **5**, 102, 119
U.S. National Defense Education Act, **3**, 43, 60; **5**, 158; **8**, 312
U.S. National Historical Publications Commission, **3**, 246, 249, 257, 259, 260
U.S. National Indian Education Act, **8**, 171
U.S. National Library of Medicine, **1**, 10; **2**, 28, 48–62, 64, 66, 69, 77–78, 84; **3**, 170, 251; **5**, 36–37, 174
U.S. National Science Foundation, **2**, 17, 26; **3**, 251; **4**, 33; **5**, 174; **6**, 99
U.S. National Vocational Student Loan Insurance Act, **3**, 43
U.S. Navy, **2**, 176
U.S. Office for Civil Rights, **8**, 84, 86
U.S. Office for Economic Opportunity, **2**, 256; **4**, 86; **5**, 166
U.S. Office of Education, **3**, 53, 58, 160–161;

4, 28; **5**, 116, 157–159, 161, 164, 167, 174–175; **6**, 17
U.S. Office of Education, Educational Resources and Information Centers, **2**, 30; **3**, 7; **4**, 33; **5**, 33; **8**, 84, 101, 262, 284, 297, 311, 313
U.S. Presidential Commission on Obscenity and Pornography, **2**, 244–246
U.S. President's Science Advisory Committee, **2**, 31
U.S. Public Broadcasting Act, **5**, 245
U.S. Public Law, **2**, 19, 480
U.S. Smithsonian Institution, **2**, 17
U.S. Social Security Administration, **2**, 286
U.S. State Technical Services Act, **2**, 35
U.S. Supreme Court, **2**, 237–238, 244
U.S. Vietnam Era Veterans Readjustment Act, **8**, 85
U.S. Vocational Education Act, **3**, 43; **5**, 158; **8**, 312
U.S. Vocational Rehabilitation Act, **8**, 85
U.S. War on Poverty, **4**, 85–88
Unit records in acquisitions, **1**, 41
Universal Bibliographic Control 1, **5**, 3
Universal Decimal Classification, **7**, 45, 54–56, 76–77
Universal System for Information in Science and Technology, **5**, 3–5, 7, 9, 11, 21, 24, 30–31, 34, 42, 44–45, 49, 51, 82
University, **10**, 97–98
University College, **6**, 221–224
University Grants Committee, **3**, 109–112, 117
University guidelines in budget formulation, **10**, 111–112
University libraries, **8**, 1–40
University microfilms, **2**, 175
Upward Bound, **3**, 9
User fees, **9**, 38–56
User needs, **10**, 19–21
User satisfaction, **9**, 108–109
User studies, **9**, 126–127
Utah University Library, **3**, 121–122, 124
Utley, George B., **7**, 152

V

Vanderbilt University, **3**, 123, 128; **5**, 324, 340, 344, 349
Venezuela, **5**, 81–82, 101
Vermont, **2**, 191; **3**, 142, 144
Video viewers, **3**, 124
Vincennes University, **5**, 219
VINITI, **5**, 36, 39
Violence, **6**, 172–176
Vision, **4**, 198–200
Vocabulary control, **7**, 2–35
Vocational education, **3**, 42
Voigt, Melvin J., **1**, 115

W

Wales National Library, **3**, 170
Warsaw Adult Education Section, **4**, 152
Warwick University Library, **3**, 116
Washington Association for Educational Communications and Technology, **5**, 219
Washington, D.C., **3**, 25
Washington State University, **1**, 50–52; **3**, 121, 124; **5**, 216–217
Washington University (St. Louis) Library, **3**, 120–121, 131
Washington University School of Librarianship, **3**, 270
Washington University School of Medicine Library, **2**, 66–67, 131, 134
Waterloo University Library, **3**, 120, 123, 173
Wayne State University libraries, **3**, 123, 129, 274
WEAL Education and Legal Defense Fund, **8**, 89
Weeding, **8**, 29–30
Weinberg report, **2**, 25, 31
Weizmann Institute, **5**, 81
Wells College Library, **3**, 129
Welsford, Percy, **7**, 153
Wentworth Institute Library, **3**, 66
Western Association of Schools and Colleges, **3**, 57
Western Interstate Commission for Higher Education, **8**, 290
Western Interstate Library Coordinating Organization, **8**, 291
Western Ontario University, **8**, 203, 213
Western Reserve University, **5**, 330–331
Western State College Library, **3**, 121
Western Union, **5**, 222–223
Westmont College Library, **3**, 121
Who's Who in America, **3**, 257

Williamson, Charles C., **7**, 165
Williamson Report, **7**, 166–168
Wilson Library Bulletin, **7**, 162
Window Rock Public Schools, **8**, 161
Windsor University Library, **3**, 91
Winsor, Justin, **7**, 151, 152
Winterthur Museum, **3**, 268
Wisconsin, **8**, 164–165
Wisconsin Department of Public Instruction, **6**, 16
Wisconsin University libraries, **2**, 86, 262; **3**, 120, 121, 123, 128, 141, 253, 274; **4**, 29; **5**, 167
Wisconsin Valley Library Service, **8**, 165
Women, **4**, 106–107, 122, 128, 138–140, 141; **8**, 90–94, 110
Women employment, **8**, 90–94
Women Library Workers, **8**, 88
Women's Bureau, **8**, 81
Women's History Research Center, **4**, 140
Women's Press Club, **4**, 122
Word Recognition, **4**, 184–197, 209–212
Workload indicators, **9**, 125
World Intellectual Property Organization, **2**, 330; **5**, 25–26
World Meteorological Organization, **5**, 28
World War II, **9**, 150–151
World War II veterans, **3**, 36
World Weather Watch, **5**, 28
Writing, **9**, 14–16
Writing systems, **4**, 178–180
Wyer, J. I., **7**, 152

X

Xerox Bibliographies, **4**, 49
Xerox Corporation, **2**, 176

Y

Yale University, **1**, 48; **3**, 184, 207–208, 210–211; **4**, 69; **7**, 316
Yates, James, **7**, 150
York University Library, **3**, 116
Youth, **3**, 15–26

Z

Zuni Public Library, **8**, 163